THE HARVARD CLASSICS
EDITED BY CHARLES W. ELIOT, LL.D.

The Apology, Phædo *and* Crito *of* Plato

TRANSLATED BY BENJAMIN JOWETT

The Golden Sayings *of* Epictetus

TRANSLATED BY HASTINGS CROSSLEY

The Meditations *of* Marcus Aurelius

TRANSLATED BY GEORGE LONG

With *Introductions and* Notes

V*olume* 2

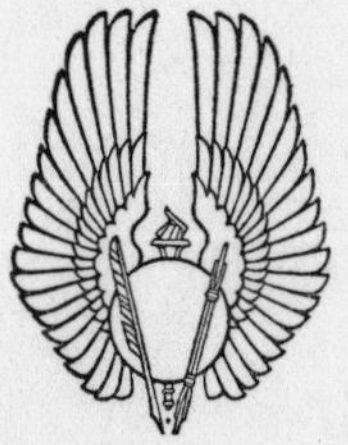

P. F. Collier & Son Company
NEW YORK

MANUFACTURED IN U. S. A.

THE HARVARD CLASSICS

The Five-Foot Shelf of Books

CONTENTS

INTRODUCTORY NOTE

SOCRATES, the son of an Athenian sculptor, was born in 469 B.C. He was trained in his father's art, but gave it up early to devote his time to the search for truth and virtue. He took his part as a citizen both in war and in peace, and bore the hardships of poverty and a shrewish wife with calm indifference. He did not give formal instruction after the fashion of other philosophers of his time, but went about engaging people in conversation, seeking, chiefly by questions, to induce his contemporaries, and especially the young men, to think clearly and to act reasonably. He made profession of no knowledge except of his own ignorance, and the famous "Socratic irony" was shown in his attitude of apparent willingness to learn from anyone who professed to know. The inevitable result of such conversations, however, was the reduction of the would-be instructor to a state either of irritation at the unmasking of his pretensions, or of humility and eagerness to be instructed by his questioner. It was natural that such a habit should create enemies, and Socrates was finally accused of introducing new gods and of corrupting the youth. His defense, as will be seen from the "Apology," was conducted with his customary firm adherence to his convictions, and with entire fearlessness of consequences. He could, in all probability, have easily escaped the death sentence had he been willing to take a conciliatory tone, but he died (B.C. 399) a martyr to his unswerving devotion to truth. Socrates wrote nothing, and we learn what we know of his teachings chiefly from his disciples, Xenophon and Plato.

Plato was also an Athenian, born in 428 B.C. of a distinguished family. He became a disciple of Socrates at the age of twenty, and after the death of his master he traveled in Egypt, Sicily, and elsewhere, returning to Athens about 388. Here he established his school of philosophy in a garden near a gymnasium, called the Academy, and here he spent the last forty years of his life, numbering among his pupils his great rival in philosophical renown, Aristotle. Unlike Socrates, Plato took no part in the civic life of Athens, but he was much interested in political philosophy, and is said to have been consulted by statesmen both at home and abroad.

All the works of Plato have been preserved, and they include, besides those here printed, the "Republic," "Symposium," "Phædrus," "Protagoras," "Theætetus," "Gorgias," and many others. They take the form of dialogues, in which Plato himself appears, if at all, only as a listener, and in which the chief speaker is Socrates. As Plato developed the philosophy of Socrates, especially on speculative lines, far beyond the point reached by Socrates himself, it is impossible to judge with any exactness precisely how much of the teaching is the master's, how much the pupil's.

The philosophy of these dialogues has remained for over two thousand years one of the great intellectual influences of the civilized world; and they are as admirable from the point of view of literature as of philosophy. The style is not only beautiful in itself, but is adapted with great dramatic skill to the large variety of speakers; and the suggestion of situation and the drawing of character are the work of a great artist. The three dialogues here given are at once favorable examples of the literary skill of Plato and intimate pictures of the personality of his master.

THE APOLOGY OF SOCRATES

HOW you have felt, O men of Athens, at hearing the speeches of my accusers, I cannot tell; but I know that their persuasive words almost made me forget who I was, such was the effect of them; and yet they have hardly spoken a word of truth. But many as their falsehoods were, there was one of them which quite amazed me: I mean when they told you to be upon your guard, and not to let yourself be deceived by the force of my eloquence. They ought to have been ashamed of saying this, because they were sure to be detected as soon as I opened my lips and displayed my deficiency; they certainly did appear to be most shameless in saying this, unless by the force of eloquence they mean the force of truth: for then I do indeed admit that I am eloquent. But in how different a way from theirs! Well, as I was saying, they have hardly uttered a word, or not more than a word, of truth; but you shall hear from me the whole truth: not, however, delivered after their manner, in a set oration duly ornamented with words and phrases. No, indeed! but I shall use the words and arguments which occur to me at the moment; for I am certain that this is right, and that at my time of life I ought not to be appearing before you, O men of Athens, in the character of a juvenile orator: let no one expect this of me. And I must beg of you to grant me one favor, which is this—if you hear me using the same words in my defence which I have been in the habit of using, and which most of you may have heard in the *agora,* and at the tables of the money-changers, or anywhere else, I would ask you not to be surprised at this, and not to interrupt me. For I am more than seventy years of age, and this is the first time that I have ever appeared in a court of law, and I am quite a stranger to the ways of the place; and therefore I would have you regard me as if I were really a stranger, whom you would excuse if he spoke in his native tongue, and after the fashion of his country: that I think is not an unfair request. Never mind the manner, which may or may not be good; but think only of the justice of my cause, and give heed to that: let the judge decide justly and the speaker speak truly.

And first, I have to reply to the older charges and to my first accusers, and then I will go to the later ones. For I have had many accusers, who accused me of old, and their false charges have continued during many years; and I am more afraid of them than of Anytus and his associates, who are dangerous, too, in their own way. But far more dangerous are these, who began when you were children, and took possession of your minds with their falsehoods, telling of one Socrates, a wise man, who speculated about the heaven above, and searched into the earth beneath, and made the worse appear the better cause. These are the accusers whom I dread; for they are the circulators of this rumor, and their hearers are too apt to fancy that speculators of this sort do not believe in the gods. And they are many, and their charges against me are of ancient date, and they made them in days when you were impressible—in childhood, or perhaps in youth—and the cause when heard went by default, for there was none to answer. And, hardest of all, their names I do not know and cannot tell; unless in the chance of a comic poet. But the main body of these slanderers who from envy and malice have wrought upon you—and there are some of them who are convinced themselves, and impart their convictions to others—all these, I say, are most difficult to deal with; for I cannot have them up here, and examine them, and therefore I must simply fight with shadows in my own defence, and examine when there is no one who answers. I will ask you then to assume with me, as I was saying, that my opponents are of two kinds—one recent, the other ancient; and I hope that you will see the propriety of my answering the latter first, for these accusations you heard long before the others, and much oftener.

Well, then, I will make my defence, and I will endeavor in the short time which is allowed to do away with this evil opinion of me which you have held for such a long time; and I hope I may succeed, if this be well for you and me, and that my words may find favor with you. But I know that to accomplish this is not easy—I quite see the nature of the task. Let the event be as God wills: in obedience to the law I make my defence.

I will begin at the beginning, and ask what the accusation is which has given rise to this slander of me, and which has encouraged Meletus to proceed against me. What do the slanderers say? They shall be my prosecutors, and I will sum up their words in an affidavit: "Socrates is an evil-doer, and a curious person, who searches into things under the earth and in heaven, and he makes the worse appear the better cause; and he teaches the aforesaid doctrines to others." That is the nature of the accusation, and that is what you have seen yourselves in the comedy of Aristophanes; who has introduced a man whom he calls Socrates, going about and saying that he can walk in the air, and talking a deal of nonsense concerning matters of which I do not pretend to know either much or little—not that I mean to say anything disparaging of anyone who is a student of natural philosophy. I should be very sorry if Meletus could lay that to my charge. But the simple truth is, O Athenians, that I have nothing to do with these studies. Very many of those here present are witnesses to the truth of this, and to them I appeal. Speak then, you who have heard me, and tell your neighbors whether any of you have ever known me hold forth in few words or in many upon matters of this sort. . . . You hear their answer. And from what they say of this you will be able to judge of the truth of the rest.

As little foundation is there for the report that I am a teacher, and take money; that is no more true than the other. Although, if a man is able to teach, I honor him for being paid. There is Gorgias of Leontium, and Prodicus of Ceos, and Hippias of Elis, who go the round of the cities, and are able to persuade the young men to leave their own citizens, by whom they might be taught for nothing, and come to them, whom they not only pay, but are thankful if they may be allowed to pay them. There is actually a Parian philosopher residing in Athens, of whom I have heard; and I came to hear of him in this way: I met a man who has spent a world of money on the Sophists, Callias the son of Hipponicus, and knowing that he had sons, I asked him: "Callias," I said, "if your two sons were foals or calves, there would be no difficulty in finding someone to put over them; we should hire a trainer of horses or a farmer probably who would improve and perfect them in their own proper virtue and excellence; but as they are human beings, whom are you thinking of placing over them? Is there anyone who understands human and political virtue? You must have thought about this as you have sons; is there anyone?" "There is," he said. "Who is he?" said I, "and of what country? and what does he charge?" "Evenus the Parian," he replied; "he is the man, and his charge is five minæ." Happy is Evenus, I said to myself, if he really has this wisdom, and teaches at such a modest charge. Had I the same, I should have been very proud and conceited; but the truth is that I have no knowledge of the kind, O Athenians.

I dare say that someone will ask the question, "Why is this, Socrates, and what is the origin of these accusations of you: for there must have been something strange which you have been doing? All this great fame and talk about you would never have arisen if you had been like other men: tell us, then, why this is, as we should be sorry to judge hastily of you." Now I regard this as a fair challenge, and I will endeavor to explain to you the origin of this name of "wise," and of this evil fame. Please to attend then. And although some of you may think I am joking, I declare that I will tell you the entire truth. Men of Athens, this reputation of mine has come of a certain sort of wisdom which I possess. If you ask me what kind of wisdom, I reply, such wisdom as is attainable by man, for to that extent I am inclined to believe that I am wise; whereas the persons of whom I was speaking have a superhuman wisdom, which I may fail to describe, because I have it not myself; and he who says that I have, speaks falsely, and is taking away my character. And here, O men of Athens, I must beg you not to interrupt me, even if I seem to say something extravagant. For the word which I will speak is not mine. I will refer you to a witness who is worthy of credit, and will tell you about my wisdom—whether I have any, and of what sort—and that witness shall be the god of Delphi. You must have known Chærephon; he was early a friend of mine, and also a friend of yours, for he shared in the exile of the people, and returned with you. Well, Chærephon, as you know, was very impetuous in all his doings, and he went to Delphi and boldly asked the oracle to tell him whether—as I was saying, I must beg you not to interrupt—he asked the oracle to tell him whether there was anyone wiser than I was, and the Pythian prophetess answered that there was no man wiser. Chærephon is dead himself, but his brother, who is in court, will confirm the truth of this story.

Why do I mention this? Because I am going to explain to you why I have such an evil name. When I heard the answer, I said to myself, What can the god mean? and what is the interpretation of this riddle? for I know that I have no wisdom, small or great. What can he mean when he says that I am the wisest of men? And yet he is a god and cannot lie; that would be against his nature. After a long consideration, I at last thought of a method of trying the question. I reflected that if I could only find a man wiser than myself, then I might go to the god with a refutation in my hand. I should say to him, "Here is a man who is wiser than I am; but you said that I was the wisest." Accordingly I went to one who had the reputation of wisdom, and observed to him—his name I need not mention; he was a politician whom I selected for examination—and the result was as follows: When I began to talk with him, I could not help thinking that he was not really wise, although he was thought wise by many, and wiser still by himself; and I went and tried to explain to him that he thought himself wise, but was not really wise; and the consequence was that he hated me, and his enmity was shared by several who were present and heard me. So I left him, saying to myself, as I went away: Well, although I do not suppose that either of us knows anything really beautiful and good, I am better off than he is—for he knows nothing, and thinks that he knows. I neither know nor think that I know. In this latter particular, then, I seem to have slightly the advantage of him. Then I went to another, who had still higher philosophical pretensions, and my conclusion was exactly the same. I made another enemy of him, and of many others besides him.

After this I went to one man after another, being not unconscious of the enmity which I provoked, and I lamented and feared this: but necessity was laid upon me—the word of God, I thought, ought to be considered first. And I said to myself, Go I must to all who appear to know, and find out the meaning of the oracle. And I swear to you, Athenians, by the dog I swear!—for I must tell you the truth—the result of my mission was just this: I found that the men most in repute were all but the most foolish; and that some inferior men were really wiser and better. I will tell you the tale of my wanderings and of the "Herculean" labors, as I may call them, which I endured only to find at last the oracle irrefutable. When I left the politicians, I went to the poets; tragic, dithyrambic, and all sorts. And there, I said to myself, you will be detected; now you will find out that you are more ignorant than they are. Accordingly, I took them some of the most elaborate passages in their own writings, and asked what was the meaning of them—thinking that they would teach me something. Will you believe me? I am almost ashamed to speak of this, but still I must say that there is hardly a person present who would not have talked better about their poetry than they did themselves. That showed me in an instant that not by wisdom do poets write poetry, but by a sort of genius and inspiration; they are like diviners or soothsayers who also say many fine things, but do not understand the meaning of them. And the poets appeared to me to be much in the same case; and I further observed that upon the strength of their poetry they believed themselves to be the wisest of men in other things in which they were not wise. So I departed, conceiving myself to be superior to them for the same reason that I was superior to the politicians.

At last I went to the artisans, for I was conscious that I knew nothing at all, as I may say, and I was sure that they knew many fine things; and in this I was not mistaken, for they did know many things of which I was ignorant, and in this they certainly were wiser than I was. But I observed that even the good artisans fell into the same error as the poets; because they were good workmen they thought that they also knew all sorts of high matters, and this defect in them overshadowed their wisdom—therefore I asked myself on behalf of the oracle, whether I would like to be as I was, neither having their knowledge nor their ignorance, or like them in both; and I made answer to myself and the oracle that I was better off as I was.

This investigation has led to my having many enemies of the worst and most dangerous kind, and has given occasion also to many calumnies, and I am called wise, for my hearers always imagine that I myself possess the wisdom which I find wanting in others: but the truth is, O men of Athens, that God only is wise; and in this oracle he means to say that the wisdom of men is little or nothing; he is not speaking of Socrates, he is only using my name as an illustration, as if he said, He, O men, is the wisest, who, like Socrates, knows that his wisdom is in truth worth nothing. And so I go my way, obedient to the god, and make inquisition into the wisdom of anyone, whether citizen or stranger, who appears to be wise; and if he is not wise, then in vindication of the oracle I show him that he is not wise; and this occupation quite absorbs me, and I have no time to give either to any public matter of interest or to any concern of my own, but I am in utter poverty by reason of my devotion to the god.

There is another thing:—young men of the richer classes, who have not much to do, come about me of their own accord; they like to hear the pretenders examined, and they often imitate me, and examine others themselves; there are plenty of persons, as they soon enough discover, who think that they know something, but really know little or nothing: and then those who are examined by them instead of being angry with themselves are angry with me: This confounded Socrates, they say; this villainous misleader of youth!—and then if somebody asks them, Why, what evil does he practise or teach? they do not know, and cannot tell; but in order that they may not appear to be at a loss, they repeat the ready-made charges which are used against all philosophers about teaching things up in the clouds and under the earth, and having no gods, and making the worse appear the better cause; for they do not like to confess that their pretence of knowledge has been detected—which is the truth: and as they are numerous and ambitious and energetic, and are all in battle array and have persuasive tongues, they have filled your ears with their loud and inveterate calumnies. And this is the reason why my three accusers, Meletus and Anytus and Lycon, have set upon me; Meletus, who has a quarrel with me on behalf of the poets; Anytus, on behalf of the craftsmen; Lycon, on behalf of the rhetoricians: and as I said at the beginning, I cannot expect to get rid of this mass of calumny all in a moment. And this, O men of Athens, is the truth and the whole truth; I have concealed nothing, I have dissembled nothing. And yet I know that this plainness of speech makes them hate me, and what is their hatred but a proof that I am speaking the truth?—this is the occasion and reason of their slander of me, as you will find out either in this or in any future inquiry.

I have said enough in my defence against the first class of my accusers; I turn to the second class, who are headed by Meletus, that good and patriotic man, as he calls himself. And now I will try to defend myself against them: these new accusers must also have their affidavit read. What do they say? Something of this sort: That Socrates is a doer of evil, and corrupter of the youth, and he does not believe in the gods of the State, and has other new divinities of his own. That is the sort of charge; and now let us examine the particular counts. He says that I am a doer of evil, who corrupt the youth; but I say, O men of Athens, that Meletus is a doer of evil, and the evil is that he makes a joke of a serious matter, and is too ready at bringing other men to trial from a pretended zeal and interest about matters in which he really never had the smallest interest. And the truth of this I will endeavor to prove.

Come hither, Meletus, and let me ask a question of you. You think a great deal about the improvement of youth?

Yes, I do.

Tell the judges, then, who is their improver; for you must know, as you have taken the pains to discover their corrupter, and are citing and accusing me before them. Speak, then, and tell the judges who their improver is. Observe, Meletus, that you are silent, and have nothing to say. But is not this rather disgraceful, and a very considerable proof of what I was saying, that you have no interest in the matter? Speak up, friend, and tell us who their improver is.

The laws.

But that, my good sir, is not my meaning. I want to know who the person is, who, in the first place, knows the laws.

The judges, Socrates, who are present in court.

What do you mean to say, Meletus, that they are able to instruct and improve youth?

Certainly they are.

What, all of them, or some only and not others?

All of them.

By the goddess Here, that is good news! There are plenty of improvers, then. And what do you say of the audience—do they improve them?

Yes, they do.

And the Senators?

Yes, the Senators improve them.

But perhaps the ecclesiasts corrupt them?—or do they too improve them?

They improve them.

Then every Athenian improves and elevates them; all with the exception of myself; and I alone am their corrupter? Is that what you affirm?

That is what I stoutly affirm.

I am very unfortunate if that is true. But suppose I ask you a question: Would you say that this also holds true in the case of horses? Does one man do them harm and all the world good? Is not the exact opposite of this true? One man is able to do them good, or at least not many; the trainer of horses, that is to say, does them good, and others who have to do with them rather injure them? Is not that true, Meletus, of horses, or any other animals? Yes, certainly. Whether you and Anytus say yes or no, that is no matter. Happy indeed would be the condition of youth if they had one corrupter only, and all the rest of the world were their improvers. And you, Meletus, have sufficiently shown that you never had a thought about the young: your carelessness is seen in your not caring about matters spoken of in this very indictment.

And now, Meletus, I must ask you another question: Which is better, to live among bad citizens, or among good ones? Answer, friend, I say; for that is a question which may be easily answered. Do not the good do their neighbors good, and the bad do them evil?

Certainly.

And is there anyone who would rather be injured than benefited by those who live with him? Answer, my good friend; the law requires you to answer—does anyone like to be injured?

Certainly not.

And when you accuse me of corrupting and deteriorating the youth, do you allege that I corrupt them intentionally or unintentionally?

Intentionally, I say.

But you have just admitted that the good do their neighbors good, and the evil do them evil. Now is that a truth which your superior wisdom has recognized thus early in life, and am I, at my age, in such darkness and ignorance as not to know that if a man with whom I have to live is corrupted by me, I am very likely to be harmed by him, and yet I corrupt him, and intentionally, too? that is what you are saying, and of that you will never persuade me or any other human being. But either I do not corrupt them, or I corrupt them unintentionally, so that on either view of the case you lie. If my offence is unintentional, the law has no cognizance of unintentional offences: you ought to have taken me privately, and warned and admonished me; for if I had been better advised, I should have left off doing what I only did unintentionally—no doubt I should; whereas you hated to converse with me or teach me, but you indicted me in this court, which is a place not of instruction, but of punishment.

I have shown, Athenians, as I was saying, that Meletus has no care at all, great or small, about the matter. But still I should like to know, Meletus, in what I am affirmed to corrupt the young. I suppose you mean, as I infer from your indictment, that I teach them not to acknowledge the gods which the State acknowledges, but some other new divinities or spiritual agencies in their stead. These are the lessons which corrupt the youth, as you say.

Yes, that I say emphatically.

Then, by the gods, Meletus, of whom we are speaking, tell me and the court, in somewhat plainer terms, what you mean! for I do not as yet understand whether you affirm that I teach others to acknowledge some gods, and therefore do believe in gods and am not an entire atheist—this you do not lay to my charge; but only that they are not the same gods which the city recognizes—the charge is that they are different gods. Or, do you mean to say that I am an atheist simply, and a teacher of atheism?

I mean the latter—that you are a complete atheist.

That is an extraordinary statement, Meletus. Why do you say that? Do you mean that I do not believe in the god-head of the sun or moon, which is the common creed of all men?

I assure you, judges, that he does not believe in them; for he says that the sun is stone, and the moon earth.

Friend Meletus, you think that you are accusing Anaxagoras; and you have but a bad opinion of the judges, if you fancy them ignorant to such a degree as not to know that those doctrines are found in the books of Anaxagoras the Clazomenian, who is full of them. And these are the doctrines which the youth are said to learn of Socrates, when there are not unfrequently exhibitions of them at the theatre (price of admission one drachma at the most); and they might cheaply purchase them, and laugh at Socrates if he pretends to father such eccentricities. And so, Meletus, you really think that I do not believe in any god?

I swear by Zeus that you believe absolutely in none at all.

You are a liar, Meletus, not believed even by yourself. For I cannot help thinking, O men of Athens, that Meletus is reckless and impudent, and that he has written this indictment in a spirit of mere wantonness and youthful bravado. Has he not compounded a riddle, thinking to try me? He said to himself: I shall see whether this wise Socrates will discover my ingenious contradiction, or whether I shall be able to deceive him and the rest of them. For he certainly does appear to me to contradict himself in the indictment as much as if he said that Socrates is guilty of not believing in the gods, and yet of believing in them—but this surely is a piece of fun.

I should like you, O men of Athens, to join me in examining what I conceive to be his inconsistency; and do you, Meletus, answer. And I must remind you that you are not to interrupt me if I speak in my accustomed manner.

Did ever man, Meletus, believe in the existence of human things, and not of human beings? . . . I wish, men of Athens, that he would answer, and not be always trying to get up an interruption. Did ever any man believe in horsemanship, and not in horses? or in flute-playing, and not in flute-players? No, my friend; I will answer to you and to the court, as you refuse to answer for yourself.

There is no man who ever did. But now please to answer the next question: Can a man believe in spiritual and divine agencies, and not in spirits or demigods?

He cannot.

I am glad that I have extracted that answer, by the assistance of the court; nevertheless you swear in the indictment that I teach and believe in divine or spiritual agencies (new or old, no matter for that); at any rate, I believe in spiritual agencies, as you say and swear in the affidavit; but if I believe in divine beings, I must believe in spirits or demigods; is not that true? Yes, that is true, for I may assume that your silence gives assent to that. Now what are spirits or demigods? are they not either gods or the sons of gods? Is that true?

Yes, that is true.

But this is just the ingenious riddle of which I was speaking: the demigods or spirits are gods, and you say first that I don't believe in gods, and then again that I do believe in gods; that is, if I believe in demigods. For if the demigods are the illegitimate sons of gods, whether by the Nymphs or by any other mothers, as is thought, that, as all men will allow, necessarily implies the existence of their parents. You might as well affirm the existence of mules, and deny that of horses and asses. Such nonsense, Meletus, could only have been intended by you as a trial of me. You have put this into the indictment because you had nothing real of which to accuse me. But no one who has a particle of understanding will ever be convinced by you that the same man can believe in divine and superhuman things, and yet not believe that there are gods and demigods and heroes.

I have said enough in answer to the charge of Meletus: any elaborate defence is unnecessary; but as I was saying before, I certainly have many enemies, and this is what will be my destruction if I am destroyed; of that I am certain; not Meletus, nor yet Anytus, but the envy and detraction of the world, which has been the death of many good men, and will probably be the death of many more; there is no danger of my being the last of them.

Someone will say: And are you not ashamed, Socrates, of a course of life which is likely to bring you to an untimely end? To him I may fairly answer: There you are mistaken: a man who is good for anything ought not to calculate the chance of living or dying; he ought only to consider whether in doing anything he is doing right or wrong—acting the part of a good man or of a bad. Whereas, according to your view, the heroes who fell at Troy were not good for much, and the son of Thetis above all, who altogether despised danger in comparison with disgrace; and when his goddess mother said to him, in his eagerness to slay Hector, that if he avenged his companion Patroclus, and slew Hector, he would die himself—"Fate," as she said, "waits upon you next after Hector"; he, hearing this, utterly despised danger and death, and instead of fearing them, feared rather to live in dishonor, and not to avenge his friend. "Let me die next," he replies, "and be avenged of my enemy, rather than abide here by the beaked ships, a scorn and a burden of the earth." Had Achilles any thought of death and danger? For wherever a man's place is, whether the place which he has chosen or that in which he has been placed by a commander, there he ought to remain in the hour of danger; he should not think of death or of anything, but of disgrace. And this, O men of Athens, is a true saying.

Strange, indeed, would be my conduct, O men of Athens, if I who, when I was ordered by the generals whom you chose to command me at Potidæa and Amphipolis and Delium, remained where they placed me, like any other man, facing death—if, I say, now, when, as I conceive and imagine, God orders me to fulfil the philosopher's mission of searching into myself and other men, I were to desert my post through fear of death, or any other fear; that would indeed be strange, and I might justly be arraigned in court for denying the existence of the gods, if I disobeyed the oracle because I was afraid of death: then I should be fancying that I was wise when I was not wise. For this fear of death is indeed the pretence of wisdom, and not real wisdom, being the appearance of knowing the unknown; since no one knows whether death, which they in their fear apprehend to be the greatest evil, may not be the greatest good. Is there not here conceit of knowledge, which is a disgraceful sort of ignorance? And this is the point in which, as I think, I am superior to men in general, and in which I might perhaps fancy myself wiser than other men—that whereas I know but little of the world below, I do not suppose that I know: but I do know that injustice and disobedience to a better, whether God or man, is evil and dishonorable, and I will never fear or avoid a possible good rather than a certain evil. And therefore if you let me go now, and reject the counsels of Anytus, who said that if I were not put to death I ought not to have been prosecuted, and that if I escape now, your sons will all be utterly ruined by listening to my words—if you say to me, Socrates, this time we will not mind Anytus, and will let you off, but upon one condition, that you are not to inquire and speculate in this way any more, and that if you are caught doing this again you shall die—if this was the condition on which you let me go, I should reply: Men of Athens, I honor and love you; but I shall obey God rather than you, and while I have life and strength I shall never cease from the practice and teaching of philosophy, exhorting anyone whom I meet after my manner, and convincing him, saying: O my friend, why do you who are a citizen of the great and mighty and wise city of Athens, care so much about laying up the greatest amount of money and honor and reputation, and so little about wisdom and truth and the greatest improvement of the soul, which you never regard or heed at all? Are you not ashamed of this? And if the person with whom I am arguing says: Yes, but I do care; I do not depart or let him go at once; I interrogate and examine and cross-examine him, and if I think that he has no virtue, but only says that he has, I reproach him with undervaluing the greater, and overvaluing the less. And this I should say to everyone whom I meet, young and old, citizen and alien, but especially to the citizens, inasmuch as they are my brethren. For this is the command of God, as I would have you know; and I believe that to this day no greater good has ever happened in the State than my service to the God. For I do nothing but go about persuading you all, old and young alike, not to take thought for your persons and your properties, but first and chiefly to care about the greatest improvement of the soul. I tell you that virtue is not given by money, but that from virtue come money and every other good of man, public as well as private. This is my teaching, and if this is the doctrine which corrupts the youth, my influence is ruinous indeed. But if anyone says that this is not my teaching, he is speaking an untruth. Wherefore, O men of Athens, I say to you, do as Anytus bids or not as Anytus bids, and either acquit me or not; but whatever you do, know that I shall never alter my ways, not even if I have to die many times.

Men of Athens, do not interrupt, but hear me; there was an agreement between us that you should hear me out. And I think that what I am going to say will do you good: for I have something more to say, at which you may be inclined to cry out; but I beg that you will not do this. I would have you know that, if you kill such a one as I am, you will injure yourselves more than you will injure me. Meletus and Anytus will not injure me: they cannot; for it is not in the nature of things that a bad man should injure a better than himself. I do not deny that he may, perhaps, kill him, or drive him into exile, or deprive him of civil rights; and he may imagine, and others may imagine, that he is doing him a great injury: but in that I do not agree with him; for the evil of doing as Anytus is doing—of unjustly taking away another man's life—is greater far. And now, Athenians, I am not going to argue for my own sake, as you may think, but for yours, that you may not sin against the God, or lightly reject his boon by condemning me. For if you kill me you will not easily find another like me, who, if I may use such a ludicrous figure of speech, am a sort of gadfly, given to the State by the God; and the State is like a great and noble steed who is tardy in his motions owing to his very size, and requires to be stirred into life. I am that gadfly which God has given the State and all day long and in all places am always fastening upon you, arousing and persuading and reproaching you. And as you will not easily find another like me, I would advise you to spare me. I dare say that you may feel irritated at being suddenly awakened when you are caught napping; and you may think that if you were to strike me dead, as Anytus advises, which you easily might, then you would sleep on for the remainder of your lives, unless God in his care of you gives you another gadfly. And that I am given to you by God is proved by this: that if I had been like other men, I should not have neglected all my own concerns, or patiently seen the neglect of them during all these years, and have been doing yours, coming to you individually, like a father or elder brother, exhorting you to regard virtue; this, I say, would not be like human nature. And had I gained anything, or if my exhortations had been paid, there would have been some sense in that: but now, as you will perceive, not even the impudence of my accusers dares to say that I have ever exacted or sought pay of anyone; they have no witness of that. And I have a witness of the truth of what I say; my poverty is a sufficient witness.

Someone may wonder why I go about in private, giving advice and busying myself with the concerns of others, but do not venture to come forward in public and advise the State. I will tell you the reason of this. You have often heard me speak of an oracle or sign which comes to me, and is the divinity which Meletus ridicules in the indictment. This sign I have had ever since I was a child. The sign is a voice which comes to me and always forbids me to do something which I am going to do, but never commands me to do anything, and this is what stands in the way of my being a politician. And rightly, as I think. For I am certain, O men of Athens, that if I had engaged in politics, I should have perished long ago and done no good either to you or to myself. And don't be offended at my telling you the truth: for the truth is that no man who goes to war with you or any other multitude, honestly struggling against the commission of unrighteousness and wrong in the State, will save his life; he who will really fight for the right, if he would live even for a little while, must have a private station and not a public one.

I can give you as proofs of this, not words only, but deeds, which you value more than words. Let me tell you a passage of my own life, which will prove to you that I should never have yielded to injustice from any fear of death, and that if I had not yielded I should have died at once. I will tell you a story—tasteless, perhaps, and commonplace, but nevertheless true. The only office of State which I ever held, O men of Athens, was that of Senator; the tribe Antiochis, which is my tribe, had the presidency at the trial of the generals who had not taken up the bodies of the slain after the battle of Arginusæ; and you proposed to try them all together, which was illegal, as you all thought afterwards; but at the time I was the only one of the Prytanes who was opposed to the illegality, and I gave my vote against you; and when the orators threatened to impeach and arrest me, and have me taken away, and you called and shouted, I made up my mind that I would run the risk, having law and justice with me, rather than take part in your injustice because I feared imprisonment and death. This happened in the days of the democracy. But when the oligarchy of the Thirty was in power, they sent for me and four others into the rotunda, and bade us bring Leon the Salaminian from Salamis, as they wanted to execute him. This was a specimen of the sort of commands which they were always giving with the view of implicating as many as possible in their crimes; and then I showed, not in words only, but in deed, that, if I may be allowed to use such an expression, I cared not a straw for death, and that my only fear was the fear of doing an unrighteous or unholy thing. For the strong arm of that oppressive power did not frighten me into doing wrong; and when we came out of the rotunda the other four went to Salamis and fetched Leon, but I went quietly home. For which I might have lost my life, had not the power of the Thirty shortly afterwards come to an end. And to this many will witness.

Now do you really imagine that I could have survived all these years, if I had led a public life, supposing that like a good man I had always supported the right and had made justice, as I ought, the first thing? No, indeed, men of Athens, neither I nor any other. But I have been always the same in all my actions, public as well as private, and never have I yielded any base compliance to those who are slanderously termed my disciples or to any other. For the truth is that I have no regular disciples: but if anyone likes to come and hear me while I am pursuing my mission, whether he be young or old, he may freely come. Nor do I converse with those who pay only, and not with those who do not pay; but anyone, whether he be rich or poor, may ask and answer me and listen to my words; and whether he turns out to be a bad man or a good one, that cannot be justly laid to my charge, as I never taught him anything. And if anyone says that he has ever learned or heard anything from me in private which all the world has not heard, I should like you to know that he is speaking an untruth.

But I shall be asked, Why do people delight in continually conversing with you? I have told you already, Athenians, the whole truth about this: they like to hear the cross-examination of the pretenders to wisdom; there is amusement in this. And this is a duty which the God has imposed upon me, as I am assured by oracles, visions, and in every sort of way in which the will of divine power was ever signified to anyone. This is true, O Athenians; or, if not true, would be soon refuted. For if I am really corrupting the youth, and have corrupted some of them already, those of them who have grown up and have become sensible that I gave them bad advice in the days of their youth should come forward as accusers and take their revenge; and if they do not like to come themselves, some of their relatives, fathers, brothers, or other kinsmen, should say what evil their families suffered at my hands. Now is their time. Many of them I see in the court. There is Crito, who is of the same age and of the same *deme* with myself; and there is Critobulus his son, whom I also see. Then again there is Lysanias of Sphettus, who is the father of Æschines—he is present; and also there is Antiphon of Cephisus, who is the father of Epignes; and there are the brothers of several who have associated with me. There is Nicostratus the son of Theosdotides, and the brother of Theodotus (now Theodotus himself is dead, and therefore he, at any rate, will not seek to stop him); and there is Paralus the son of Demodocus, who had a brother Theages; and Adeimantus the son of Ariston, whose brother Plato is present; and Æantodorus, who is the brother of Apollodorus, whom I also see. I might mention a great many others, any of whom Meletus should have produced as witnesses in the course of his speech; and let him still produce them, if he has forgotten; I will make way for him. And let him say, if he has any testimony of the sort which he can produce. Nay, Athenians, the very opposite is the truth. For all these are ready to witness on behalf of the corrupter, of the destroyer of their kindred, as Meletus and Anytus call me; not the corrupted youth only—there might have been a motive for that—but their uncorrupted elder relatives. Why should they too support me with their testimony? Why, indeed, except for the sake of truth and justice, and because they know that I am speaking the truth, and that Meletus is lying.

Well, Athenians, this and the like of this is nearly all the defence which I have to offer. Yet a word more. Perhaps there may be someone who is offended at me, when he calls to mind how he himself, on a similar or even a less serious occasion, had recourse to prayers and supplications with many tears, and how he produced his children in court, which was a moving spectacle, together with a posse of his relations and friends; whereas I, who am probably in danger of my life, will do none of these things. Perhaps this may come into his mind, and he may be set against me, and vote in anger because he is displeased at this. Now if there be such a person among you, which I am far from affirming, I may fairly reply to him: My friend, I am a man, and like other men, a creature of flesh and blood, and not of wood or stone, as Homer says; and I have a family, yes, and sons, O Athenians, three in number, one of whom is growing up, and the two others are still young; and yet I will not bring any of them hither in order to petition you for an acquittal. And why not? Not from any self-will or disregard of you. Whether I am or am not afraid of death is another question, of which I will not now speak. But my reason simply is that I feel such conduct to be discreditable to myself, and you, and the whole State. One who has reached my years, and who has a name for wisdom, whether deserved or not, ought not to debase himself. At any rate, the world has decided that Socrates is in some way superior to other men. And if those among you who are said to be superior in wisdom and courage, and any other virtue, demean themselves in this way, how shameful is their conduct! I have seen men of reputation, when they have been condemned, behaving in the strangest manner: they seemed to fancy that they were going to suffer something dreadful if they died, and that they could be immortal if you only allowed them to live; and I think that they were a dishonor to the State, and that any stranger coming in would say of them that the most eminent men of Athens, to whom the Athenians themselves give honor and command, are no better than women. And I say that these things ought not to be done by those of us who are of reputation; and if they are done, you ought not to permit them; you ought rather to show that you are more inclined to condemn, not the man who is quiet, but the man who gets up a doleful scene, and makes the city ridiculous.

But, setting aside the question of dishonor, there seems to be something wrong in petitioning a judge, and thus procuring an acquittal instead of informing and convincing him. For his duty is, not to make a present of justice, but to give judgment; and he has sworn that he will judge according to the laws, and not according to his own good pleasure; and neither he nor we should get into the habit of perjuring ourselves—there can be no piety in that. Do not then require me to do what I consider dishonorable and impious and wrong, especially now, when I am being tried for impiety on the indictment of Meletus. For if, O men of Athens, by force of persuasion and entreaty, I could overpower your oaths, then I should be teaching you to believe that there are no gods, and convict myself, in my own defence, of not believing in them. But that is not the case; for I do believe that there are gods, and in a far higher sense than that in which any of my accusers believe in them. And to you and to God I commit my cause, to be determined by you as is best for you and me.

THERE are many reasons why I am not grieved, O men of Athens, at the vote of condemnation. I expected this, and am only surprised that the votes are so nearly equal; for I had thought that the majority against me would have been far larger; but now, had thirty votes gone over to the other side, I should have been acquitted. And I may say that I have escaped Meletus. And I may say more; for without the assistance of Anytus and Lycon, he would not have had a fifth part of the votes, as the law requires, in which case he would have incurred a fine of a thousand drachmæ, as is evident.

And so he proposes death as the penalty. And what shall I propose on my part, O men of Athens? Clearly that which is my due. And what is that which I ought to pay or to receive? What shall be done to the man who has never had the wit to be idle during his whole life; but has been careless of what the many care about—wealth, and family interests, and military offices, and speaking in the assembly, and magistracies, and plots, and parties. Reflecting that I was really too honest a man to follow in this way and live, I did not go where I could do no good to you or to myself; but where I could do the greatest good privately to everyone of you, thither

I went, and sought to persuade every man among you that he must look to himself, and seek virtue and wisdom before he looks to his private interests, and look to the State before he looks to the interests of the State; and that this should be the order which he observes in all his actions. What shall be done to such a one? Doubtless some good thing, O men of Athens, if he has his reward; and the good should be of a kind suitable to him. What would be a reward suitable to a poor man who is your benefactor, who desires leisure that he may instruct you? There can be no more fitting reward than maintenance in the Prytaneum, O men of Athens, a reward which he deserves far more than the citizen who has won the prize at Olympia in the horse or chariot race, whether the chariots were drawn by two horses or by many. For I am in want, and he has enough; and he only gives you the appearance of happiness, and I give you the reality. And if I am to estimate the penalty justly, I say that maintenance in the Prytaneum is the just return.

Perhaps you may think that I am braving you in saying this, as in what I said before about the tears and prayers. But that is not the case. I speak rather because I am convinced that I never intentionally wronged anyone, although I cannot convince you of that—for we have had a short conversation only; but if there were a law at Athens, such as there is in other cities, that a capital cause should not be decided in one day, then I believe that I should have convinced you; but now the time is too short. I cannot in a moment refute great slanders; and, as I am convinced that I never wronged another, I will assuredly not wrong myself. I will not say of myself that I deserve any evil, or propose any penalty. Why should I? Because I am afraid of the penalty of death which Meletus proposes? When I do not know whether death is a good or an evil, why should I propose a penalty which would certainly be an evil? Shall I say imprisonment? And why should I live in prison, and be the slave of the magistrates of the year—of the Eleven? Or shall the penalty be a fine, and imprisonment until the fine is paid? There is the same objection. I should have to lie in prison, for money I have none, and I cannot pay. And if I say exile (and this may possibly be the penalty which you will affix), I must indeed be blinded by the love of life if I were to consider that when you, who are my own citizens, cannot endure my discourses and words, and have found them so grievous and odious that you would fain have done with them, others are likely to endure me. No, indeed, men of Athens, that is not very likely. And what a life should I lead, at my age, wandering from city to city, living in ever-changing exile, and always being driven out! For I am quite sure that into whatever place I go, as here so also there, the young men will come to me; and if I drive them away, their elders will drive me out at their desire: and if I let them come, their fathers and friends will drive me out for their sakes. Someone will say: Yes, Socrates, but cannot you hold your tongue, and then you may go into a foreign city, and no one will interfere with you? Now I have great difficulty in making you understand my answer to this. For if I tell you that this would be a disobedience to a divine command, and therefore that I cannot hold my tongue, you will not believe that I am serious; and if I say again that the greatest good of man is daily to converse about virtue, and all that concerning which you hear me examining myself and others, and that the life which is unexamined is not worth living—that you are still less likely to believe. And yet what I say is true, although a thing of which it is hard for me to persuade you. Moreover, I am not accustomed to think that I deserve any punishment. Had I money I might have proposed to give you what I had, and have been none the worse. But you see that I have none, and can only ask you to proportion the fine to my means. However, I think that I could afford a mina, and therefore I propose that penalty; Plato, Crito, Critobulus, and Apollodorus, my friends here, bid me say thirty minæ, and they will be the sureties. Well then, say thirty minæ, let that be the penalty; for that they will be ample security to you.

Not much time will be gained, O Athenians, in return for the evil name which you will get from the detractors of the city, who will say that you killed Socrates, a wise man; for they will call me wise even although I am not wise when they want to reproach you. If you had waited a little while, your desire would have been fulfilled in the course of nature. For I am far advanced in years, as you may perceive, and not far from death. I am speaking now only to those of you who have condemned me to death. And I have another thing to say to them: You think that I was convicted through deficiency of words—I mean, that if I had thought fit to leave nothing undone, nothing unsaid, I might have gained an acquittal. Not so; the deficiency which led to my conviction was not of words—certainly not. But I had not the boldness or impudence or inclination to address you as you would have liked me to address you, weeping and wailing and lamenting, and saying and doing many things which you have been accustomed to hear from others, and which, as I say, are unworthy of me. But I thought that I ought not to do anything common or mean in the hour of danger: nor do I now repent of the manner of my defence, and I would rather die having spoken after my manner, than speak in your manner and live. For neither in war nor yet at law ought any man to use every way of escaping death. For often in battle there is no doubt that if a man will throw away his arms, and fall on his knees before his pursuers, he may escape death; and in other dangers there are other ways of escaping death, if a man is willing to say and do anything. The difficulty, my friends, is not in avoiding death, but in avoiding unrighteousness; for that runs faster than death. I am old and move slowly, and the slower runner has overtaken me, and my accusers are keen and quick, and the faster runner, who is unrighteousness, has overtaken them. And now I depart hence condemned by you to suffer the penalty of death, and they, too, go their ways condemned by the truth to suffer the penalty of villainy and wrong; and I must abide by my award—let them abide by theirs. I suppose that these things may be regarded as fated—and I think that they are well.

And now, O men who have condemned me, I would fain prophesy to you; for I am about to die, and that is the hour in which men are gifted with prophetic power. And I prophesy to you who are my murderers, that immediately after my death punishment far heavier than you have inflicted on me will surely await you. Me you have killed because you wanted to escape the accuser, and not to give an account of your lives. But that will not be as you suppose: far otherwise. For I say that there will be more accusers of you than there are now; accusers whom hitherto I have restrained: and as they are younger they will be more severe with you, and you will be more offended at them. For if you think that by killing men you can avoid the accuser censuring your lives, you are mistaken; that is not a way of escape which is either possible or honorable; the easiest and noblest way is not to be crushing others, but to be improving yourselves. This is the prophecy which I utter before my departure, to the judges who have condemned me.

Friends, who would have acquitted me, I would like also to talk with you about this thing which has happened, while the magistrates are busy, and before I go to the place at which I must die. Stay then awhile, for we may as well talk with one another while there is time. You are my friends, and I should like to show you the meaning of this event which has happened to me. O my judges—for you I may truly call judges—I should like to tell you of a wonderful circumstance. Hitherto the familiar oracle within me has constantly been in the habit of opposing me even about trifles, if I was going to make a slip or error about anything; and now as you see there has come upon me that which may be thought, and is generally believed to be, the last and worst evil. But the oracle made no sign of opposition, either as I was leaving my house and going out in the morning, or when I was going up into this court, or while I was speaking, at anything which I was going to say; and yet I have often been stopped in the middle of a speech; but now in nothing I either said or did touching this matter has the oracle opposed me. What do I take to be the explanation of this? I will tell you. I regard this as a proof that what has happened to me is a good, and that those of us who think that death is an evil are in error. This is a great proof to me of what I am saying, for the customary sign would surely have opposed me had I been going to evil and not to good.

Let us reflect in another way, and we shall see that there is great reason to hope that death is a good, for one of two things: either death is a state of nothingness and utter unconsciousness, or, as men say, there is a change and migration of the soul from this world to another. Now if you suppose that there is no consciousness, but a sleep like the sleep of him who is undisturbed even by the sight of dreams, death will be an unspeakable gain. For if a person were to select the night in which his sleep was undisturbed even by dreams, and were to compare with this the other days and nights of his life, and then were to tell us how many days and nights he had passed in the course of his life better and more pleasantly than this one, I think that any man, I will not say a private man, but even the great king, will not find many such days or nights, when compared with the others. Now if death is like this, I say that to die is gain; for eternity is then only a single night. But if death is the journey to another place, and there, as men say, all the dead are, what good, O my friends and judges, can be greater than this? If indeed when the pilgrim arrives in the world below, he is delivered from the professors of justice in this world, and finds the true judges who are said to give judgment there, Minos and Rhadamanthus and Æacus and Triptolemus, and other sons of God who were righteous in their own life, that pilgrimage will be worth making. What would not a man give if he might converse with Orpheus and Musæus and Hesiod and Homer? Nay, if this be true, let me die again and again. I, too, shall have a wonderful interest in a place where I can converse with Palamedes, and Ajax the son of Telamon, and other heroes of old, who have suffered death through an unjust judgment; and there will be no small pleasure, as I think, in comparing my own sufferings with theirs. Above all, I shall be able to continue my search into true and false knowledge; as in this world, so also in that; I shall find out who is wise, and who pretends to be wise, and is not. What would not a man give, O judges, to be able to examine the leader of the great Trojan expedition; or Odysseus or Sisyphus, or numberless others, men and women too! What infinite delight would there be in conversing with them and asking them questions! For in that world they do not put a man to death for this; certainly not. For besides being happier in that world than in this, they will be immortal, if what is said is true.

Wherefore, O judges, be of good cheer about death, and know this of a truth—that no evil can happen to a good man, either in life or after death. He and his are not neglected by the gods; nor has my own approaching end happened by mere chance. But I see clearly that to die and be released was better for me; and therefore the oracle gave no sign. For which reason also, I am not angry with my accusers, or my condemners; they have done me no harm, although neither of them meant to do me any good; and for this I may gently blame them.

Still I have a favor to ask of them. When my sons are grown up, I would ask you, O my friends, to punish them; and I would have you trouble them, as I have troubled you, if they seem to care about riches, or anything, more than about virtue; or if they pretend to be something when they are really nothing—then reprove them, as I have reproved you, for not caring about that for which they ought to care, and thinking that they are something when they are really nothing. And if you do this, I and my sons will have received justice at your hands.

The hour of departure has arrived, and we go our ways—I to die, and you to live. Which is better, God only knows.

CRITO

PERSONS OF THE DIALOGUE

Socrates   Crito

Scene: *The Prison of Socrates*

Socrates

WHY have you come at this hour, Crito? it must be quite early.

Crito. Yes, certainly.

Soc. What is the exact time?

Cr. The dawn is breaking.

Soc. I wonder the keeper of the prison would let you in.

Cr. He knows me because I often come, Socrates; moreover, I have done him a kindness.

Soc. And are you only just come?

Cr. No, I came some time ago.

Soc. Then why did you sit and say nothing, instead of awakening me at once?

Cr. Why, indeed, Socrates, I myself would rather not have all this sleeplessness and sorrow. But I have been wondering at your peaceful slumbers, and that was the reason why I did not awaken you, because I wanted you to be out of pain. I have always thought you happy in the calmness of your temperament; but never did I see the like of the easy, cheerful way in which you bear this calamity.

Soc. Why, Crito, when a man has reached my age he ought not to be repining at the prospect of death.

Cr. And yet other old men find themselves in similar misfortunes, and age does not prevent them from repining.

Soc. That may be. But you have not told me why you come at this early hour.

Cr. I come to bring you a message which is sad and painful; not, as I believe, to yourself, but to all of us who are your friends, and saddest of all to me.

Soc. What! I suppose that the ship has come from Delos, on the arrival of which I am to die?

Cr. No, the ship has not actually arrived, but she will probably be here to-day, as persons who have come from Sunium tell me that they have left her there; and therefore to-morrow, Socrates, will be the last day of your life.

Soc. Very well, Crito; if such is the will of God, I am willing; but my belief is that there will be a delay of a day.

Cr. Why do you say this?

Soc. I will tell you. I am to die on the day after the arrival of the ship?

Cr. Yes; that is what the authorities say.

Soc. But I do not think that the ship will be here until to-morrow; this I gather from a vision which I had last night, or rather only just now, when you fortunately allowed me to sleep.

Cr. And what was the nature of the vision?

Soc. There came to me the likeness of a woman, fair and comely, clothed in white raiment, who called to me and said: O Socrates—

"The third day hence, to Phthia shalt thou go."

Cr. What a singular dream, Socrates!

Soc. There can be no doubt about the meaning Crito, I think.

Cr. Yes: the meaning is only too clear. But, O! my beloved Socrates, let me entreat you once more to take my advice and escape. For if you die I shall not only lose a friend who can never be replaced, but there is another evil: people who do not know you and me will believe that I might have saved you if I had been willing to give money, but that I did not care. Now, can there be a worse disgrace than this—that I should be thought to value money more than the life of a friend? For the many will not be persuaded that I wanted you to escape, and that you refused.

Soc. But why, my dear Crito, should we care about the opinion of the many? Good men, and they are the only persons who are worth considering, will think of these things truly as they happened.

Cr. But do you see, Socrates, that the opinion of the many must be regarded, as is evident in your own case, because they can do the very greatest evil to anyone who has lost their good opinion?

Soc. I only wish, Crito, that they could; for then they could also do the greatest good, and that would be well. But the truth is, that they can do neither good nor evil: they cannot make a man wise or make him foolish; and whatever they do is the result of chance.

Cr. Well, I will not dispute about that; but please to tell me, Socrates, whether you are not acting out of regard to me and your other friends: are you not afraid that if you escape hence we may get into trouble with the informers for having stolen you away, and lose either the whole or a great part of our property; or that even a worse evil may happen to us? Now, if this is your fear, be at ease; for in order to save you, we ought surely to run this or even a greater risk; be persuaded, then, and do as I say.

Soc. Yes, Crito, that is one fear which you mention, but by no means the only one.

Cr. Fear not. There are persons who at no great cost are willing to save you and bring you out of prison; and as for the informers, you may observe that they are far from being exorbitant in their demands; a little money will satisfy them. My means, which, as I am sure, are ample, are at your service, and if you have a scruple about spending all mine, here are strangers who will give you the use of theirs; and one of them, Simmias the Theban, has brought a sum of money for this very purpose; and Cebes and many others are willing to spend their money too. I say, therefore, do not on that account hesitate about making your escape, and do not say, as you did in the court, that you will have a difficulty in knowing what to do with yourself if you escape. For men will love you in other places to which you may go, and not in Athens only; there are friends of mine in Thessaly, if you like to go to them, who will value and protect you, and no Thessalian will give you any trouble. Nor can I think that you are justified, Socrates, in betraying your own life when you might be saved; this is playing into the hands of your enemies and destroyers; and moreover I should say that you were betraying your children; for you might bring them up and educate them; instead of which you go away and leave them, and they will have to take their chance; and if they do not meet with the usual fate of orphans, there will be small thanks to you. No man should bring children into the world who is unwilling to persevere to the end in their nurture and education. But you are choosing the easier part, as I think, not the better and manlier, which would rather have become one who professes virtue in all his actions, like yourself. And, indeed, I am ashamed not only of you, but of us who are your friends, when I reflect that this entire business of yours will be attributed to our want of courage. The trial need never have come on, or might have been brought to another issue; and the end of all, which is the crowning absurdity, will seem to have been permitted by us, through cowardice and baseness, who might have saved you, as you might have saved yourself, if we had been good for anything (for there was no difficulty in escaping); and we did not see how disgraceful, Socrates, and also miserable all this will be to us as well as to you. Make your mind up then, or rather have your mind already made up, for the time of deliberation is over, and there is only one thing to be done, which must be done, if at all, this very night, and which any delay will render all but impossible; I beseech you therefore, Socrates, to be persuaded by me, and to do as I say.

Soc. Dear Crito, your zeal is invaluable, if a right one; but if wrong, the greater the zeal the greater the evil; and therefore we ought to consider whether these things shall be done or not. For I am and always have been one of those natures who must be guided by reason, whatever the reason may be which upon reflection appears to me to be the best; and now that this fortune has come upon me, I cannot put away the reasons which I have before given: the principles which I have hitherto honored and revered I still honor, and unless we can find other and better principles on the instant, I am certain not to agree with you; no, not even if the power of the multitude could inflict many more imprisonments, confiscations, deaths, frightening us like children with hobgoblin terrors. But what will be the fairest way of considering the question? Shall I return to your old argument about the opinions of men, some of which are to be regarded, and others, as we were saying, are not to be regarded? Now were we right in maintaining this before I was condemned? And has the argument which was once good now proved to be talk for the sake of talking; in fact an amusement only, and altogether vanity? That is what I want to consider with your help, Crito: whether, under my present circumstances, the argument appears to be in any way different or not; and is to be allowed by me or disallowed. That argument, which, as I believe, is maintained by many who assume to be authorities, was to the effect, as I was saying, that the opinions of some men are to be regarded, and of other men not to be regarded. Now you, Crito, are a disinterested person who are not going to die to-morrow—at least, there is no human probability of this, and you are therefore not liable to be deceived by the circumstances in which you are placed. Tell me, then, whether I am right in saying that some opinions, and the opinions of some men only, are to be valued, and other opinions, and the opinions of other men, are not to be valued. I ask you whether I was right in maintaining this?

Cr. Certainly.

Soc. The good are to be regarded, and not the bad?

Cr. Yes.

Soc. And the opinions of the wise are good, and the opinions of the unwise are evil?

Cr. Certainly.

Soc. And what was said about another matter? Was the disciple in gymnastics supposed to attend to the praise and blame and opinion of every man, or of one man only—his physician or trainer, whoever that was?

Cr. Of one man only.

Soc. And he ought to fear the censure and welcome the praise of that one only, and not of the many?

Cr. That is clear.

Soc. And he ought to live and train, and eat and drink in the way which seems good to his single master who has understanding, rather than according to the opinion of all other men put together?

Cr. True.

Soc. And if he disobeys and disregards the opinion and approval of the one, and regards the opinion of the many who have no understanding, will he not suffer evil?

Cr. Certainly he will.

Soc. And what will the evil be, whither tending and what affecting, in the disobedient person?

Cr. Clearly, affecting the body; that is what is destroyed by the evil.

Soc. Very good; and is not this true, Crito, of other things which we need not separately enumerate? In the matter of just and unjust, fair and foul, good and evil, which are the subjects of our present consultation, ought we to follow the opinion of the many and to fear them; or the opinion of the one man who has understanding, and whom we ought to fear and reverence more than all the rest of the world: and whom deserting we shall destroy and injure that principle in us which may be assumed to be improved by justice and deteriorated by injustice; is there not such a principle?

Cr. Certainly there is, Socrates.

Soc. Take a parallel instance; if, acting under the advice of men who have no understanding, we destroy that which is improvable by health and deteriorated by disease—when that has been destroyed, I say, would life be worth having? And that is—the body?

Cr. Yes.

Soc. Could we live, having an evil and corrupted body?

Cr. Certainly not.

Soc. And will life be worth having, if that higher part of man be depraved, which is improved by justice and deteriorated by injustice? Do we suppose that principle, whatever it may be in man, which has to do with justice and injustice, to be inferior to the body?

Cr. Certainly not.

Soc. More honored, then?

Cr. Far more honored.

Soc. Then, my friend, we must not regard what the many say of us: but what he, the one man who has understanding of just and unjust, will say, and what the truth will say. And therefore you begin in error when you suggest that we should regard the opinion of the many about just and unjust, good and evil, honorable and dishonorable. Well, someone will say, "But the many can kill us."

Cr. Yes, Socrates; that will clearly be the answer.

Soc. That is true; but still I find with surprise that the old argument is, as I conceive, unshaken as ever. And I should like to know whether I may say the same of another proposition—that not life, but a good life, is to be chiefly valued?

Cr. Yes, that also remains.

Soc. And a good life is equivalent to a just and honorable one—that holds also?

Cr. Yes, that holds.

Soc. From these premises I proceed to argue the question whether I ought or ought not to try to escape without the consent of the Athenians: and if I am clearly right in escaping, then I will make the attempt; but if not, I will abstain. The other considerations which you mention, of money and loss of character, and the duty of educating children, are, I fear, only the doctrines of the multitude, who would be as ready to call people to life, if they were able, as they are to put them to death—and with as little reason. But now, since the argument has thus far prevailed, the only question which remains to be considered is, whether we shall do rightly either in escaping or in suffering others to aid in our escape and paying them in money and thanks, or whether we shall not do rightly; and if the latter, then death or any other calamity which may ensue on my remaining here must not be allowed to enter into the calculation.

Cr. I think that you are right, Socrates; how then shall we proceed?

Soc. Let us consider the matter together, and do you either refute me if you can, and I will be convinced; or else cease, my dear friend, from repeating to me that I ought to escape against the wishes of the Athenians: for I am extremely desirous to be persuaded by you, but not against my own better judgment. And now please to consider my first position, and do your best to answer me.

Cr. I will do my best.

Soc. Are we to say that we are never intentionally to do wrong, or that in one way we ought and in another way we ought not to do wrong, or is doing wrong always evil and dishonorable, as I was just now saying, and as has been already acknowledged by us? Are all our former admissions which were made within a few days to be thrown away? And have we, at our age, been earnestly discoursing with one another all our life long only to discover that we are no better than children? Or are we to rest assured, in spite of the opinion of the many, and in spite of consequences whether better or worse, of the truth of what was then said, that injustice is always an evil and dishonor to him who acts unjustly? Shall we affirm that?

Cr. Yes.

Soc. Then we must do no wrong?

Cr. Certainly not.

Soc. Nor when injured injure in return, as the many imagine; for we must injure no one at all?

Cr. Clearly not.

Soc. Again, Crito, may we do evil?

Cr. Surely not, Socrates.

Soc. And what of doing evil in return for evil, which is the morality of the many—is that just or not?

Cr. Not just.

Soc. For doing evil to another is the same as injuring him?

Cr. Very true.

Soc. Then we ought not to retaliate or render evil for evil to anyone, whatever evil we may have suffered from him. But I would have you consider, Crito, whether you really mean what you are saying. For this opinion has never been held, and never will be held, by any considerable number of persons; and those who are agreed and those who are not agreed upon this point have no common ground, and can only despise one another, when they see how widely they differ. Tell me, then, whether you agree with and assent to my first principle, that neither injury nor retaliation nor warding off evil by evil is ever right. And shall that be the premise of our agreement? Or do you decline and dissent from this? For this has been of old and is still my opinion; but, if you are of another opinion, let me hear what you have to say. If, however, you remain of the same mind as formerly, I will proceed to the next step.

Cr. You may proceed, for I have not changed my mind.

Soc. Then I will proceed to the next step, which may be put in the form of a question: Ought a man to do what he admits to be right, or ought he to betray the right?

Cr. He ought to do what he thinks right.

Soc. But if this is true, what is the application? In leaving the prison against the will of the Athenians, do I wrong any? or rather do I not wrong those whom I ought least to wrong? Do I not desert the principles which were acknowledged by us to be just? What do you say?

Cr. I cannot tell, Socrates, for I do not know.

Soc. Then consider the matter in this way: Imagine that I am about to play truant (you may call the proceeding by any name which you like), and the laws and the government come and interrogate me: "Tell us, Socrates," they say; "what are you about? are you going by an act of yours to overturn us—the laws and the whole State, as far as in you lies? Do you imagine that a State can subsist and not be overthrown, in which the decisions of law have no power, but are set aside and overthrown by individuals?" What will be our answer, Crito, to these and the like words? Anyone, and especially a clever rhetorician, will have a good deal to urge about the evil of setting aside the law which requires a sentence to be carried out; and we might reply, "Yes; but the State has injured us and given an unjust sentence." Suppose I say that?

Cr. Very good, Socrates.

Soc. "And was that our agreement with you?" the law would say; "or were you to abide by the sentence of the State?" And if I were to express astonishment at their saying this, the law would probably add: "Answer, Socrates, instead of opening your eyes: you are in the habit of asking and answering questions. Tell us what complaint you have to make against us which justifies you in attempting to destroy us and the State? In the first place did we not bring you into existence? Your father married your mother by our aid and begat you. Say whether you have any objection to urge against those of us who regulate marriage?" None, I should reply. "Or against those of us who regulate the system of nurture and education of children in which you were trained? Were not the laws, who have the charge of this, right in commanding your father to train you in music and gymnastic?" Right, I should reply. "Well, then, since you were brought into the world and nurtured and educated by us, can you deny in the first place that you are our child and slave, as your fathers were before you? And if this is true you are not on equal terms with us; nor can you think that you have a right to do to us what we are doing to you. Would you have any right to strike or revile or do any other evil to a father or to your master, if you had one, when you have been struck or reviled by him, or received some other evil at his hands?—you would not say this? And because we think right to destroy you, do you think that you have any right to destroy us in return, and your country as far as in you lies? And will you, O professor of true virtue, say that you are justified in this? Has a philosopher like you failed to discover that our country is more to be valued and higher and holier far than mother or father or any ancestor, and more to be regarded in the eyes of the gods and of men of understanding? also to be soothed, and gently and reverently entreated when angry, even more than a father, and if not persuaded, obeyed? And when we are punished by her, whether with imprisonment or stripes, the punishment is to be endured in silence; and if she leads us to wounds or death in battle, thither we follow as is right; neither may anyone yield or retreat or leave his rank, but whether in battle or in a court of law, or in any other place, he must do what his city and his country order him; or he must change their view of what is just: and if he may do no violence to his father or mother, much less may he do violence to his country." What answer shall we make to this, Crito? Do the laws speak truly, or do they not?

Cr. I think that they do.

Soc. Then the laws will say: "Consider, Socrates, if this is true, that in your present attempt you are going to do us wrong. For, after having brought you into the world, and nurtured and educated you, and given you and every other citizen a share in every good that we had to give, we further proclaim and give the right to every Athenian, that if he does not like us when he has come of age and has seen the ways of the city, and made our acquaintance, he may go where he pleases and take his goods with him; and none of us laws will forbid him or interfere with him. Any of you who does not like us and the city, and who wants to go to a colony or to any other city, may go where he likes, and take his goods with him. But he who has experience of the manner in which we order justice and administer the State, and still remains, has entered into an implied contract that he will do as we command him. And he who disobeys us is, as we maintain, thrice wrong: first, because in disobeying us he is disobeying his parents; secondly, because we are the authors of his education; thirdly, because he has made an agreement with us that he will duly obey our commands; and he neither obeys them nor convinces us that our commands are wrong; and we do not rudely impose them, but give him the alternative of obeying or convincing us; that is what we offer, and he does neither. These are the sort of accusations to which, as we were saying, you, Socrates, will be exposed if you accomplish your intentions; you, above all other Athenians." Suppose I ask, why is this? they will justly retort upon me that I above all other men have acknowledged the agreement. "There is clear proof," they will say, "Socrates, that we and the city were not displeasing to you. Of all Athenians you have been the most constant resident in the city, which, as you never leave, you may be supposed to love. For you never went out of the city either to see the games, except once when you went to the Isthmus, or to any other place unless when you were on military service; nor did you travel as other men do. Nor had you any curiosity to know other States or their laws: your affections did not go beyond us and our State; we were your especial favorites, and you acquiesced in our government of you; and this is the State in which you begat your children, which is a proof of your satisfaction. Moreover, you might, if you had liked, have fixed the penalty at banishment in the course of the trial—the State which refuses to let you go now would have let you go then. But you pretended that you preferred death to exile, and that you were not grieved at death. And now you have forgotten these fine sentiments, and pay no respect to us, the laws, of whom you are the destroyer; and are doing what only a miserable slave would do, running away and turning your back upon the compacts and agreements which you made as a citizen. And first of all answer this very question: Are we right in saying that you agreed to be governed according to us in deed, and not in word only? Is that true or not?" How shall we answer that, Crito? Must we not agree?

Cr. There is no help, Socrates.

Soc. Then will they not say: "You, Socrates, are breaking the covenants and agreements which you made with us at your leisure, not in any haste or under any compulsion or deception, but having had seventy years to think of them, during which time you were at liberty to leave the city, if we were not to your mind, or if our covenants appeared to you to be unfair. You had your choice, and might have gone either to Lacedæmon or Crete, which you often praise for their good government, or to some other Hellenic or foreign State. Whereas you, above all other Athenians, seemed to be so fond of the State, or, in other words, of us her laws (for who would like a State that has no laws?), that you never stirred out of her: the halt, the blind, the maimed, were not more stationary in her than you were. And now you run away and forsake your agreements. Not so, Socrates, if you will take our advice; do not make yourself ridiculous by escaping out of the city.

"For just consider, if you transgress and err in this sort of way, what good will you do, either to yourself or to your friends? That your friends will be driven into exile and deprived of citizenship, or will lose their property, is tolerably certain; and you yourself, if you fly to one of the neighboring cities, as, for example, Thebes or Megara, both of which are well-governed cities, will come to them as an enemy, Socrates, and their government will be against you, and all patriotic citizens will cast an evil eye upon you as a subverter of the laws, and you will confirm in the minds of the judges the justice of their own condemnation of you. For he who is a corrupter of the laws is more than likely to be corrupter of the young and foolish portion of mankind. Will you then flee from well-ordered cities and virtuous men? and is existence worth having on these terms? Or will you go to them without shame, and talk to them, Socrates? And what will you say to them? What you say here about virtue and justice and institutions and laws being the best things among men? Would that be decent of you? Surely not. But if you go away from well-governed States to Crito's friends in Thessaly, where there is great disorder and license, they will be charmed to have the tale of your escape from prison, set off with ludicrous particulars of the manner in which you were wrapped in a goatskin or some other disguise, and metamorphosed as the fashion of runaways is—that is very likely; but will there be no one to remind you that in your old age you violated the most sacred laws from a miserable desire of a little more life? Perhaps not, if you keep them in a good temper; but if they are out of temper you will hear many degrading things; you will live, but how?—as the flatterer of all men, and the servant of all men; and doing what?—eating and drinking in Thessaly, having gone abroad in order that you may get a dinner. And where will be your fine sentiments about justice and virtue then? Say that you wish to live for the sake of your children, that you may bring them up and educate them—will you take them into Thessaly and deprive them of Athenian citizenship? Is that the benefit which you would confer upon them? Or are you under the impression that they will be better cared for and educated here if you are still alive, although absent from them; for that your friends will take care of them? Do you fancy that if you are an inhabitant of Thessaly they will take care of them, and if you are an inhabitant of the other world they will not take care of them? Nay; but if they who call themselves friends are truly friends, they surely will.

"Listen, then, Socrates, to us who have brought you up. Think not of life and children first, and of justice afterwards, but of justice first, that you may be justified before the princes of the world below. For neither will you nor any that belong to you be happier or holier or juster in this life, or happier in another, if you do as Crito bids. Now you depart in innocence, a sufferer and not a doer of evil; a victim, not of the laws, but of men. But if you go forth, returning evil for evil, and injury for injury, breaking the covenants and agreements which you have made with us, and wronging those whom you ought least to wrong, that is to say, yourself, your friends, your country, and us, we shall be angry with you while you live, and our brethren, the laws in the world below, will receive you as an enemy; for they will know that you have done your best to destroy us. Listen, then, to us and not to Crito."

This is the voice which I seem to hear murmuring in my ears, like the sound of the flute in the ears of the mystic; that voice, I say, is humming in my ears, and prevents me from hearing any other. And I know that anything more which you will say will be in vain. Yet speak, if you have anything to say.

Cr. I have nothing to say, Socrates.

Soc. Then let me follow the intimations of the will of God.

PHÆDO

PERSONS OF THE DIALOGUE

PHÆDO, *who is the narrator of the dialogue to* ECHECRATES *of Phlius*

SOCRATES

APOLLODORUS

SIMMIAS

CEBES

CRITO

ATTENDANT OF THE PRISON

SCENE: *The Prison of Socrates*

PLACE OF THE NARRATION: *Phlius*

Echecrates

WERE you yourself, Phædo, in the prison with Socrates on the day when he drank the poison?

Phædo. Yes, Echecrates, I was.

Ech. I wish that you would tell me about his death. What did he say in his last hours? We were informed that he died by taking poison, but no one knew anything more; for no Phliasian ever goes to Athens now, and a long time has elapsed since any Athenian found his way to Phlius, and therefore we had no clear account.

Phæd. Did you not hear of the proceedings at the trial?

Ech. Yes; someone told us about the trial, and we could not understand why, having been condemned, he was put to death, as appeared, not at the time, but long afterwards. What was the reason of this?

Phæd. An accident, Echecrates. The reason was that the stern of the ship which the Athenians send to Delos happened to have been crowned on the day before he was tried.

Ech. What is this ship?

Phæd. This is the ship in which, as the Athenians say, Theseus went to Crete when he took with him the fourteen youths, and was the saviour of them and of himself. And they were said to have vowed to Apollo at the time, that if they were saved they would make an annual pilgrimage to Delos. Now this custom still continues, and the whole period of the voyage to and from Delos, beginning when the priest of Apollo crowns the stern of the ship, is a holy season, during which the city is not allowed to be polluted by public executions; and often, when the vessel is detained by adverse winds, there may be a very considerable delay. As I was saying, the ship was crowned on the day before the trial, and this was the reason why Socrates lay in prison and was not put to death until long after he was condemned.

Ech. What was the manner of his death, Phædo? What was said or done? And which of his friends had he with him? Or were they not allowed by the authorities to be present? And did he die alone?

Phæd. No; there were several of his friends with him.

Ech. If you have nothing to do, I wish that you would tell me what passed, as exactly as you can.

Phæd. I have nothing to do, and will try to gratify your wish. For to me, too, there is no greater pleasure than to have Socrates brought to my recollection, whether I speak myself or hear another speak of him.

Ech. You will have listeners who are of the same mind with you, and I hope that you will be as exact as you can.

Phæd. I remember the strange feeling which came over me at being with him. For I could hardly believe that I was present at the death of a friend, and therefore I did not pity him, Echecrates; his mien and his language were so noble and fearless in the hour of death that to me he appeared blessed. I thought that in going to the other world he could not be without a divine call, and that he would be happy, if any man ever was, when he arrived there, and therefore I did not pity him as might seem natural at such a time. But neither could I feel the pleasure which I usually felt in philosophical discourse (for philosophy was the theme of which we spoke). I was pleased, and I was also pained, because I knew that he was soon to die, and this strange mixture of feeling was shared by us all; we were laughing and weeping by turns, especially the excitable Apollodorus—you know the sort of man?

Ech. Yes.

Phæd. He was quite overcome; and I myself and all of us were greatly moved.

Ech. Who were present?

Phæd. Of native Athenians there were, besides Apollodorus, Critobulus and his father Crito, Hermogenes, Epigenes, Æschines, and Antisthenes; likewise Ctesippus of the *deme* of Pæania, Menexenus, and some others; but Plato, if I am not mistaken, was ill.

Ech. Were there any strangers?

Phæd. Yes, there were; Simmias the Theban, and Cebes, and Phædondes; Euclid and Terpison, who came from Megara.

Ech. And was Aristippus there, and Cleombrotus?

Phæd. No, they were said to be in Ægina.

Ech. Anyone else?

Phæd. I think that these were about all.

Ech. And what was the discourse of which you spoke?

Phæd. I will begin at the beginning, and endeavor to repeat the entire conversation. You must understand that we had been previously in the habit of assembling early in the morning at the court in which the trial was held, and which is not far from the prison. There we remained talking with one another until the opening of the prison doors (for they were not opened very early), and then went in and generally passed the day with Socrates. On the last morning the meeting was earlier than usual; this was owing to our having heard on the previous evening that the sacred ship had arrived from Delos, and therefore we agreed to meet very early at the accustomed place. On our going to the prison, the jailer who answered the door, instead of admitting us, came out and bade us wait and he would call us. "For the Eleven," he said, "are now with Socrates; they are taking off his chains, and giving orders that he is to die to-day." He soon returned and said that we might come in. On entering we found Socrates just released from chains, and Xanthippe, whom you know, sitting by him, and holding his child in her arms. When she saw us she uttered a cry and said, as women will: "O Socrates, this is the last time that either you will converse with your friends, or they with you." Socrates turned to Crito and said: "Crito, let someone take her home." Some of Crito's people accordingly led her away, crying out and beating herself. And when she was gone, Socrates, sitting up on the couch, began to bend and rub his leg, saying, as he rubbed: "How singular is the thing called pleasure, and how curiously related to pain, which might be thought to be the opposite of it; for they never come to a man together, and yet he who pursues either of them is generally compelled to take the other. They are two, and yet they grow together out of one head or stem; and I cannot help thinking that if Æsop had noticed them, he would have made a fable about God trying to reconcile their strife, and when he could not, he fastened their heads together; and this is the reason why when one comes the other follows, as I find in my own case pleasure comes following after the pain in my leg, which was caused by the chain."

Upon this Cebes said: I am very glad indeed, Socrates, that you mentioned the name of Æsop. For that reminds me of a question which has been asked by others, and was asked of me only the day before yesterday by Evenus the poet, and as he will be sure to ask again, you may as well tell me what I should say to him, if you would like him to have an answer. He wanted to know why you who never before wrote a line of poetry, now that you are in prison are putting Æsop into verse, and also composing that hymn in honor of Apollo.

Tell him, Cebes, he replied, that I had no idea of rivalling him or his poems; which is the truth, for I knew that I could not do that. But I wanted to see whether I could purge away a scruple which I felt about certain dreams. In the course of my life I have often had intimations in dreams "that I should make music." The same dream came to me sometimes in one form, and sometimes in another, but always saying the same or nearly the same words: Make and cultivate music, said the dream. And hitherto I had imagined that this was only intended to exhort and encourage me in the study of philosophy, which has always been the pursuit of my life, and is the noblest and best of music. The dream was bidding me to do what I was already doing, in the same way that the competitor in a race is bidden by the spectators to run when he is already running. But I was not certain of this, as the dream might have meant music in the popular sense of the word, and being under sentence of death, and the festival giving me a respite, I thought that I should be safer if I satisfied the scruple, and, in obedience to the dream, composed a few verses before I departed. And first I made a hymn in honor of the god of the festival, and then considering that a poet, if he is really to be a poet or maker, should not only put words together but make stories, and as I have no invention, I took some fables of Æsop, which I had ready at hand and knew, and turned them into verse. Tell Evenus this, and bid him be of good cheer; say that I would have him come after me if he be a wise man, and not tarry; and that to-day I am likely to be going, for the Athenians say that I must.

Simmias said: What a message for such a man! having been a frequent companion of his, I should say that, as far as I know him, he will never take your advice unless he is obliged.

Why, said Socrates,—is not Evenus a philosopher?

I think that he is, said Simmias.

Then he, or any man who has the spirit of philosophy, will be willing to die, though he will not take his own life, for that is held not to be right.

Here he changed his position, and put his legs off the couch on to the ground, and during the rest of the conversation he remained sitting.

Why do you say, inquired Cebes, that a man ought not to take his own life, but that the philosopher will be ready to follow the dying?

Socrates replied: And have you, Cebes and Simmias, who are acquainted with Philolaus, never heard him speak of this?

I never understood him, Socrates.

My words, too, are only an echo; but I am very willing to say what I have heard: and indeed, as I am going to another place, I ought to be thinking and talking of the nature of the pilgrimage which I am about to make. What can I do better in the interval between this and the setting of the sun?

Then tell me, Socrates, why is suicide held not to be right? as I have certainly heard Philolaus affirm when he was staying with us at Thebes: and there are others who say the same, although none of them has ever made me understand him.

But do your best, replied Socrates, and the day may come when you will understand. I suppose that you wonder why, as most things which are evil may be accidentally good, this is to be the only exception (for may not death, too, be better than life in some cases?), and why, when a man is better dead, he is not permitted to be his own benefactor, but must wait for the hand of another.

By Jupiter! yes, indeed, said Cebes, laughing, and speaking in his native Doric.

I admit the appearance of inconsistency, replied Socrates, but there may not be any real inconsistency after all in this. There is a doctrine uttered in secret that man is a prisoner who has no right to open the door of his prison and run away; this is a great mystery which I do not quite understand. Yet I, too, believe that the gods are our guardians, and that we are a possession of theirs. Do you not agree?

Yes, I agree to that, said Cebes.

And if one of your own possessions, an ox or an ass, for example took the liberty of putting himself out of the way when you had given no intimation of your wish that he should die, would you not be angry with him, and would you not punish him if you could?

Certainly, replied Cebes.

Then there may be reason in saying that a man should wait, and not take his own life until God summons him, as he is now summoning me.

Yes, Socrates, said Cebes, there is surely reason in that. And yet how can you reconcile this seemingly true belief that God is our guardian and we his possessions, with that willingness to die which we were attributing to the philosopher? That the wisest of men should be willing to leave this service in which they are ruled by the gods who are the best of rulers is not reasonable, for surely no wise man thinks that when set at liberty he can take better care of himself than the gods take of him. A fool may perhaps think this—he may argue that he had better run away from his master, not considering that his duty is to remain to the end, and not to run away from the good, and that there is no sense in his running away. But the wise man will want to be ever with him who is better than himself. Now this, Socrates, is the reverse of what was just now said; for upon this view the wise man should sorrow and the fool rejoice at passing out of life.

The earnestness of Cebes seemed to please Socrates. Here, said he, turning to us, is a man who is always inquiring, and is not to be convinced all in a moment, nor by every argument.

And in this case, added Simmias, his objection does appear to me to have some force. For what can be the meaning of a truly wise man wanting to fly away and lightly leave a master who is better than himself? And I rather imagine that Cebes is referring to you; he thinks that you are too ready to leave us, and too ready to leave the gods who, as you acknowledge, are our good rulers.

Yes, replied Socrates; there is reason in that. And this indictment you think that I ought to answer as if I were in court?

That is what we should like, said Simmias.

Then I must try to make a better impression upon you than I did when defending myself before the judges. For I am quite ready to acknowledge, Simmias and Cebes, that I ought to be grieved at death, if I were not persuaded that I am going to other gods who are wise and good (of this I am as certain as I can be of anything of the sort) and to men departed (though I am not so certain of this), who are better than those whom I leave behind; and therefore I do not grieve as I might have done, for I have good hope that there is yet something remaining for the dead, and, as has been said of old, some far better thing for the good than for the evil.

But do you mean to take away your thoughts with you, Socrates? said Simmias. Will you not communicate them to us?—the benefit is one in which we too may hope to share. Moreover, if you succeed in convincing us, that will be an answer to the charge against yourself.

I will do my best, replied Socrates. But you must first let me hear what Crito wants; he was going to say something to me.

Only this, Socrates, replied Crito: the attendant who is to give you the poison has been telling me that you are not to talk much, and he wants me to let you know this; for that by talking heat is increased, and this interferes with the action of the poison; those who excite themselves are sometimes obliged to drink the poison two or three times.

Then, said Socrates, let him mind his business and be prepared to give the poison two or three times, if necessary; that is all.

I was almost certain that you would say that, replied Crito; but I was obliged to satisfy him.

Never mind him, he said.

And now I will make answer to you, O my judges, and show that he who has lived as a true philosopher has reason to be of good cheer when he is about to die, and that after death he may hope to receive the greatest good in the other world. And how this may be, Simmias and Cebes, I will endeavor to explain. For I deem that the true disciple of philosophy is likely to be misunderstood by other men; they do not perceive that he is ever pursuing death and dying; and if this is true, why, having had the desire of death all his life long, should he repine at the arrival of that which he has been always pursuing and desiring?

Simmias laughed and said: Though not in a laughing humor, I swear that I cannot help laughing when I think what the wicked world will say when they hear this. They will say that this is very true, and our people at home will agree with them in saying that the life which philosophers desire is truly death, and that they have found them out to be deserving of the death which they desire.

And they are right, Simmias, in saying this, with the exception of the words "They have found them out"; for they have not found out what is the nature of this death which the true philosopher desires, or how he deserves or desires death. But let us leave them and have a word with ourselves: Do we believe that there is such a thing as death?

To be sure, replied Simmias.

And is this anything but the separation of soul and body? And being dead is the attainment of this separation; when the soul exists in herself, and is parted from the body and the body is parted from the soul—that is death?

Exactly: that and nothing else, he replied.

And what do you say of another question, my friend, about which I should like to have your opinion, and the answer to which will probably throw light on our present inquiry: Do you think that the philosopher ought to care about the pleasures—if they are to be called pleasures—of eating and drinking?

Certainly not, answered Simmias.

And what do you say of the pleasures of love—should he care about them?

By no means.

And will he think much of the other ways of indulging the body—for example, the acquisition of costly raiment, or sandals, or other adornments of the body? Instead of caring about them, does he not rather despise anything more than nature needs? What do you say?

I should say the true philosopher would despise them.

Would you not say that he is entirely concerned with the soul and not with the body? He would like, as far as he can, to be quit of the body and turn to the soul.

That is true.

In matters of this sort philosophers, above all other men, may be observed in every sort of way to dissever the soul from the body.

That is true.

Whereas, Simmias, the rest of the world are of opinion that a life which has no bodily pleasures and no part in them is not worth having; but that he who thinks nothing of bodily pleasures is almost as though he were dead.

That is quite true.

What again shall we say of the actual acquirement of knowledge?—is the body, if invited to share in the inquiry, a hinderer or a helper? I mean to say, have sight and hearing any truth in them? Are they not, as the poets are always telling us, inaccurate witnesses? and yet, if even they are inaccurate and indistinct, what is to be said of the other senses?—for you will allow that they are the best of them?

Certainly, he replied.

Then when does the soul attain truth?—for in attempting to consider anything in company with the body she is obviously deceived.

Yes, that is true.

Then must not existence be revealed to her in thought, if at all?

Yes.

And thought is best when the mind is gathered into herself and none of these things trouble her—neither sounds nor sights nor pain nor any pleasure—when she has as little as possible to do with the body, and has no bodily sense or feeling, but is aspiring after being?

That is true.

And in this the philosopher dishonors the body; his soul runs away from the body and desires to be alone and by herself?

That is true.

Well, but there is another thing, Simmias: Is there or is there not an absolute justice?

Assuredly there is.

And an absolute beauty and absolute good?

Of course.

But did you ever behold any of them with your eyes?

Certainly not.

Or did you ever reach them with any other bodily sense? (and I speak not of these alone, but of absolute greatness, and health, and strength, and of the essence or true nature of everything). Has the reality of them ever been perceived by you through the bodily organs? or rather, is not the nearest approach to the knowledge of their several natures made by him who so orders his intellectual vision as to have the most exact conception of the essence of that which he considers?

Certainly.

And he attains to the knowledge of them in their highest purity who goes to each of them with the mind alone, not allowing when in the act of thought the intrusion or introduction of sight or any other sense in the company of reason, but with the very light of the mind in her clearness penetrates into the very light of truth in each; he has got rid, as far as he can, of eyes and ears and of the whole body, which he conceives of only as a disturbing element, hindering the soul from the acquisition of knowledge when in company with her—is not this the sort of man who, if ever man did, is likely to attain the knowledge of existence?

There is admirable truth in that, Socrates, replied Simmias.

And when they consider all this, must not true philosophers make a reflection, of which they will speak to one another in such words as these: We have found, they will say, a path of speculation which seems to bring us and the argument to the conclusion that while we are in the body, and while the soul is mingled with this mass of evil, our desire will not be satisfied, and our desire is of the truth.

For the body is a source of endless trouble to us by reason of the mere requirement of food; and also is liable to diseases which overtake and impede us in the search after truth: and by filling us so full of loves, and lusts, and fears, and fancies, and idols, and every sort of folly, prevents our ever having, as people say, so much as a thought. For whence come wars, and fightings, and factions? whence but from the body and the lusts of the body? For wars are occasioned by the love of money, and money has to be acquired for the sake and in the service of the body; and in consequence of all these things the time which ought to be given to philosophy is lost. Moreover, if there is time and an inclination toward philosophy, yet the body introduces a turmoil and confusion and fear into the course of speculation, and hinders us from seeing the truth: and all experience shows that if we would have pure knowledge of anything we must be quit of the body, and the soul in herself must behold all things in themselves: then I suppose that we shall attain that which we desire, and of which we say that we are lovers, and that is wisdom, not while we live, but after death, as the argument shows; for if while in company with the body the soul cannot have pure knowledge, one of two things seems to follow—either knowledge is not to be attained at all, or, if at all, after death. For then, and not till then, the soul will be in herself alone and without the body. In this present life, I reckon that we make the nearest approach to knowledge when we have the least possible concern or interest in the body, and are not saturated with the bodily nature, but remain pure until the hour when God himself is pleased to release us. And then the foolishness of the body will be cleared away and we shall be pure and hold converse with other pure souls, and know of ourselves the clear light everywhere; and this is surely the light of truth. For no impure thing is allowed to approach the pure. These are the sort of words, Simmias, which the true lovers of wisdom cannot help saying to one another, and thinking. You will agree with me in that?

Certainly, Socrates.

But if this is true, O my friend, then there is great hope that, going whither I go, I shall there be satisfied with that which has been the chief concern of you and me in our past lives. And now that the hour of departure is appointed to me, this is the hope with which I depart, and not I only, but every man who believes that he has his mind purified.

Certainly, replied Simmias.

And what is purification but the separation of the soul from the body, as I was saying before; the habit of the soul gathering and collecting herself into herself, out of all the courses of the body; the dwelling in her own place alone, as in another life, so also in this, as far as she can; the release of the soul from the chains of the body?

Very true, he said.

And what is that which is termed death, but this very separation and release of the soul from the body?

To be sure, he said.

And the true philosophers, and they only, study and are eager to release the soul. Is not the separation and release of the soul from the body their especial study?

That is true.

And as I was saying at first, there would be a ridiculous contradiction in men studying to live as nearly as they can in a state of death, and yet repining when death comes.

Certainly.

Then, Simmias, as the true philosophers are ever studying death, to them, of all men, death is the least terrible. Look at the matter in this way: how inconsistent of them to have been always enemies of the body, and wanting to have the soul alone, and when this is granted to them, to be trembling and repining; instead of rejoicing at their departing to that place where, when they arrive, they hope to gain that which in life they loved (and this was wisdom), and at the same time to be rid of the company of their enemy. Many a man has been willing to go to the world below in the hope of seeing there an earthly love, or wife, or son, and conversing with them. And will he who is a true lover of wisdom, and is persuaded in like manner that only in the world below he can worthily enjoy her, still repine at death? Will he not depart with joy? Surely he will, my friend, if he be a true philosopher. For he will have a firm conviction that there only, and nowhere else, he can find wisdom in her purity. And if this be true, he would be very absurd, as I was saying, if he were to fear death.

He would, indeed, replied Simmias.

And when you see a man who is repining at the approach of death, is not his reluctance a sufficient proof that he is not a lover of wisdom, but a lover of the body, and probably at the same time a lover of either money or power, or both?

That is very true, he replied.

There is a virtue, Simmias, which is named courage. Is not that a special attribute of the philosopher?

Certainly.

Again, there is temperance. Is not the calm, and control, and disdain of the passions which even the many call temperance, a quality belonging only to those who despise the body and live in philosophy?

That is not to be denied.

For the courage and temperance of other men, if you will consider them, are really a contradiction.

How is that, Socrates?

Well, he said, you are aware that death is regarded by men in general as a great evil.

That is true, he said.

And do not courageous men endure death because they are afraid of yet greater evils?

That is true.

Then all but the philosophers are courageous only from fear, and because they are afraid; and yet that a man should be courageous from fear, and because he is a coward, is surely a strange thing.

Very true.

And are not the temperate exactly in the same case? They are temperate because they are intemperate—which may seem to be a contradiction, but is nevertheless the sort of thing which happens with this foolish temperance. For there are pleasures which they must have, and are afraid of losing; and therefore they abstain from one class of pleasures because they are overcome by another: and whereas intemperance is defined as "being under the dominion of pleasure," they overcome only because they are overcome by pleasure. And that is what I mean by saying that they are temperate through intemperance.

That appears to be true.

Yet the exchange of one fear or pleasure or pain for another fear or pleasure or pain, which are measured like coins, the greater with the less, is not the exchange of virtue. O my dear Simmias, is there not one true coin for which all things ought to exchange?—and that is wisdom; and only in exchange for this, and in company with this, is anything truly bought or sold, whether courage or temperance or justice. And is not all true virtue the companion of wisdom, no matter what fears or pleasures or other similar goods or evils may or may not attend her? But the virtue which is made up of these goods, when they are severed from wisdom and exchanged with one another, is a shadow of virtue only, nor is there any freedom or health or truth in her; but in the true exchange there is a purging away of all these things, and temperance, and justice, and courage, and wisdom herself are a purgation of them. And I conceive that the founders of the mysteries had a real meaning and were not mere triflers when they intimated in a figure long ago that he who passes unsanctified and uninitiated into the world below will live in a slough, but that he who arrives there after initiation and purification will dwell with the gods. For "many," as they say in the mysteries, "are the thyrsus bearers, but few are the mystics,"—meaning, as I interpret the words, the true philosophers. In the number of whom I have been seeking, according to my ability, to find a place during my whole life; whether I have sought in a right way or not, and whether I have succeeded or not, I shall truly know in a little while, if God will, when I myself arrive in the other world: that is my belief. And now, Simmias and Cebes, I have answered those who charge me with not grieving or repining at parting from you and my masters in this world; and I am right in not repining, for I believe that I shall find other masters and friends who are as good in the world below. But all men cannot believe this, and I shall be glad if my words have any more success with you than with the judges of the Athenians.

Cebes answered: I agree, Socrates, in the greater part of what you say. But in what relates to the soul, men are apt to be incredulous; they fear that when she leaves the body her place may be nowhere, and that on the very day of death she may be destroyed and perish—immediately on her release from the body, issuing forth like smoke or air and vanishing away into nothingness. For if she could only hold together and be herself after she was released from the evils of the body, there would be good reason to hope, Socrates, that what you say is true. But much persuasion and many arguments are required in order to prove that when the man is dead the soul yet exists, and has any force of intelligence.

True, Cebes, said Socrates; and shall I suggest that we talk a little of the probabilities of these things?

I am sure, said Cebes, that I should greatly like to know your opinion about them.

I reckon, said Socrates, that no one who heard me now, not even if he were one of my old enemies, the comic poets, could accuse me of idle talking about matters in which I have no concern. Let us, then, if you please, proceed with the inquiry.

Whether the souls of men after death are or are not in the world below, is a question which may be argued in this manner: The ancient doctrine of which I have been speaking affirms that they go from this into the other world, and return hither, and are born from the dead. Now if this be true, and the living come from the dead, then our souls must be in the other world, for if not, how could they be born again? And this would be conclusive, if there were any real evidence that the living are only born from the dead; but if there is no evidence of this, then other arguments will have to be adduced.

That is very true, replied Cebes.

Then let us consider this question, not in relation to man only, but in relation to animals generally, and to plants, and to everything of which there is generation, and the proof will be easier. Are not all things which have opposites generated out of their opposites? I mean such things as good and evil, just and unjust—and there are innumerable other opposites which are generated out of opposites. And I want to show that this holds universally of all opposites; I mean to say, for example, that anything which becomes greater must become greater after being less.

True.

And that which becomes less must have been once greater and then become less.

Yes.

And the weaker is generated from the stronger, and the swifter from the slower.

Very true.

And the worse is from the better, and the more just is from the more unjust.

Of course.

And is this true of all opposites? and are we convinced that all of them are generated out of opposites?

Yes.

And in this universal opposition of all things, are there not also two intermediate processes which are ever going on, from one to the other, and back again; where there is a greater and a less there is also an intermediate process of increase and diminution, and that which grows is said to wax, and that which decays to wane?

Yes, he said.

And there are many other processes, such as division and composition, cooling and heating, which equally involve a passage into and out of one another. And this holds of all opposites, even though not always expressed in words—they are generated out of one another, and there is a passing or process from one to the other of them?

Very true, he replied.

Well, and is there not an opposite of life, as sleep is the opposite of waking?

True, he said.

And what is that?

Death, he answered.

And these, then, are generated, if they are opposites, the one from the other, and have there their two intermediate processes also?

Of course.

Now, said Socrates, I will analyze one of the two pairs of opposites which I have mentioned to you, and also its intermediate processes, and you shall analyze the other to me. The state of sleep is opposed to the state of waking, and out of sleeping waking is generated, and out of waking, sleeping, and the process of generation is in the one case falling asleep, and in the other waking up. Are you agreed about that?

Quite agreed.

Then suppose that you analyze life and death to me in the same manner. Is not death opposed to life?

Yes.

And they are generated one from the other?

Yes.

What is generated from life?

Death.

And what from death?

I can only say in answer—life.

Then the living, whether things or persons, Cebes, are generated from the dead?

That is clear, he replied.

Then the inference is, that our souls are in the world below?

That is true.

And one of the two processes or generations is visible—for surely the act of dying is visible?

Surely, he said.

And may not the other be inferred as the complement of nature, who is not to be supposed to go on one leg only? And if not, a corresponding process of generation in death must also be assigned to her?

Certainly, he replied.

And what is that process?

Revival.

And revival, if there be such a thing, is the birth of the dead into the world of the living?

Quite true.

Then there is a new way in which we arrive at the inference that the living come from the dead, just as the dead come from the living; and if this is true, then the souls of the dead must be in some place out of which they come again. And this, as I think, has been satisfactorily proved.

Yes, Socrates, he said; all this seems to flow necessarily out of our previous admissions.

And that these admissions are not unfair, Cebes, he said, may be shown, as I think, in this way: If generation were in a straight line only, and there were no compensation or circle in nature, no turn or return into one another, then you know that all things would at last have the same form and pass into the same state, and there would be no more generation of them.

What do you mean? he said.

A simple thing enough, which I will illustrate by the case of sleep, he replied. You know that if there were no compensation of sleeping and waking, the story of the sleeping Endymion would in the end have no meaning, because all other things would be asleep, too, and he would not be thought of. Or if there were composition only, and no division of substances, then the chaos of Anaxagoras would come again. And in like manner, my dear Cebes, if all things which partook of life were to die, and after they were dead remained in the form of death, and did not come to life again, all would at last die, and nothing would be alive—how could this be otherwise? For if the living spring from any others who are not the dead, and they die, must not all things at last be swallowed up in death?

There is no escape from that, Socrates, said Cebes; and I think that what you say is entirely true.

Yes, he said, Cebes, I entirely think so, too; and we are not walking in a vain imagination; but I am confident in the belief that there truly is such a thing as living again, and that the living spring from the dead, and that the souls of the dead are in existence, and that the good souls have a better portion than the evil.

Cebes added: Your favorite doctrine, Socrates, that knowledge is simply recollection, if true, also necessarily implies a previous time in which we learned that which we now recollect. But this would be impossible unless our soul was in some place before existing in the human form; here, then, is another argument of the soul's immortality.

But tell me, Cebes, said Simmias, interposing, what proofs are given of this doctrine of recollection? I am not very sure at this moment that I remember them.

One excellent proof, said Cebes, is afforded by questions. If you put a question to a person in a right way, he will give a true answer of himself; but how could he do this unless there were knowledge and right reason already in him? And this is most clearly shown when he is taken to a diagram or to anything of that sort.

But if, said Socrates, you are still incredulous, Simmias, I would ask you whether you may not agree with me when you look at the matter in another way; I mean, if you are still incredulous as to whether knowledge is recollection.

Incredulous, I am not, said Simmias; but I want to have this doctrine of recollection brought to my own recollection, and, from what Cebes has said, I am beginning to recollect and be convinced; but I should still like to hear what more you have to say.

This is what I would say, he replied: We should agree, if I am not mistaken, that what a man recollects he must have known at some previous time.

Very true.

And what is the nature of this recollection? And, in asking this, I mean to ask whether, when a person has already seen or heard or in any way perceived anything, and he knows not only that, but something else of which he has not the same, but another knowledge, we may not fairly say that he recollects that which comes into his mind. Are we agreed about that?

What do you mean?

I mean what I may illustrate by the following instance: The knowledge of a lyre is not the same as the knowledge of a man?

True.

And yet what is the feeling of lovers when they recognize a lyre, or a garment, or anything else which the beloved has been in the habit of using? Do not they, from knowing the lyre, form in the mind's eye an image of the youth to whom the lyre belongs? And this is recollection: and in the same way anyone who sees Simmias may remember Cebes; and there are endless other things of the same nature.

Yes, indeed, there are—endless, replied Simmias.

And this sort of thing, he said, is recollection, and is most commonly a process of recovering that which has been forgotten through time and inattention.

Very true, he said.

Well; and may you not also from seeing the picture of a horse or a lyre remember a man? and from the picture of Simmias, you may be led to remember Cebes?

True.

Or you may also be led to the recollection of Simmias himself?

True, he said.

And in all these cases, the recollection may be derived from things either like or unlike?

That is true.

And when the recollection is derived from like things, then there is sure to be another question, which is, whether the likeness of that which is recollected is in any way defective or not.

Very true, he said.

And shall we proceed a step further, and affirm that there is such a thing as equality, not of wood with wood, or of stone with stone, but that, over and above this, there is equality in the abstract? Shall we affirm this?

Affirm, yes, and swear to it, replied Simmias, with all the confidence in life.

And do we know the nature of this abstract essence?

To be sure, he said.

And whence did we obtain this knowledge? Did we not see equalities of material things, such as pieces of wood and stones, and gather from them the idea of an equality which is different from them?—you will admit that? Or look at the matter again in this way: Do not the same pieces of wood or stone appear at one time equal, and at another time unequal?

That is certain.

But are real equals ever unequal? or is the idea of equality ever inequality?

That surely was never yet known, Socrates.

Then these (so-called) equals are not the same with the idea of equality?

I should say, clearly not, Socrates.

And yet from these equals, although differing from the idea of equality, you conceived and attained that idea?

Very true, he said.

Which might be like, or might be unlike them?

Yes.

But that makes no difference; whenever from seeing one thing you conceived another, whether like or unlike, there must surely have been an act of recollection?

Very true.

But what would you say of equal portions of wood and stone, or other material equals? and what is the impression produced by them? Are they equals in the same sense as absolute equality? or do they fall short of this in a measure?

Yes, he said, in a very great measure, too.

And must we not allow that when I or anyone look at any object, and perceive that the object aims at being some other thing, but falls short of, and cannot attain to it—he who makes this observation must have had previous knowledge of that to which, as he says, the other, although similar, was inferior?

Certainly.

And has not this been our case in the matter of equals and of absolute equality?

Precisely.

Then we must have known absolute equality previously to the time when we first saw the material equals, and reflected that all these apparent equals aim at this absolute equality, but fall short of it?

That is true.

And we recognize also that this absolute equality has only been known, and can only be known, through the medium of sight or touch, or of some other sense. And this I would affirm of all such conceptions.

Yes, Socrates, as far as the argument is concerned, one of them is the same as the other.

And from the senses, then, is derived the knowledge that all sensible things aim at an idea of equality of which they fall short—is not that true?

Yes.

Then before we began to see or hear or perceive in any way, we must have had a knowledge of absolute equality, or we could not have referred to that the equals which are derived from the senses—for to that they all aspire, and of that they fall short?

That, Socrates, is certainly to be inferred from the previous statements.

And did we not see and hear and acquire our other senses as soon as we were born?

Certainly.

Then we must have acquired the knowledge of the ideal equal at some time previous to this?

Yes.

That is to say, before we were born, I suppose?

True.

And if we acquired this knowledge before we were born, and were born having it, then we also knew before we were born and at the instant of birth not only equal or the greater or the less, but all other ideas; for we are not speaking only of equality absolute, but of beauty, goodness, justice, holiness, and all which we stamp with the name of essence in the dialectical process, when we ask and answer questions. Of all this we may certainly affirm that we acquired the knowledge before birth?

That is true.

But if, after having acquired, we have not forgotten that which we acquired, then we must always have been born with knowledge, and shall always continue to know as long as life lasts—for knowing is the acquiring and retaining knowledge and not forgetting. Is not forgetting, Simmias, just the losing of knowledge?

Quite true, Socrates.

But if the knowledge which we acquired before birth was lost by us at birth, and afterwards by the use of the senses we recovered that which we previously knew, will not that which we call learning be a process of recovering our knowledge, and may not this be rightly termed recollection by us?

Very true.

For this is clear, that when we perceived something, either by the help of sight or hearing, or some other sense, there was no difficulty in receiving from this a conception of some other thing like or unlike which had been forgotten and which was associated with this; and therefore, as I was saying, one of two alternatives follows: either we had this knowledge at birth, and continued to know through life; or, after birth, those who are said to learn only remember, and learning is recollection only.

Yes, that is quite true, Socrates.

And which alternative, Simmias, do you prefer? Had we the knowledge at our birth, or did we remember afterwards the things which we knew previously to our birth?

I cannot decide at the moment.

At any rate you can decide whether he who has knowledge ought or ought not to be able to give a reason for what he knows.

Certainly, he ought.

But do you think that every man is able to give a reason about these very matters of which we are speaking?

I wish that they could, Socrates, but I greatly fear that to-morrow at this time there will be no one able to give a reason worth having.

Then you are not of opinion, Simmias, that all men know these things?

Certainly not.

Then they are in process of recollecting that which they learned before.

Certainly.

But when did our souls acquire this knowledge?—not since we were born as men?

Certainly not.

And therefore previously?

Yes.

Then, Simmias, our souls must have existed before they were in the form of man—without bodies, and must have had intelligence.

Unless indeed you suppose, Socrates, that these notions were given us at the moment of birth; for this is the only time that remains.

Yes, my friend, but when did we lose them? for they are not in us when we are born—that is admitted. Did we lose them at the moment of receiving them, or at some other time?

No, Socrates, I perceive that I was unconsciously talking nonsense.

Then may we not say, Simmias, that if, as we are always repeating, there is an absolute beauty, and goodness, and essence in general, and to this, which is now discovered to be a previous condition of our being, we refer all our sensations, and with this compare them—assuming this to have a prior existence, then our souls must have had a prior existence, but if not, there would be no force in the argument? There can be no doubt that if these absolute ideas existed before we were born, then our souls must have existed before we were born, and if not the ideas, then not the souls.

Yes, Socrates; I am convinced that there is precisely the same necessity for the existence of the soul before birth, and of the essence of which you are speaking: and the argument arrives at a result which happily agrees with my own notion. For there is nothing which to my mind is so evident as that beauty, goodness, and other notions of which you were just now speaking have a most real and absolute existence; and I am satisfied with the proof.

Well, but is Cebes equally satisfied? for I must convince him too.

I think, said Simmias, that Cebes is satisfied: although he is the most incredulous of mortals, yet I believe that he is convinced of the existence of the soul before birth. But that after death the soul will continue to exist is not yet proven even to my own satisfaction. I cannot get rid of the feeling of the many to which Cebes was referring—the feeling that when the man dies the soul may be scattered, and that this may be the end of her. For admitting that she may be generated and created in some other place, and may have existed before entering the human body, why after having entered in and gone out again may she not herself be destroyed and come to an end?

Very true, Simmias, said Cebes; that our soul existed before we were born was the first half of the argument, and this appears to have been proven; that the soul will exist after death as well as before birth is the other half of which the proof is still wanting, and has to be supplied.

But that proof, Simmias and Cebes, has been already given, said Socrates, if you put the two arguments together—I mean this and the former one, in which we admitted that everything living is born of the dead. For if the soul existed before birth, and in coming to life and being born can be born only from death and dying, must she not after death continue to exist, since she has to be born again? surely the proof which you desire has been already furnished. Still I suspect that you and Simmias would be glad to probe the argument further; like children, you are haunted with a fear that when the soul leaves the body, the wind may really blow her away and scatter her; especially if a man should happen to die in stormy weather and not when the sky is calm.

Cebes answered with a smile: Then, Socrates, you must argue us out of our fears—and yet, strictly speaking, they are not our fears, but there is a child within us to whom death is a sort of hobgoblin; him too we must persuade not to be afraid when he is alone with him in the dark.

Socrates said: Let the voice of the charmer be applied daily until you have charmed him away.

And where shall we find a good charmer of our fears, Socrates, when you are gone?

Hellas, he replied, is a large place, Cebes, and has many good men, and there are barbarous races not a few: seek for him among them all, far and wide, sparing neither pains nor money; for there is no better way of using your money. And you must not forget to seek for him among yourselves too; for he is nowhere more likely to be found.

The search, replied Cebes, shall certainly be made. And now, if you please, let us return to the point of the argument at which we digressed.

By all means, replied Socrates; what else should I please?

Very good, he said.

Must we not, said Socrates, ask ourselves some question of this sort?—What is that which, as we imagine, is liable to be scattered away, and about which we fear? and what again is that about which we have no fear? And then we may proceed to inquire whether that which suffers dispersion is or is not of the nature of soul—our hopes and fears as to our own souls will turn upon that.

That is true, he said.

Now the compound or composite may be supposed to be naturally capable of being dissolved in like manner as of being compounded; but that which is uncompounded, and that only, must be, if anything is, indissoluble.

Yes; that is what I should imagine, said Cebes.

And the uncompounded may be assumed to be the same and unchanging, where the compound is always changing and never the same?

That I also think, he said.

Then now let us return to the previous discussion. Is that idea or essence, which in the dialectical process we define as essence of true existence—whether essence of equality, beauty, or anything else: are these essences, I say, liable at times to some degree of change? or are they each of them always what they are, having the same simple, self-existent and unchanging forms, and not admitting of variation at all, or in any way, or at any time?

They must be always the same, Socrates, replied Cebes.

And what would you say of the many beautiful—whether men or horses or garments or any other things which may be called equal or beautiful—are they all unchanging and the same always, or quite the reverse? May they not rather be described as almost always changing and hardly ever the same either with themselves or with one another?

The latter, replied Cebes; they are always in a state of change.

And these you can touch and see and perceive with the senses, but the unchanging things you can only perceive with the mind—they are invisible and are not seen?

That is very true, he said.

Well, then, he added, let us suppose that there are two sorts of existences, one seen, the other unseen.

Let us suppose them.

The seen is the changing, and the unseen is the unchanging.

That may be also supposed.

And, further, is not one part of us body, and the rest of us soul?

To be sure.

And to which class may we say that the body is more alike and akin?

Clearly to the seen: no one can doubt that.

And is the soul seen or not seen?

Not by man, Socrates.

And by "seen" and "not seen" is meant by us that which is or is not visible to the eye of man?

Yes, to the eye of man.

And what do we say of the soul? is that seen or not seen?

Not seen.

Unseen then?

Yes.

Then the soul is more like to the unseen, and the body to the seen?

That is most certain, Socrates.

And were we not saying long ago that the soul when using the body as an instrument of perception, that is to say, when using the sense of sight or hearing or some other sense (for the meaning of perceiving through the body is perceiving through the senses)—were we not saying that the soul too is then dragged by the body into the region of the changeable, and wanders and is confused; the world spins round her, and she is like a drunkard when under their influence?

Very true.

But when returning into herself she reflects; then she passes into the realm of purity, and eternity, and immortality, and unchangeableness, which are her kindred, and with them she ever lives, when she is by herself and is not let or hindered; then she ceases from her erring ways, and being in communion with the unchanging is unchanging. And this state of the soul is called wisdom?

That is well and truly said, Socrates, he replied.

And to which class is the soul more nearly alike and akin, as far as may be inferred from this argument, as well as from the preceding one?

I think, Socrates, that, in the opinion of everyone who follows the argument, the soul will be infinitely more like the unchangeable—even the most stupid person will not deny that.

And the body is more like the changing?

Yes.

Yet once more consider the matter in this light: When the soul and the body are united, then nature orders the soul to rule and govern, and the body to obey and serve.

Now which of these two functions is akin to the divine? and which to the mortal? Does not the divine appear to you to be that which naturally orders and rules, and the mortal that which is subject and servant?

True.

And which does the soul resemble?

The soul resembles the divine and the body the mortal—there can be no doubt of that, Socrates.

Then reflect, Cebes: is not the conclusion of the whole matter this?—that the soul is in the very likeness of the divine, and immortal, and intelligible, and uniform, and indissoluble, and unchangeable; and the body is in the very likeness of the human, and mortal, and unintelligible, and multiform, and dissoluble, and changeable. Can this, my dear Cebes, be denied?

No, indeed.

But if this is true, then is not the body liable to speedy dissolution? and is not the soul almost or altogether indissoluble?

Certainly.

And do you further observe, that after a man is dead, the body, which is the visible part of man, and has a visible framework, which is called a corpse, and which would naturally be dissolved and decomposed and dissipated, is not dissolved or decomposed at once, but may remain for a good while, if the constitution be sound at the time of death, and the season of the year favorable? For the body when shrunk and embalmed, as is the custom in Egypt, may remain almost entire through infinite ages; and even in decay, still there are some portions, such as the bones and ligaments, which are practically indestructible. You allow that?

Yes.

And are we to suppose that the soul, which is invisible, in passing to the true Hades, which like her is invisible, and pure, and noble, and on her way to the good and wise God, whither, if God will, my soul is also soon to go—that the soul, I repeat, if this be her nature and origin, is blown away and perishes immediately on quitting the body as the many say? That can never be, dear Simmias and

Cebes. The truth rather is that the soul which is pure at departing draws after her no bodily taint, having never voluntarily had connection with the body, which she is ever avoiding, herself gathered into herself (for such abstraction has been the study of her life). And what does this mean but that she has been a true disciple of philosophy and has practised how to die easily? And is not philosophy the practice of death?

Certainly.

That soul, I say, herself invisible, departs to the invisible world—to the divine and immortal and rational: thither arriving, she lives in bliss and is released from the error and folly of men, their fears and wild passions and all other human ills, and forever dwells, as they say of the initiated, in company with the gods. Is not this true, Cebes?

Yes, said Cebes, beyond a doubt.

But the soul which has been polluted, and is impure at the time of her departure, and is the companion and servant of the body always, and is in love with and fascinated by the body and by the desires and pleasures of the body, until she is led to believe that the truth only exists in a bodily form, which a man may touch and see and taste and use for the purposes of his lusts—the soul, I mean, accustomed to hate and fear and avoid the intellectual principle, which to the bodily eye is dark and invisible, and can be attained only by philosophy—do you suppose that such a soul as this will depart pure and unalloyed?

That is impossible, he replied.

She is engrossed by the corporeal, which the continual association and constant care of the body have made natural to her.

Very true.

And this, my friend, may be conceived to be that heavy, weighty, earthy element of sight by which such a soul is depressed and dragged down again into the visible world, because she is afraid of the invisible and of the world below—prowling about tombs and sepulchres, in the neighborhood of which, as they tell us, are seen certain ghostly apparitions of souls which have not departed pure, but are cloyed with sight and therefore visible.

That is very likely, Socrates.

Yes, that is very likely, Cebes; and these must be the souls, not of the good, but of the evil, who are compelled to wander about such places in payment of the penalty of their former evil way of life; and they continue to wander until the desire which haunts them is satisfied and they are imprisoned in another body. And they may be supposed to be fixed in the same natures which they had in their former life.

What natures do you mean, Socrates?

I mean to say that men who have followed after gluttony, and wantonness, and drunkenness, and have had no thought of avoiding them, would pass into asses and animals of that sort. What do you think?

I think that exceedingly probable.

And those who have chosen the portion of injustice, and tyranny, and violence, will pass into wolves, or into hawks and kites; whither else can we suppose them to go?

Yes, said Cebes; that is doubtless the place of natures such as theirs.

And there is no difficulty, he said, in assigning to all of them places answering to their several natures and propensities?

There is not, he said.

Even among them some are happier than others; and the happiest both in themselves and their place of abode are those who have practised the civil and social virtues which are called temperance and justice, and are acquired by habit and attention without philosophy and mind.

Why are they the happiest?

Because they may be expected to pass into some gentle, social nature which is like their own, such as that of bees or ants, or even back again into the form of man, and just and moderate men spring from them.

That is not impossible.

But he who is a philosopher or lover of learning, and is entirely pure at departing, is alone permitted to reach the gods. And this is the reason, Simmias and Cebes, why the true votaries of philosophy abstain from all fleshly lusts, and endure and refuse to give themselves up to them—not because they fear poverty or the ruin of their families, like the lovers of money, and the world in general; nor like the lovers of power and honor, because they dread the dishonor or disgrace of evil deeds.

No, Socrates, that would not become them, said Cebes.

No, indeed, he replied; and therefore they who have a care of their souls, and do not merely live in the fashions of the body, say farewell to all this; they will not walk in the ways of the blind: and when philosophy offers them purification and release from evil, they feel that they ought not to resist her influence, and to her they incline, and whither she leads they follow her.

What do you mean, Socrates?

I will tell you, he said. The lovers of knowledge are conscious that their souls, when philosophy receives them, are simply fastened and glued to their bodies: the soul is only able to view existence through the bars of a prison, and not in her own nature; she is wallowing in the mire of all ignorance; and philosophy, seeing the terrible nature of her confinement, and that the captive through desire is led to conspire in her own captivity (for the lovers of knowledge are aware that this was the original state of the soul, and that when she was in this state philosophy received and gently counseled her, and wanted to release her, pointing out to her that the eye is full of deceit, and also the ear and other senses, and persuading her to retire from them in all but the necessary use of them and to be gathered up and collected into herself, and to trust only to herself and her own intuitions of absolute existence, and mistrust that which comes to her through others and is subject to vicissitude)—philosophy shows her that this is visible and tangible, but that what she sees in her own nature is intellectual and invisible. And the soul of the true philosopher thinks that she ought not to resist this deliverance, and therefore abstains from pleasures and desires and pains and fears, as far as she is able; reflecting that when a man has great joys or sorrows or fears or desires he suffers from them, not the sort of evil which might be anticipated—as, for example, the loss of his health or property, which he has sacrificed to his lusts—but he has suffered an evil greater far, which is the greatest and worst of all evils, and one of which he never thinks.

And what is that, Socrates? said Cebes.

Why, this: When the feeling of pleasure or pain in the soul is most intense, all of us naturally suppose that the object of this intense feeling is then plainest and truest: but this is not the case.

Very true.

And this is the state in which the soul is most enthralled by the body.

How is that?

Why, because each pleasure and pain is a sort of nail which nails and rivets the soul to the body, and engrosses her and makes her believe that to be true which the body affirms to be true; and from agreeing with the body and having the same delights she is obliged to have the same habits and ways, and is not likely ever to be pure at her departure to the world below, but is always saturated with the body; so that she soon sinks into another body and there germinates and grows, and has therefore no part in the communion of the divine and pure and simple.

That is most true, Socrates, answered Cebes.

And this, Cebes, is the reason why the true lovers of knowledge are temperate and brave; and not for the reason which the world gives.

Certainly not.

Certainly not! For not in that way does the soul of a philosopher reason; she will not ask philosophy to release her in order that when released she may deliver herself up again to the thraldom of pleasures and pains, doing a work only to be undone again, weaving instead of unweaving her Penelope's web. But she will make herself a calm of passion and follow Reason, and dwell in her, beholding the true and divine (which is not matter of opinion), and thence derive nourishment. Thus she seeks to live while she lives, and after death she hopes to go to her own kindred and to be freed from human ills. Never fear, Simmias and Cebes, that a soul which has been thus nurtured and has had these pursuits, will at her departure from the body be scattered and blown away by the winds and be nowhere and nothing.

When Socrates had done speaking, for a considerable time there was silence; he himself and most of us appeared to be meditating on what had been said; only Cebes and Simmias spoke a few words to one another. And Socrates observing this asked them what they thought of the argument, and whether there was anything wanting? For, said he, much is still open to suspicion and attack, if anyone were disposed to sift the matter thoroughly. If you are talking of something else I would rather not interrupt you, but if you are still doubtful about the argument do not hesitate to say exactly what you think, and let us have anything better which you can suggest; and if I am likely to be of any use, allow me to help you.

Simmias said: I must confess, Socrates, that doubts did arise in our minds, and each of us was urging and inciting the other to put the question which he wanted to have answered and which neither of us liked to ask, fearing that our importunity might be troublesome under present circumstances.

Socrates smiled and said: O Simmias, how strange that is; I am not very likely to persuade other men that I do not regard my present situation as a misfortune, if I am unable to persuade you, and you will keep fancying that I am at all more troubled now than at any other time. Will you not allow that I have as much of the spirit of prophecy in me as the swans? For they, when they perceive that they must die, having sung all their life long, do then sing more than ever, rejoicing in the thought that they are about to go away to the god whose ministers they are. But men, because they are themselves afraid of death, slanderously affirm of the swans that they sing a lament at the last, not considering that no bird sings when cold, or hungry, or in pain, not even the nightingale, nor the swallow, nor yet the hoopoe; which are said indeed to tune a lay of sorrow, although I do not believe this to be true of them any more than of the swans. But because they are sacred to Apollo and have the gift of prophecy and anticipate the good things of another world, therefore they sing and rejoice in that day more than they ever did before. And I, too, believing myself to be the consecrated servant of the same God, and the fellow servant of the swans, and thinking that I have received from my master gifts of prophecy which are not inferior to theirs, would not go out of life less merrily than the swans. Cease to mind then about this, but speak and ask anything which you like, while the eleven magistrates of Athens allow.

Well, Socrates, said Simmias, then I will tell you my difficulty, and Cebes will tell you his. For I dare say that you, Socrates, feel, as I do, how very hard or almost impossible is the attainment of any certainty about questions such as these in the present life. And yet I should deem him a coward who did not prove what is said about them to the uttermost, or whose heart failed him before he had examined them on every side. For he should persevere until he has attained one of two things: either he should discover or learn the truth about them; or, if this is impossible, I would have him take the best and most irrefragable of human notions, and let this be the raft upon which he sails through life—not without risk, as I admit, if he cannot find some word of God which will more surely and safely carry him. And now, as you bid me, I will venture to question you, as I should not like to reproach myself hereafter with not having said at the time what I think. For when I consider the matter either alone or with Cebes, the argument does certainly appear to me, Socrates, to be not sufficient.

Socrates answered: I dare say, my friend, that you may be right, but I should like to know in what respect the argument is not sufficient.

In this respect, replied Simmias: Might not a person use the same argument about harmony and the lyre—might he not say that harmony is a thing invisible, incorporeal, fair, divine, abiding in the lyre which is harmonized, but that the lyre and the strings are matter and material, composite, earthy, and akin to mortality? And when someone breaks the lyre, or cuts and rends the strings, then he who takes this view would argue as you do, and on the same analogy, that the harmony survives and has not perished; for you cannot imagine, as we would say, that the lyre without the strings, and the broken strings themselves, remain, and yet that the harmony, which is of heavenly and immortal nature and kindred, has perished—and perished too before the mortal. The harmony, he would say, certainly exists somewhere, and the wood and strings will decay before that decays. For I suspect, Socrates, that the notion of the soul which we are all of us inclined to entertain, would also be yours, and that you too would conceive the body to be strung up, and held together, by the elements of hot and cold, wet and dry, and the like, and that the soul is the harmony or due proportionate admixture of them. And, if this is true, the inference clearly is that when the strings of the body are unduly loosened or overstrained through disorder or other injury, then the soul, though most divine, like other harmonies of music or of the works of art, of course perishes at once, although the material remains of the body may last for a considerable time, until they are either decayed or burnt. Now if anyone maintained that the soul, being the harmony of the elements of the body, first perishes in that which is called death, how shall we answer him?

Socrates looked round at us as his manner was, and said, with a smile: Simmias has reason on his side; and why does not some one of you who is abler than myself answer him? for there is force in his attack upon me. But perhaps, before we answer him, we had better also hear what Cebes has to say against the argument—this will give us time for reflection, and when both of them have spoken, we may either assent to them if their words appear to be in consonance with the truth, or if not, we may take up the other side, and argue with them. Please to tell me then, Cebes, he said, what was the difficulty which troubled you?

Cebes said: I will tell you. My feeling is that the argument is still in the same position, and open to the same objections which were urged before; for I am ready to admit that the existence of the soul before entering into the bodily form has been very ingeniously, and, as I may be allowed to say, quite sufficiently proven; but the existence of the soul after death is still, in my judgment, unproven. Now my objection is not the same as that of Simmias; for I am not disposed to deny that the soul is stronger and more lasting than the body, being of opinion that in all such respects the soul very far excels the body. Well, then, says the argument to me, why do you remain unconvinced? When you see that the weaker is still in existence after the man is dead, will you not admit that the more lasting must also survive during the same period of time? Now I, like Simmias, must employ a figure; and I shall ask you to consider whether the figure is to the point. The parallel which I will suppose is that of an old weaver, who dies, and after his death somebody says: He is not dead, he must be alive; and he appeals to the coat which he himself wove and wore, and which is still whole and undecayed. And then he proceeds to ask of someone who is incredulous, whether a man lasts longer, or the coat which is in use and wear; and when he is answered that a man lasts far longer, thinks that he has thus certainly demonstrated the survival of the man, who is the more lasting, because the less lasting remains. But that, Simmias, as I would beg you to observe, is not the truth; everyone sees that he who talks thus is talking nonsense. For the truth is that this weaver, having worn and woven many such coats, though he outlived several of them, was himself outlived by the last; but this is surely very far from proving that a man is slighter and weaker than a coat. Now the relation of the body to the soul may be expressed in a similar figure; for you may say with reason that the soul is lasting, and the body weak and short-lived in comparison. And every soul may be said to wear out many bodies, especially in the course of a long life. For if while the man is alive the body deliquesces and decays, and yet the soul always weaves her garment anew and repairs the waste, then of course, when the soul perishes, she must have on her last garment, and this only will survive her; but then again when the soul is dead the body will at last show its native weakness, and soon pass into decay. And therefore this is an argument on which I would rather not rely as proving that the soul exists after death. For suppose that we grant even more than you affirm as within the range of possibility, and besides acknowledging that the soul existed before birth admit also that after death the souls of some are existing still, and will exist, and will be born and die again and again, and that there is a natural strength in the soul which will hold out and be born many times—for all this, we may be still inclined to think that she will weary in the labors of successive births, and may at last succumb in one of her deaths and utterly perish; and this death and dissolution of the body which brings destruction to the soul may be unknown to any of us, for no one of us can have had any experience of it: and if this be true, then I say that he who is confident in death has but a foolish confidence, unless he is able to prove that the soul is altogether immortal and imperishable. But if he is not able to prove this, he who is about to die will always have reason to fear that when the body is disunited, the soul also may utterly perish.

All of us, as we afterwards remarked to one another, had an

unpleasant feeling at hearing them say this. When we had been so firmly convinced before, now to have our faith shaken seemed to introduce a confusion and uncertainty, not only into the previous argument, but into any future one; either we were not good judges, or there were no real grounds of belief.

Ech. There I feel with you—indeed I do, Phædo, and when you were speaking, I was beginning to ask myself the same question: What argument can I ever trust again? For what could be more convincing than the argument of Socrates, which has now fallen into discredit? That the soul is a harmony is a doctrine which has always had a wonderful attraction for me, and, when mentioned, came back to me at once, as my own original conviction. And now I must begin again and find another argument which will assure me that when the man is dead the soul dies not with him. Tell me, I beg, how did Socrates proceed? Did he appear to share the unpleasant feeling which you mention? or did he receive the interruption calmly and give a sufficient answer? Tell us, as exactly as you can, what passed.

Phæd. Often, Echecrates, as I have admired Socrates, I never admired him more than at that moment. That he should be able to answer was nothing, but what astonished me was, first, the gentle and pleasant and approving manner in which he regarded the words of the young men, and then his quick sense of the wound which had been inflicted by the argument, and his ready application of the healing art. He might be compared to a general rallying his defeated and broken army, urging them to follow him and return to the field of argument.

Ech. How was that?

Phæd. You shall hear, for I was close to him on his right hand, seated on a sort of stool, and he on a couch which was a good deal higher. Now he had a way of playing with my hair, and then he smoothed my head, and pressed the hair upon my neck, and said: To-morrow, Phædo, I suppose that these fair locks of yours will be severed.

Yes, Socrates, I suppose that they will, I replied.

Not so if you will take my advice.

What shall I do with them? I said.

To-day, he replied, and not to-morrow, if this argument dies and cannot be brought to life again by us, you and I will both shave our locks; and if I were you, and could not maintain my ground against Simmias and Cebes, I would myself take an oath, like the Argives, not to wear hair any more until I had renewed the conflict and defeated them.

Yes, I said, but Heracles himself is said not to be a match for two.

Summon me then, he said, and I will be your Iolaus until the sun goes down.

I summon you rather, I said, not as Heracles summoning Iolaus, but as Iolaus might summon Heracles.

That will be all the same, he said. But first let us take care that we avoid a danger.

And what is that? I said.

The danger of becoming misologists, he replied, which is one of the very worst things that can happen to us. For as there are misanthropists or haters of men, there are also misologists or haters of ideas, and both spring from the same cause, which is ignorance of the world. Misanthropy arises from the too great confidence of inexperience; you trust a man and think him altogether true and good and faithful, and then in a little while he turns out to be false and knavish; and then another and another, and when this has happened several times to a man, especially within the circle of his most trusted friends, as he deems them, and he has often quarreled with them, he at last hates all men, and believes that no one has any good in him at all. I dare say that you must have observed this.

Yes, I said.

And is not this discreditable? The reason is that a man, having to deal with other men, has no knowledge of them; for if he had knowledge he would have known the true state of the case, that few are the good and few the evil, and that the great majority are in the interval between them.

How do you mean? I said.

I mean, he replied, as you might say of the very large and very small, that nothing is more uncommon than a very large or a very small man; and this applies generally to all extremes, whether of great and small, or swift and slow, or fair and foul, or black and white: and whether the instances you select be men or dogs or anything else, few are the extremes, but many are in the mean between them. Did you never observe this?

Yes, I said, I have.

And do you not imagine, he said, that if there were a competition of evil, the first in evil would be found to be very few?

Yes, that is very likely, I said.

Yes, that is very likely, he replied; not that in this respect arguments are like men—there I was led on by you to say more than I had intended; but the point of comparison was that when a simple man who has no skill in dialectics believes an argument to be true which he afterwards imagines to be false, whether really false or not, and then another and another, he has no longer any faith left, and great disputers, as you know, come to think, at last that they have grown to be the wisest of mankind; for they alone perceive the utter unsoundness and instability of all arguments, or, indeed, of all things, which, like the currents in the Euripus, are going up and down in never-ceasing ebb and flow.

That is quite true, I said.

Yes, Phædo, he replied, and very melancholy too, if there be such a thing as truth or certainty or power of knowing at all, that a man should have lighted upon some argument or other which at first seemed true and then turned out to be false, and instead of blaming himself and his own want of wit, because he is annoyed, should at last be too glad to transfer the blame from himself to arguments in general; and forever afterwards should hate and revile them, and lose the truth and knowledge of existence.

Yes, indeed, I said; that is very melancholy.

Let us, then, in the first place, he said, be careful of admitting into our souls the notion that there is no truth or health or soundness in any arguments at all; but let us rather say that there is as yet no health in us, and that we must quit ourselves like men and do our best to gain health—you and all other men with a view to the whole of your future life, and I myself with a view to death. For at this moment I am sensible that I have not the temper of a philosopher; like the vulgar, I am only a partisan. For the partisan, when he is engaged in a dispute, cares nothing about the rights of the question, but is anxious only to convince his hearers of his own assertions. And the difference between him and me at the present moment is only this—that whereas he seeks to convince his hearers that what he says is true, I am rather seeking to convince myself; to convince my hearers is a secondary matter with me. And do but see how much I gain by this. For if what I say is true, then I do well to be persuaded of the truth, but if there be nothing after death, still, during the short time that remains, I shall save my friends from lamentations, and my ignorance will not last, and therefore no harm will be done. This is the state of mind, Simmias and Cebes, in which I approach the argument. And I would ask you to be thinking of the truth and not of Socrates: agree with me, if I seem to you to be speaking the truth; or if not, withstand me might and main, that I may not deceive you as well as myself in my enthusiasm, and, like the bee, leave my sting in you before I die.

And now let us proceed, he said. And first of all let me be sure that I have in my mind what you were saying. Simmias, if I remember rightly, has fears and misgivings whether the soul, being in the form of harmony, although a fairer and diviner thing than the body, may not perish first. On the other hand, Cebes appeared to grant that the soul was more lasting than the body, but he said that no one could know whether the soul, after having worn out many bodies, might not perish herself and leave her last body behind her; and that this is death, which is the destruction not of the body but of the soul, for in the body the work of destruction is ever going on. Are not these, Simmias and Cebes, the points which we have to consider?

They both agreed to this statement of them.

He proceeded: And did you deny the force of the whole preceding argument, or of a part only?

Of a part only, they replied.

And what did you think, he said, of that part of the argument in which we said that knowledge was recollection only, and inferred from this that the soul must have previously existed somewhere else before she was enclosed in the body? Cebes said that he had been wonderfully impressed by that part of the argument, and that his conviction remained unshaken. Simmias agreed, and added that he himself could hardly imagine the possibility of his ever thinking differently about that.

But, rejoined Socrates, you will have to think differently, my Theban friend, if you still maintain that harmony is a compound, and that the soul is a harmony which is made out of strings set in the frame of the body; for you will surely never allow yourself to say that a harmony is prior to the elements which compose the harmony.

No, Socrates, that is impossible.

But do you not see that you *are* saying this when you say that the soul existed before she took the form and body of man, and was made up of elements which as yet had no existence? For harmony is not a sort of thing like the soul, as you suppose; but first the lyre, and the strings, and the sounds exist in a state of discord, and then harmony is made last of all, and perishes first. And how can such a notion of the soul as this agree with the other?

Not at all, replied Simmias.

And yet, he said, there surely ought to be harmony when harmony is the theme of discourse.

There ought, replied Simmias.

But there is no harmony, he said, in the two propositions that knowledge is recollection, and that the soul is a harmony. Which of them, then, will you retain?

I think, he replied, that I have a much stronger faith, Socrates, in the first of the two, which has been fully demonstrated to me, than in the latter, which has not been demonstrated at all, but rests only on probable and plausible grounds; and I know too well that these arguments from probabilities are impostors, and unless great caution is observed in the use of them they are apt to be deceptive—in geometry, and in other things too. But the doctrine of knowledge and recollection has been proven to me on trustworthy grounds; and the proof was that the soul must have existed before she came into the body, because to her belongs the essence of which the very name implies existence. Having, as I am convinced, rightly accepted this conclusion, and on sufficient grounds, I must, as I suppose, cease to argue or allow others to argue that the soul is a harmony.

Let me put the matter, Simmias, he said, in another point of view: Do you imagine that a harmony or any other composition can be in a state other than that of the elements out of which it is compounded?

Certainly not.

Or do or suffer anything other than they do or suffer?

He agreed.

Then a harmony does not lead the parts or elements which make up the harmony, but only follows them.

He assented.

For harmony cannot possibly have any motion, or sound, or other quality which is opposed to the parts.

That would be impossible, he replied.

And does not every harmony depend upon the manner in which the elements are harmonized?

I do not understand you, he said.

I mean to say that a harmony admits of degrees, and is more of a harmony, and more completely a harmony, when more completely harmonized, if that be possible; and less of a harmony, and less completely a harmony, when less harmonized.

True.

But does the soul admit of degrees? or is one soul in the very least degree more or less, or more or less completely, a soul than another?

Not in the least.

Yet surely one soul is said to have intelligence and virtue, and to be good, and another soul is said to have folly and vice, and to be an evil soul: and this is said truly?

Yes, truly.

But what will those who maintain the soul to be a harmony say of this presence of virtue and vice in the soul?—will they say that there is another harmony, and another discord, and that the virtuous soul is harmonized, and herself being a harmony has another harmony within her, and that the vicious soul is inharmonical and has no harmony within her?

I cannot say, replied Simmias; but I suppose that something of that kind would be asserted by those who take this view.

And the admission is already made that no soul is more a soul than another; and this is equivalent to admitting that harmony is not more or less harmony, or more or less completely a harmony?

Quite true.

And that which is not more or less a harmony is not more or less harmonized?

True.

And that which is not more or less harmonized cannot have more or less of harmony, but only an equal harmony?

Yes, an equal harmony.

Then one soul not being more or less absolutely a soul than another, is not more or less harmonized?

Exactly.

And therefore has neither more nor less of harmony or of discord?

She has not.

And having neither more nor less of harmony or of discord, one soul has no more vice or virtue than another, if vice be discord and virtue harmony?

Not at all more.

Or speaking more correctly, Simmias, the soul, if she is a harmony, will never have any vice; because a harmony, being absolutely a harmony, has no part in the inharmonical?

No.

And therefore a soul which is absolutely a soul has no vice?

How can she have, consistently with the preceding argument?

Then, according to this, if the souls of all animals are equally and absolutely souls, they will be equally good?

I agree with you, Socrates, he said.

And can all this be true, think you? he said; and are all these consequences admissible—which nevertheless seem to follow from the assumption that the soul is a harmony?

Certainly not, he said.

Once more, he said, what ruling principle is there of human things other than the soul, and especially the wise soul? Do you know of any?

Indeed, I do not.

And is the soul in agreement with the affections of the body? or is she at variance with them? For example, when the body is hot and thirsty, does not the soul incline us against drinking? and when the body is hungry, against eating? And this is only one instance out of ten thousand of the opposition of the soul to the things of the body.

Very true.

But we have already acknowledged that the soul, being a harmony, can never utter a note at variance with the tensions and relaxations and vibrations and other affections of the strings out of which she is composed; she can only follow, she cannot lead them?

Yes, he said, we acknowledged that, certainly.

And yet do we not now discover the soul to be doing the exact opposite—leading the elements of which she is believed to be composed; almost always opposing and coercing them in all sorts of ways throughout life, sometimes more violently with the pains of medicine and gymnastic; then again more gently; threatening and also reprimanding the desires, passions, fears, as if talking to a thing which is not herself, as Homer in the "Odyssey" represents Odysseus doing in the words,

> "He beat his breast, and thus reproached his heart:
> Endure, my heart; far worse hast thou endured!"

Do you think that Homer could have written this under the idea that the soul is a harmony capable of being led by the affections of the body, and not rather of a nature which leads and masters them; and herself a far diviner thing than any harmony?

Yes, Socrates, I quite agree to that.

Then, my friend, we can never be right in saying that the soul is a harmony, for that would clearly contradict the divine Homer as well as ourselves.

True, he said.

Thus much, said Socrates, of Harmonia, your Theban goddess, Cebes, who has not been ungracious to us, I think; but what shall I say to the Theban Cadmus, and how shall I propitiate him?

I think that you will discover a way of propitiating him, said Cebes; I am sure that you have answered the argument about harmony in a manner that I could never have expected. For when

Simmias mentioned his objection, I quite imagined that no answer could be given to him, and therefore I was surprised at finding that his argument could not sustain the first onset of yours; and not impossibly the other, whom you call Cadmus, may share a similar fate.

Nay, my good friend, said Socrates, let us not boast, lest some evil eye should put to flight the word which I am about to speak. That, however, may be left in the hands of those above, while I draw near in Homeric fashion, and try the mettle of your words. Briefly, the sum of your objection is as follows: You want to have proven to you that the soul is imperishable and immortal, and you think that the philosopher who is confident in death has but a vain and foolish confidence, if he thinks that he will fare better than one who has led another sort of life, in the world below, unless he can prove this; and you say that the demonstration of the strength and divinity of the soul, and of her existence prior to our becoming men, does not necessarily imply her immortality. Granting that the soul is long-lived, and has known and done much in a former state, still she is not on that account immortal; and her entrance into the human form may be a sort of disease which is the beginning of dissolution, and may at last, after the toils of life are over, end in that which is called death. And whether the soul enters into the body once only or many times, that, as you would say, makes no difference in the fears of individuals. For any man, who is not devoid of natural feeling, has reason to fear, if he has no knowledge or proof of the soul's immortality. That is what I suppose you to say, Cebes, which I designedly repeat, in order that nothing may escape us, and that you may, if you wish, add or subtract anything.

But, said Cebes, as far as I can see at present, I have nothing to add or subtract; you have expressed my meaning.

Socrates paused awhile, and seemed to be absorbed in reflection. At length he said: This is a very serious inquiry which you are raising, Cebes, involving the whole question of generation and corruption, about which I will, if you like, give you my own experience; and you can apply this, if you think that anything which I say will avail towards the solution of your difficulty.

I should very much like, said Cebes, to hear what you have to say.

Then I will tell you, said Socrates. When I was young, Cebes, I had a prodigious desire to know that department of philosophy which is called Natural Science; this appeared to me to have lofty aims, as being the science which has to do with the causes of things, and which teaches why a thing is, and is created and destroyed; and I was always agitating myself with the consideration of such questions as these: Is the growth of animals the result of some decay which the hot and cold principle contracts, as some have said? Is the blood the element with which we think, or the air, or the fire? or perhaps nothing of this sort—but the brain may be the originating power of the perceptions of hearing and sight and smell, and memory and opinion may come from them, and science may be based on memory and opinion when no longer in motion, but at rest. And then I went on to examine the decay of them, and then to the things of heaven and earth, and at last I concluded that I was wholly incapable of these inquiries, as I will satisfactorily prove to you. For I was fascinated by them to such a degree that my eyes grew blind to things that I had seemed to myself, and also to others, to know quite well; and I forgot what I had before thought to be self-evident, that the growth of man is the result of eating and drinking; for when by the digestion of food flesh is added to flesh and bone to bone, and whenever there is an aggregation of congenial elements, the lesser bulk becomes larger and the small man greater. Was not that a reasonable notion?

Yes, said Cebes, I think so.

Well; but let me tell you something more. There was a time when I thought that I understood the meaning of greater and less pretty well; and when I saw a great man standing by a little one I fancied that one was taller than the other by a head; or one horse would appear to be greater than another horse: and still more clearly did I seem to perceive that ten is two more than eight, and that two cubits are more than one, because two is twice one.

And what is now your notion of such matters? said Cebes.

I should be far enough from imagining, he replied, that I knew the cause of any of them, indeed I should, for I cannot satisfy myself that when one is added to one, the one to which the addition is made becomes two, or that the two units added together make two by reason of the addition. For I cannot understand how, when separated from the other, each of them was one and not two, and now, when they are brought together, the mere juxtaposition of them can be the cause of their becoming two: nor can I understand how the division of one is the way to make two; for then a different cause would produce the same effect—as in the former instance the addition and juxtaposition of one to one was the cause of two, in this the separation and subtraction of one from the other would be the cause. Nor am I any longer satisfied that I understand the reason why one or anything else either is generated or destroyed or is at all, but I have in my mind some confused notion of another method, and can never admit this.

Then I heard someone who had a book of Anaxagoras, as he said, out of which he read that mind was the disposer and cause of all, and I was quite delighted at the notion of this, which appeared admirable, and I said to myself: If mind is the disposer, mind will dispose all for the best, and put each particular in the best place; and I argued that if anyone desired to find out the cause of the generation or destruction or existence of anything, he must find out what state of being or suffering or doing was best for that thing, and therefore a man had only to consider the best for himself and others, and then he would also know the worse, for that the same science comprised both. And I rejoiced to think that I had found in Anaxagoras a teacher of the causes of existence such as I desired, and I imagined that he would tell me first whether the earth is flat or round; and then he would further explain the cause and the necessity of this, and would teach me the nature of the best and show that this was best; and if he said that the earth was in the centre, he would explain that this position was the best, and I should be satisfied if this were shown to me, and not want any other sort of cause. And I thought that I would then go and ask him about the sun and moon and stars, and that he would explain to me their comparative swiftness, and their returnings and various states, and how their several affections, active and passive, were all for the best. For I could not imagine that when he spoke of mind as the disposer of them, he would give any other account of their being as they are, except that this was best; and I thought when he had explained to me in detail the cause of each and the cause of all, he would go on to explain to me what was best for each and what was best for all. I had hopes which I would not have sold for much, and I seized the books and read them as fast as I could in my eagerness to know the better and the worse.

What hopes I had formed, and how grievously was I disappointed! As I proceeded, I found my philosopher altogether forsaking mind or any other principle of order, but having recourse to air, and ether, and water, and other eccentricities. I might compare him to a person who began by maintaining generally that mind is the cause of the actions of Socrates, but who, when he endeavored to explain the causes of my several actions in detail, went on to show that I sit here because my body is made up of bones and muscles; and the bones, as he would say, are hard and have ligaments which divide them, and the muscles are elastic, and they cover the bones, which have also a covering or environment of flesh and skin which contains them; and as the bones are lifted at their joints by the contraction or relaxation of the muscles, I am able to bend my limbs, and this is why I am sitting here in a curved posture: that is what he would say, and he would have a similar explanation of my talking to you, which he would attribute to sound, and air, and hearing, and he would assign ten thousand other causes of the same sort, forgetting to mention the true cause, which is that the Athenians have thought fit to condemn me, and accordingly I have thought it better and more right to remain here and undergo my sentence; for I am inclined to think that these muscles and bones of mine would have gone off to Megara or Bœotia—by the dog of Egypt they would, if they had been guided only by their own idea of what was best, and if I had not chosen as the better and nobler part, instead of playing truant and running away, to undergo any punishment which the State inflicts. There is surely a strange confusion of causes and conditions in all this. It may be said, indeed, that without bones and muscles and the other parts of the body I cannot execute my purposes. But to say that I do as I do because of them, and that this is the way in which mind acts, and not from the choice of the best, is a very careless and idle mode of speaking. I wonder that they cannot distinguish the cause from the condition, which the many, feeling about in the dark, are always mistaking and misnaming. And thus one man makes a vortex all round and steadies the earth by the heaven; another gives the air as a support to the earth, which is a sort of broad trough. Any power which in disposing them as they are disposes them for the best never enters into their minds, nor do they imagine that there is any superhuman strength in that; they rather expect to find another Atlas of the world who is stronger and more everlasting and more containing than the good is, and are clearly of opinion that the obligatory and containing power of the good is as nothing; and yet this is the principle which I would fain learn if anyone would teach me. But as I have failed either to discover myself or to learn of anyone else, the nature of the best, I will exhibit to you, if you like, what I have found to be the second best mode of inquiring into the cause.

I should very much like to hear that, he replied.

Socrates proceeded: I thought that as I had failed in the contemplation of true existence, I ought to be careful that I did not lose the eye of my soul; as people may injure their bodily eye by observing and gazing on the sun during an eclipse, unless they take the precaution of only looking at the image reflected in the water, or in some similar medium. That occurred to me, and I was afraid that my soul might be blinded altogether if I looked at things with my eyes or tried by the help of the senses to apprehend them. And I thought that I had better have recourse to ideas, and seek in them the truth of existence. I dare say that the simile is not perfect—for I am very far from admitting that he who contemplates existence through the medium of ideas, sees them only "through a glass darkly," any more than he who sees them in their working and effects. However, this was the method which I adopted: I first assumed some principle which I judged to be the strongest, and then I affirmed as true whatever seemed to agree with this, whether relating to the cause or to anything else; and that which disagreed I regarded as untrue. But I should like to explain my meaning clearly, as I do not think that you understand me.

No, indeed, replied Cebes, not very well.

There is nothing new, he said, in what I am about to tell you; but only what I have been always and everywhere repeating in the previous discussion and on other occasions: I want to show you the nature of that cause which has occupied my thoughts, and I shall have to go back to those familiar words which are in the mouth of everyone, and first of all assume that there is an absolute beauty and goodness and greatness, and the like; grant me this, and I hope to be able to show you the nature of the cause, and to prove the immortality of the soul.

Cebes said: You may proceed at once with the proof, as I readily grant you this.

Well, he said, then I should like to know whether you agree with me in the next step; for I cannot help thinking that if there be anything beautiful other than absolute beauty, that can only be beautiful in as far as it partakes of absolute beauty—and this I should say of everything. Do you agree in this notion of the cause?

Yes, he said, I agree.

He proceeded: I know nothing and can understand nothing of any other of those wise causes which are alleged; and if a person says to me that the bloom of color, or form, or anything else of that sort is a source of beauty, I leave all that, which is only confusing to me, and simply and singly, and perhaps foolishly, hold and am assured in my own mind that nothing makes a thing beautiful but the presence and participation of beauty in whatever way or manner obtained; for as to the manner I am uncertain, but I stoutly contend that by beauty all beautiful things become beautiful. That appears to me to be the only safe answer that I can give, either to myself or to any other, and to that I cling, in the persuasion that I shall never be overthrown, and that I may safely answer to myself or any other that by beauty beautiful things become beautiful. Do you not agree to that?

Yes, I agree.

And that by greatness only great things become great and greater greater, and by smallness the less becomes less.

True.

Then if a person remarks that A is taller by a head than B, and B less by a head than A, you would refuse to admit this, and would stoutly contend that what you mean is only that the greater is greater by, and by reason of, greatness, and the less is less only by, or by reason of, smallness; and thus you would avoid the danger of saying that the greater is greater and the less less by the measure of the head, which is the same in both, and would also avoid the monstrous absurdity of supposing that the greater man is greater by reason of the head, which is small. Would you not be afraid of that?

Indeed, I should, said Cebes, laughing.

In like manner you would be afraid to say that ten exceeded eight by, and by reason of, two; but would say by, and by reason of, number; or that two cubits exceed one cubit not by a half, but by magnitude?—that is what you would say, for there is the same danger in both cases.

Very true, he said.

Again, would you not be cautious of affirming that the addition of one to one, or the division of one, is the cause of two? And you would loudly asseverate that you know of no way in which anything comes into existence except by participation in its own proper essence, and consequently, as far as you know, the only cause of two is the participation in duality; that is the way to make two, and the participation in one is the way to make one. You would say: I will let alone puzzles of division and addition—wiser heads than mine may answer them; inexperienced as I am, and ready to start, as the proverb says, at my own shadow, I cannot afford to give up the sure ground of a principle. And if anyone assails you there, you would not mind him, or answer him until you had seen whether the consequences which follow agree with one another or not, and when you are further required to give an explanation of this principle, you would go on to assume a higher principle, and the best of the higher ones, until you found a resting-place; but you would not refuse the principle and the consequences in your reasoning like the Eristics—at least if you wanted to discover real existence. Not that this confusion signifies to them who never care or think about the matter at all, for they have the wit to be well pleased with themselves, however great may be the turmoil of their ideas. But you, if you are a philosopher, will, I believe, do as I say.

What you say is most true, said Simmias and Cebes, both speaking at once.

Ech. Yes, Phædo; and I don't wonder at their assenting. Anyone who has the least sense will acknowledge the wonderful clearness of Socrates' reasoning.

Phæd. Certainly, Echecrates; and that was the feeling of the whole company at the time.

Ech. Yes, and equally of ourselves, who were not of the company, and are now listening to your recital. But what followed?

Phæd. After all this was admitted, and they had agreed about the existence of ideas and the participation in them of the other things which derive their names from them, Socrates, if I remember rightly, said:—

This is your way of speaking; and yet when you say that Simmias is greater than Socrates and less than Phædo, do you not predicate of Simmias both greatness and smallness?

Yes, I do.

But still you allow that Simmias does not really exceed Socrates, as the words may seem to imply, because he is Simmias, but by reason of the size which he has; just as Simmias does not exceed Socrates because he is Simmias, any more than because Socrates is Socrates, but because he has smallness when compared with the greatness of Simmias?

True.

And if Phædo exceeds him in size, that is not because Phædo is Phædo, but because Phædo has greatness relatively to Simmias, who is comparatively smaller?

That is true.

And therefore Simmias is said to be great, and is also said to be small, because he is in a mean between them, exceeding the smallness of the one by his greatness, and allowing the greatness of the other to exceed his smallness. He added, laughing, I am speaking like a book, but I believe that what I am now saying is true.

Simmias assented to this.

The reason why I say this is that I want you to agree with me in thinking, not only that absolute greatness will never be great and also small, but that greatness in us or in the concrete will never admit the small or admit of being exceeded: instead of this, one of two things will happen—either the greater will fly or retire before the opposite, which is the less, or at the advance of the less will cease to exist; but will not, if allowing or admitting smallness, be changed by that; even as I, having received and admitted smallness when compared with Simmias, remain just as I was, and am the same small person. And as the idea of greatness cannot condescend ever to be or become small, in like manner the smallness in us cannot be or become great; nor can any other opposite which remains the same ever be or become its own opposite, but either passes away or perishes in the change.

That, replied Cebes, is quite my notion.

One of the company, though I do not exactly remember which of them, on hearing this, said: By Heaven, is not this the direct contrary of what was admitted before—that out of the greater came the less and out of the less the greater, and that opposites are simply generated from opposites; whereas now this seems to be utterly denied.

Socrates inclined his head to the speaker and listened. I like your courage, he said, in reminding us of this. But you do not observe that there is a difference in the two cases. For then we were speaking of opposites in the concrete, and now of the essential opposite which, as is affirmed, neither in us nor in nature can ever be at variance with itself: then, my friend, we were speaking of things in which opposites are inherent and which are called after them, but now about the opposites which are inherent in them and which give their name to them; these essential opposites will never, as we maintain, admit of generation into or out of one another. At the same time, turning to Cebes, he said: Were you at all disconcerted, Cebes, at our friend's objection?

That was not my feeling, said Cebes; and yet I cannot deny that I am apt to be disconcerted.

Then we are agreed after all, said Socrates, that the opposite will never in any case be opposed to itself?

To that we are quite agreed, he replied.

Yet once more let me ask you to consider the question from another point of view, and see whether you agree with me: There is a thing which you term heat, and another thing which you term cold?

Certainly.

But are they the same as fire and snow?

Most assuredly not.

Heat is not the same as fire, nor is cold the same as snow?

No.

And yet you will surely admit that when snow, as before said, is under the influence of heat, they will not remain snow and heat; but at the advance of the heat the snow will either retire or perish?

Very true, he replied.

And the fire too at the advance of the cold will either retire or perish; and when the fire is under the influence of the cold, they will not remain, as before, fire and cold.

That is true, he said.

And in some cases the name of the idea is not confined to the idea; but anything else which, not being the idea, exists only in the form of the idea, may also lay claim to it. I will try to make this clearer by an example: The odd number is always called by the name of odd?

Very true.

But is this the only thing which is called odd? Are there not other things which have their own name, and yet are called odd, because, although not the same as oddness, they are never without oddness?—that is what I mean to ask—whether numbers such as the number three are not of the class of odd. And there are many other examples: would you not say, for example, that three may be called by its proper name, and also be called odd, which is not the same with three? and this may be said not only of three but also of five, and every alternate number—each of them without being oddness is odd, and in the same way two and four, and the whole series of alternate numbers, has every number even, without being evenness. Do you admit that?

Yes, he said, how can I deny that?

Then now mark the point at which I am aiming: not only do essential opposites exclude one another, but also concrete things, which, although not in themselves opposed, contain opposites; these, I say, also reject the idea which is opposed to that which is contained in them, and at the advance of that they either perish or withdraw. There is the number three for example; will not that endure annihilation or anything sooner than be converted into an even number, remaining three?

Very true, said Cebes.

And yet, he said, the number two is certainly not opposed to the number three?

It is not.

Then not only do opposite ideas repel the advance of one another, but also there are other things which repel the approach of opposites.

That is quite true, he said.

Suppose, he said, that we endeavor, if possible, to determine what these are.

By all means.

Are they not, Cebes, such as compel the things of which they have possession, not only to take their own form, but also the form of some opposite?

What do you mean?

I mean, as I was just now saying, and have no need to repeat to you, that those things which are possessed by the number three must not only be three in number, but must also be odd.

Quite true.

And on this oddness, of which the number three has the impress, the opposite idea will never intrude?

No.

And this impress was given by the odd principle?

Yes.

And to the odd is opposed the even?

True.

Then the idea of the even number will never arrive at three?

No.

Then three has no part in the even?

None.

Then the triad or number three is uneven?

Very true.

To return then to my distinction of natures which are not opposites, and yet do not admit opposites: as, in this instance, three, although not opposed to the even, does not any the more admit of the even, but always brings the opposite into play on the other side;

or as two does not receive the odd, or fire the cold—from these examples (and there are many more of them) perhaps you may be able to arrive at the general conclusion that not only opposites will not receive opposites, but also that nothing which brings the opposite will admit the opposite of that which it brings in that to which it is brought. And here let me recapitulate—for there is no harm in repetition. The number five will not admit the nature of the even, any more than ten, which is the double of five, will admit the nature of the odd—the double, though not strictly opposed to the odd, rejects the odd altogether. Nor again will parts in the ratio of 3: 2, nor any fraction in which there is a half, nor again in which there is a third, admit the notion of the whole, although they are not opposed to the whole. You will agree to that?

Yes, he said, I entirely agree and go along with you in that.

And now, he said, I think that I may begin again; and to the question which I am about to ask I will beg you to give not the old safe answer, but another, of which I will offer you an example; and I hope that you will find in what has been just said another foundation which is as safe. I mean that if anyone asks you "what that is, the inherence of which makes the body hot," you will reply not heat (this is what I call the safe and stupid answer), but fire, a far better answer, which we are now in a condition to give. Or if anyone asks you "why a body is diseased," you will not say from disease, but from fever; and instead of saying that oddness is the cause of odd numbers, you will say that the monad is the cause of them: and so of things in general, as I dare say that you will understand sufficiently without my adducing any further examples.

Yes, he said, I quite understand you.

Tell me, then, what is that the inherence of which will render the body alive?

The soul, he replied.

And is this always the case?

Yes, he said, of course.

Then whatever the soul possesses, to that she comes bearing life?

Yes, certainly.

And is there any opposite to life?

There is, he said.

And what is that?

Death.

Then the soul, as has been acknowledged, will never receive the opposite of what she brings. And now, he said, what did we call that principle which repels the even?

The odd.

And that principle which repels the musical, or the just?

The unmusical, he said, and the unjust.

And what do we call the principle which does not admit of death?

The immortal, he said.

And does the soul admit of death?

No.

Then the soul is immortal?

Yes, he said.

And may we say that this is proven?

Yes, abundantly proven, Socrates, he replied.

And supposing that the odd were imperishable, must not three be imperishable?

Of course.

And if that which is cold were imperishable, when the warm principle came attacking the snow, must not the snow have retired whole and unmelted—for it could never have perished, nor could it have remained and admitted the heat?

True, he said.

Again, if the uncooling or warm principle were imperishable, the fire when assailed by cold would not have perished or have been extinguished, but would have gone away unaffected?

Certainly, he said.

And the same may be said of the immortal: if the immortal is also imperishable, the soul when attacked by death cannot perish; for the preceding argument shows that the soul will not admit of death, or ever be dead, any more than three or the odd number will admit of the even, or fire or the heat in the fire, of the cold. Yet a person may say: "But although the odd will not become even at the approach of the even, why may not the odd perish and the even take the place of the odd?" Now to him who makes this objection, we cannot answer that the odd principle is imperishable; for this has not been acknowledged, but if this had been acknowledged, there would have been no difficulty in contending that at the approach of the even the odd principle and the number three took up their departure; and the same argument would have held good of fire and heat and any other thing.

Very true.

And the same may be said of the immortal: if the immortal is also imperishable, then the soul will be imperishable as well as immortal; but if not, some other proof of her imperishableness will have to be given.

No other proof is needed, he said; for if the immortal, being eternal, is liable to perish, then nothing is imperishable.

Yes, replied Socrates, all men will agree that God, and the essential form of life, and the immortal in general, will never perish.

Yes, all men, he said—that is true; and what is more, gods, if I am not mistaken, as well as men.

Seeing then that the immortal is indestructible, must not the soul, if she is immortal, be also imperishable?

Most certainly.

Then when death attacks a man, the mortal portion of him may be supposed to die, but the immortal goes out of the way of death and is preserved safe and sound?

True.

Then, Cebes, beyond question the soul is immortal and imperishable, and our souls will truly exist in another world!

I am convinced, Socrates, said Cebes, and have nothing more to object; but if my friend Simmias, or anyone else, has any further objection, he had better speak out, and not keep silence, since I do not know how there can ever be a more fitting time to which he can defer the discussion, if there is anything which he wants to say or have said.

But I have nothing more to say, replied Simmias; nor do I see any room for uncertainty, except that which arises necessarily out of the greatness of the subject and the feebleness of man, and which I cannot help feeling.

Yes, Simmias, replied Socrates, that is well said: and more than that, first principles, even if they appear certain, should be carefully considered; and when they are satisfactorily ascertained, then, with a sort of hesitating confidence in human reason, you may, I think, follow the course of the argument; and if this is clear, there will be no need for any further inquiry.

That, he said, is true.

But then, O my friends, he said, if the soul is really immortal, what care should be taken of her, not only in respect of the portion of time which is called life, but of eternity! And the danger of neglecting her from this point of view does indeed appear to be awful. If death had only been the end of all, the wicked would have had a good bargain in dying, for they would have been happily quit not only of their body, but of their own evil together with their souls. But now, as the soul plainly appears to be immortal, there is no release or salvation from evil except the attainment of the highest virtue and wisdom. For the soul when on her progress to the world below takes nothing with her but nurture and education; which are indeed said greatly to benefit or greatly to injure the departed, at the very beginning of its pilgrimage in the other world.

For after death, as they say, the genius of each individual, to whom he belonged in life, leads him to a certain place in which the dead are gathered together for judgment, whence they go into the world below, following the guide who is appointed to conduct them from this world to the other: and when they have there received their due and remained their time, another guide brings them back again after many revolutions of ages. Now this journey to the other world is not, as Æschylus says in the "Telephus," a single and straight path—no guide would be wanted for that, and no one could miss a single path; but there are many partings of the road, and windings, as I must infer from the rites and sacrifices which are offered to the gods below in places where three ways meet on earth. The wise and orderly soul is conscious of her situation and follows in the path; but the soul which desires the body, and which, as I was relating before, has long been fluttering about the lifeless frame and the world of sight, is after many struggles and many sufferings hardly and with violence carried away by her attendant genius, and when she arrives at the place where the other souls are gathered, if she be impure and have done impure deeds, or been concerned in foul murders or other crimes which are the brothers of these, and the works of brothers in crime—from that soul everyone flees and turns away; no one will be her companion, no one her guide, but alone she wanders in extremity of evil until certain times are fulfilled, and when they are fulfilled, she is borne irresistibly to her own fitting habitation; as every pure and just soul which has passed through life in the company and under the guidance of the gods has also her own proper home.

Now the earth has divers wonderful regions, and is indeed in nature and extent very unlike the notions of geographers, as I believe on the authority of one who shall be nameless.

What do you mean, Socrates? said Simmias. I have myself heard many descriptions of the earth, but I do not know in what you are putting your faith, and I should like to know.

Well, Simmias, replied Socrates, the recital of a tale does not, I think, require the art of Glaucus; and I know not that the art of Glaucus could prove the truth of my tale, which I myself should never be able to prove, and even if I could, I fear, Simmias, that my life would come to an end before the argument was completed. I may describe to you, however, the form and regions of the earth according to my conception of them.

That, said Simmias, will be enough.

Well, then, he said, my conviction is that the earth is a round body in the center of the heavens, and therefore has no need of air or any similar force as a support, but is kept there and hindered from falling or inclining any way by the equability of the surrounding heaven and by her own equipoise. For that which, being in equipoise, is in the center of that which is equably diffused, will not incline any way in any degree, but will always remain in the same state and not deviate. And this is my first notion.

Which is surely a correct one, said Simmias.

Also I believe that the earth is very vast, and that we who dwell in the region extending from the river Phasis to the Pillars of Heracles, along the borders of the sea, are just like ants or frogs about a marsh, and inhabit a small portion only, and that many others dwell in many like places. For I should say that in all parts of the earth there are hollows of various forms and sizes, into which the water and the mist and the air collect; and that the true earth is pure and in the pure heaven, in which also are the stars—that is the heaven which is commonly spoken of as the ether, of which this is but the sediment collecting in the hollows of the earth. But we who live in these hollows are deceived into the notion that we are dwelling above on the surface of the earth; which is just as if a creature who was at the bottom of the sea were to fancy that he was on the surface of the water, and that the sea was the heaven through which he saw the sun and the other stars—he having never come to the surface by reason of his feebleness and sluggishness, and having never lifted up his head and seen, nor ever heard from one who had seen, this region which is so much purer and fairer than his own. Now this is exactly our case: for we are dwelling in a hollow of the earth, and fancy that we are on the surface; and the air we call the heaven, and in this we imagine that the stars move. But this is also owing to our feebleness and sluggishness, which prevent our reaching the surface of the air: for if any man could arrive at the exterior limit, or take the wings of a bird and fly upward, like a fish who puts his head out and sees this world, he would see a world beyond; and, if the nature of man could sustain the sight, he would acknowledge that this was the place of the true heaven and the true light and the true stars. For this earth, and the stones, and the entire region which surrounds us, are spoilt and corroded, like the things in the sea which are corroded by the brine; for in the sea too there is hardly any noble or perfect growth, but clefts only, and sand, and an endless slough of mud: and even the shore is not to be compared to the fairer sights of this world. And greater far is the superiority of the other. Now of that upper earth which is under the heaven, I can tell you a charming tale, Simmias, which is well worth hearing.

And we, Socrates, replied Simmias, shall be charmed to listen.

The tale, my friend, he said, is as follows: In the first place, the earth, when looked at from above, is like one of those balls which have leather coverings in twelve pieces, and is of divers colors, of which the colors which painters use on earth are only a sample. But there the whole earth is made up of them, and they are brighter far and clearer than ours; there is a purple of wonderful luster, also the radiance of gold, and the white which is in the earth is whiter than any chalk or snow. Of these and other colors the earth is made up, and they are more in number and fairer than the eye of man has ever seen; and the very hollows (of which I was speaking) filled with air and water are seen like light flashing amid the other colors, and have a color of their own, which gives a sort of unity to the variety of earth. And in this fair region everything that grows—trees, and flowers, and fruits—is in a like degree fairer than any here; and there are hills, and stones in them in a like degree smoother, and more transparent, and fairer in color than our highly valued emeralds and sardonyxes and jaspers, and other gems, which are but minute fragments of them: for there all the stones are like our precious stones, and fairer still. The reason of this is that they are pure, and not, like our precious stones, infected or corroded by the corrupt briny elements which coagulate among us, and which breed foulness and disease both in earth and stones, as well as in animals and plants. They are the jewels of the upper earth, which also shines with gold and silver and the like, and they are visible to sight and large and abundant and found in every region of the earth, and blessed is he who sees them. And upon the earth are animals and men, some in a middle region, others dwelling about the air as we dwell about the sea; others in islands which the air flows round, near the continent: and in a word, the air is used by them as the water and the sea are by us, and the ether is to them what the air is to us. Moreover, the temperament of their seasons is such that they have no disease, and live much longer than we do, and have sight and hearing and smell, and all the other senses, in far greater perfection, in the same degree that air is purer than water or the ether than air. Also they have temples and sacred places in which the gods really dwell, and they hear their voices and receive their answers, and are conscious of them and hold converse with them, and they see the sun, moon, and stars as they really are, and their other blessedness is of a piece with this.

Such is the nature of the whole earth, and of the things which are around the earth; and there are divers regions in the hollows on the face of the globe everywhere, some of them deeper and also wider than that which we inhabit, others deeper and with a narrower opening than ours, and some are shallower and wider; all have numerous perforations, and passages broad and narrow in the interior of the earth, connecting them with one another; and there flows into and out of them, as into basins, a vast tide of water, and huge subterranean streams of perennial rivers, and springs hot and cold, and a great fire, and great rivers of fire, and streams of liquid mud, thin or thick (like the rivers of mud in Sicily, and the lava-streams which follow them), and the regions about which they happen to flow are filled up with them. And there is a sort of swing in the interior of the earth which moves all this up and down. Now the swing is in this wise: There is a chasm which is the vastest of them all, and pierces right through the whole earth; this is that which Homer describes in the words,

> "Far off, where is the inmost depth beneath the earth";

and which he in other places, and many other poets, have called Tartarus. And the swing is caused by the streams flowing into and out of this chasm, and they each have the nature of the soil through which they flow. And the reason why the streams are always flowing in and out is that the watery element has no bed or bottom, and is surging and swinging up and down, and the surrounding wind and air do the same; they follow the water up and down, hither and thither, over the earth—just as in respiring the air is always in process of inhalation and exhalation; and the wind swinging with the water in and out produces fearful and irresistible blasts: when the waters retire with a rush into the lower parts of the earth, as they are called, they flow through the earth into those regions, and fill them up as with the alternate motion of a pump, and then when they leave those regions and rush back hither, they again fill the hollows here, and when these are filled, flow through subterranean channels and find their way to their several places, forming seas, and lakes, and rivers, and springs. Thence they again enter the earth, some of them making a long circuit into many lands, others going to few places and those not distant, and again fall into Tartarus, some at a point a good deal lower than that at which they rose, and others not much lower, but all in some degree lower than the point of issue. And some burst forth again on the opposite side, and some on the same side, and some wind round the earth with one or many folds, like the coils of a serpent, and descend as far as they can, but always return and fall into the lake. The rivers on either side can descend only to the center and no further, for to the rivers on both sides the opposite side is a precipice.

Now these rivers are many, and mighty, and diverse, and there are four principal ones, of which the greatest and outermost is that called Oceanus, which flows round the earth in a circle; and in the opposite direction flows Acheron, which passes under the earth through desert places, into the Acherusian Lake: this is the lake to the shores of which the souls of the many go when they are dead, and after waiting an appointed time, which is to some a longer and to some a shorter time, they are sent back again to be born as animals. The third river rises between the two, and near the place of rising pours into a vast region of fire, and forms a lake larger than the Mediterranean Sea, boiling with water and mud; and proceeding muddy and turbid, and winding about the earth, comes, among other places, to the extremities of the Acherusian Lake, but mingles not with the waters of the lake, and after making many coils about the earth plunges into Tartarus at a deeper level. This is that Pyriphlegethon, as the stream is called, which throws up jets of fire in all sorts of places. The fourth river goes out on the opposite side, and falls first of all into a wild and savage region, which is all of a dark-blue color, like lapis lazuli; and this is that river which is called the Stygian River, and falls into and forms the Lake Styx, and after falling into the lake and receiving strange powers in the waters, passes under the earth, winding round in the opposite direction to Pyriphlegethon, and meeting in the Acherusian Lake from the opposite side. And the water of this river too mingles with no other, but flows round in a circle and falls into Tartarus over against Pyriphlegethon, and the name of this river, as the poet says, is Cocytus.

Such is the name of the other world; and when the dead arrive at the place to which the genius of each severally conveys them, first of all they have sentence passed upon them, as they have lived well and piously or not. And those who appear to have lived neither well nor ill, go to the river Acheron, and mount such conveyances as they can get, and are carried in them to the lake, and there they dwell and are purified of their evil deeds, and suffer the penalty of the wrongs which they have done to others, and are absolved, and receive the rewards of their good deeds according to their deserts. But those who appear to be incurable by reason of the greatness of their crimes—who have committed many and terrible deeds of sacrilege, murders foul and violent, or the like—such are hurled into Tartarus, which is their suitable destiny, and they never come out. Those again who have committed crimes, which, although great, are not unpardonable—who in a moment of anger, for example, have done violence to a father or mother, and have repented for the remainder of their lives, or who have taken the life of another under like extenuating circumstances—these are plunged into Tartarus, the pains of which they are compelled to undergo for a year, but at the end of the year the wave casts them forth—mere homicides by way of Cocytus, parricides and matricides by Pyriphlegethon—and they are borne to the Acherusian Lake, and there they lift up their voices and call upon the victims whom they have slain or wronged, to have pity on them, and to receive them, and to let them come out of the river into the lake. And if they prevail, then they come forth and cease from their troubles; but if not, they are carried back again into Tartarus and from thence into the rivers unceasingly, until they obtain mercy from those whom they have wronged: for that is the sentence inflicted upon them by their judges. Those also who are remarkable for having led holy lives are released from this earthly prison, and go to their pure home which is above, and dwell in the purer earth; and those who have duly purified themselves with philosophy live henceforth altogether without the body, in mansions fairer far than these, which may not be described, and of which the time would fail me to tell.

Wherefore, Simmias, seeing all these things, what ought not we to do in order to obtain virtue and wisdom in this life? Fair is the prize, and the hope great.

I do not mean to affirm that the description which I have given of the soul and her mansions is exactly true—a man of sense ought hardly to say that. But I do say that, inasmuch as the soul is shown to be immortal, he may venture to think, not improperly or unworthily, that something of the kind is true. The venture is a glorious one, and he ought to comfort himself with words like these, which is the reason why I lengthen out the tale. Wherefore, I say, let a man be of good cheer about his soul, who has cast away the pleasures and ornaments of the body as alien to him, and rather hurtful in their effects, and has followed after the pleasures of knowledge in this life; who has adorned the soul in her own proper jewels, which are temperance, and justice, and courage, and nobility, and truth—in these arrayed she is ready to go on her journey to the world below, when her time comes. You, Simmias and Cebes, and all other men, will depart at some time or other. Me already, as the tragic poet would say, the voice of fate calls. Soon I must drink the poison; and I think that I had better repair to the bath first, in order that the women may not have the trouble of washing my body after I am dead.

When he had done speaking, Crito said: And have you any commands for us, Socrates—anything to say about your children, or any other matter in which we can serve you?

Nothing particular, he said: only, as I have always told you, I would have you look to yourselves; that is a service which you may always be doing to me and mine as well as to yourselves. And you need not make professions; for if you take no thought for yourselves, and walk not according to the precepts which I have given you, not now for the first time, the warmth of your professions will be of no avail.

We will do our best, said Crito. But in what way would you have us bury you?

In any way that you like; only you must get hold of me, and take care that I do not walk away from you. Then he turned to us, and added with a smile: I cannot make Crito believe that I am the same Socrates who have been talking and conducting the argument; he fancies that I am the other Socrates whom he will soon see, a dead body—and he asks, How shall he bury me? And though I have spoken many words in the endeavor to show that when I have drunk the poison I shall leave you and go to the joys of the blessed—these words of mine, with which I comforted you and myself, have had, I perceive, no effect upon Crito. And therefore I want you to be surety for me now, as he was surety for me at the trial: but let the promise be of another sort; for he was my surety to the judges that I would remain, but you must be my surety to him that I shall not remain, but go away and depart; and then he will suffer less at my death, and not be grieved when he sees my body being burned or buried. I would not have him sorrow at my hard lot, or say at the burial, Thus we lay out Socrates, or, Thus we follow him to the grave or bury him; for false words are not only evil in themselves, but they infect the soul with evil. Be of good cheer, then, my dear Crito, and say that you are burying my body only, and do with that as is usual, and as you think best.

When he had spoken these words, he arose and went into the bath chamber with Crito, who bade us wait; and we waited, talking and thinking of the subject of discourse, and also of the greatness of our sorrow; he was like a father of whom we were being bereaved, and we were about to pass the rest of our lives as orphans. When he had taken the bath his children were brought to him—(he had two young sons and an elder one); and the women of his family also came, and he talked to them and gave them a few directions in the presence of Crito; and he then dismissed them and returned to us.

Now the hour of sunset was near, for a good deal of time had passed while he was within. When he came out, he sat down with us again after his bath, but not much was said. Soon the jailer, who was the servant of the Eleven, entered and stood by him, saying: To you, Socrates, whom I know to be the noblest and gentlest and best of all who ever came to this place, I will not impute the angry feelings of other men, who rage and swear at me when, in obedience to the authorities, I bid them drink the poison—indeed, I am sure that you will not be angry with me; for others, as you are aware, and not I, are the guilty cause. And so fare you well, and try to bear lightly what must needs be; you know my errand. Then bursting into tears he turned away and went out.

Socrates looked at him and said: I return your good wishes, and will do as you bid. Then, turning to us, he said, How charming the man is: since I have been in prison he has always been coming to see me, and at times he would talk to me, and was as good as could be to me, and now see how generously he sorrows for me. But we must do as he says, Crito; let the cup be brought, if the poison is prepared: if not, let the attendant prepare some.

Yet, said Crito, the sun is still upon the hilltops, and many a one has taken the draught late, and after the announcement has been made to him, he has eaten and drunk, and indulged in sensual delights; do not hasten then, there is still time.

Socrates said: Yes, Crito, and they of whom you speak are right in doing thus, for they think that they will gain by the delay; but I am right in not doing thus, for I do not think that I should gain anything by drinking the poison a little later; I should be sparing and saving a life which is already gone: I could only laugh at myself for this. Please then to do as I say, and not to refuse me.

Crito, when he heard this, made a sign to the servant, and the servant went in, and remained for some time, and then returned with the jailer carrying a cup of poison. Socrates said: You, my good friend, who are experienced in these matters, shall give me directions how I am to proceed. The man answered: You have only to walk about until your legs are heavy, and then to lie down, and the poison will act. At the same time he handed the cup to Socrates, who in the easiest and gentlest manner, without the least fear or change of color or feature, looking at the man with all his eyes, Echecrates, as his manner was, took the cup and said: What do you say about making a libation out of this cup to any god? May I, or not? The man answered: We only prepare, Socrates, just so much as we deem enough. I understand, he said: yet I may and must pray to the gods to prosper my journey from this to that other world—may this, then, which is my prayer, be granted to me. Then holding the cup to his lips, quite readily and cheerfully he drank off the poison. And hitherto most of us had been able to control our sorrow; but now when we saw him drinking, and saw too that he had finished the draught, we could no longer forbear, and in spite of myself my own tears were flowing fast; so that I covered my face and wept over myself, for certainly I was not weeping over him, but at the thought of my own calamity in having lost such a companion. Nor was I the first, for Crito, when he found himself unable to restrain his tears, had got up and moved away, and I followed; and at that moment, Apollodorus, who had been weeping all the time, broke out in a loud cry which made cowards of us all. Socrates alone retained his calmness: What is this strange outcry? he said. I sent away the women mainly in order that they might not offend in this way, for I have heard that a man should die in peace. Be quiet, then, and have patience.

When we heard that, we were ashamed, and refrained our tears; and he walked about until, as he said, his legs began to fail, and then he lay on his back, according to the directions, and the man who gave him the poison now and then looked at his feet and legs; and after a while he pressed his foot hard and asked him if he could feel; and he said, no; and then his leg, and so upwards and upwards, and showed us that he was cold and stiff. And he felt them himself, and said: When the poison reaches the heart, that will be the end. He was beginning to grow cold about the groin, when he uncovered his face, for he had covered himself up, and said (they were his last words)—he said: Crito, I owe a cock to Asclepius; will you remember to pay the debt? The debt shall be paid, said Crito; is there anything else? There was no answer to this question; but in a minute or two a movement was heard, and the attendants uncovered him; his eyes were set, and Crito closed his eyes and mouth.

Such was the end, Echecrates, of our friend, whom I may truly call the wisest, and justest, and best of all the men whom I have ever known.

THE GOLDEN SAYINGS OF EPICTETUS

TRANSLATED AND ARRANGED

BY

HASTINGS CROSSLEY, M.A.

INTRODUCTORY NOTE

Epictetus was a Greek, born at Hierapolis in Phrygia, probably about the middle of the first century A.D. His early history is unknown till we find him in Rome, the slave of Epaphroditus, a freedman of Nero's. The lameness, which is the only physical characteristic of his recorded, was, according to one tradition, due to tortures inflicted by his master. He seems to have become acquainted with the principles of the Stoic philosophy through the lectures of C. Musonius Rufus; and after his emancipation he became a teacher of that system in Rome. When the Emperor Domitian banished all philosophers from Italy about 90 A.D., Epictetus went to Nicopolis in Epirus, where he continued his teaching. He left nothing in writing, and for a knowledge of his utterances we are indebted to his disciple, the Greek philosopher and historian Arrian, who compiled from his master's lectures and conversations the "Discourses and Encheiridion," from which the "Golden Sayings" are drawn. The date and circumstances of his death are unknown.

Epictetus is a main authority on Stoic morals. The points on which he laid chief stress were the importance of cultivating complete independence of external circumstances, the realization that man must find happiness within himself, and the duty of reverencing the voice of Reason in the soul. Few teachers of morals in any age are so bracing and invigorating; and the tonic quality of his utterances has been recognized ever since his own day by Pagan and Christian alike.

THE GOLDEN SAYINGS OF EPICTETUS

I

ARE these the only works of Providence in us? What words suffice to praise or set them forth? Had we but understanding, should we ever cease hymning and blessing the Divine Power, both openly and in secret, and telling of His gracious gifts? Whether digging or ploughing or eating, should we not sing the hymn to God:—

Great is God, for that He hath given us such instruments to till the ground withal:
Great is God, for that He hath given us hands, and the power of swallowing and digesting; of unconsciously growing and breathing while we sleep!

Thus should we ever have sung: yea and this, the grandest and divinest hymn of all:—

Great is God, for that He hath given us a mind to apprehend these things, and duly to use them!

What then! seeing that most of you are blinded, should there not be some one to fill this place, and sing the hymn to God on behalf of all men? What else can I that am old and lame do but sing to God? Were I a nightingale, I should do after the manner of a nightingale. Were I a swan, I should do after the manner of a swan. But now, since I am a reasonable being, I must sing to God: that is my work: I do it, nor will I desert this my post, as long as it is granted me to hold it; and upon you too I call to join in this self-same hymn.

II

How then do men act? As though one returning to his country who had sojourned for the night in a fair inn, should be so captivated thereby as to take up his abode there.

"Friend, thou hast forgotten thine intention! This was not thy destination, but only lay on the way thither."

"Nay, but it is a proper place."

"And how many more of the sort there be; only to pass through upon thy way! Thy purpose was to return to thy country; to relieve thy kinsmen's fears for thee; thyself to discharge the duties of a citizen; to marry a wife, to beget offspring, and to fill the appointed round of office. Thou didst not come to choose out what places are most pleasant; but rather to return to that wherein thou wast born and where thou wert appointed to be a citizen."

III

Try to enjoy the great festival of life with other men.

IV

But I have one whom I must please, to whom I must be subject, whom I must obey:—God, and those who come next to Him.[1] He hath entrusted me with myself: He hath made my will subject to myself alone and given me rules for the right use thereof.

V

Rufus[2] used to say, *If you have leisure to praise me, what I say is naught.* In truth he spoke in such wise, that each of us who sat there, thought that some one had accused him to Rufus:—so surely did he lay his finger on the very deeds we did: so surely display the faults of each before his very eyes.

VI

But what saith God?—"Had it been possible, Epictetus, I would have made both that body of thine and thy possessions free and unimpeded, but as it is, be not deceived:—it is not thine own; it is but finely tempered clay. Since then this I could not do, I have given thee a portion of Myself, in the power of desiring and declining and of pursuing and avoiding, and in a word the power of dealing with

[1] *I.e.,* "good and just men."
[2] C. Musonius Rufus, a Stoic philosopher, whose lectures Epictetus had attended.

the things of sense. And if thou neglect not this, but place all that thou hast therein, thou shalt never be let or hindered; thou shalt never lament; thou shalt not blame or flatter any. What then? Seemeth this to thee a little thing?"—God forbid!—"Be content then therewith!"

And so I pray the Gods.

VII

What saith Antisthenes?[3] Hast thou never heard?—

It is a kingly thing, O Cyrus, to do well and to be evil spoken of.

VIII

"Aye, but to debase myself thus were unworthy of me."

"That," said Epictetus, "is for you to consider, not for me. You know yourself what you are worth in your own eyes; and at what price you will sell yourself. For men sell themselves at various prices. This was why, when Florus was deliberating whether he should appear at Nero's shows, taking part in the performance himself, Agrippinus replied, 'Appear by all means.' And when Florus inquired, 'But why do not *you* appear?' he answered, 'Because I do not even consider the question.' For the man who has once stooped to consider such questions, and to reckon up the value of external things, is not far from forgetting what manner of man he is. Why, what is it that you ask me? Is death preferable, or life? I reply, Life. Pain or pleasure? I reply, Pleasure."

"Well, but if I do not act, I shall lose my head."

"Then go and act! But for my part I will not act."

"Why?"

"Because *you* think yourself but one among the many threads which make up the texture of the doublet. *You* should aim at being like men in general—just as your thread has no ambition either to be anything distinguished compared with the other threads. But I desire to be the purple—that small and shining part which makes the rest seem fair and beautiful. Why then do you bid me become even as the multitude? Then were I no longer the purple."

[3] The founder of the Cynic school of philosophy.

IX

If a man could be thoroughly penetrated, as he ought, with this thought, that we are all in an especial manner sprung from God, and that God is the Father of men as well as of Gods, full surely he would never conceive aught ignoble or base of himself. Whereas if Cæsar were to adopt you, your haughty looks would be intolerable; will you not be elated at knowing that you are the son of God? Now however it is not so with us: but seeing that in our birth these two things are commingled—the body which we share with the animals, and the Reason and Thought which we share with the Gods, many decline towards this unhappy kinship with the dead, few rise to the blessed kinship with the Divine. Since then every one must deal with each thing according to the view which he forms about it, those few who hold that they are born for fidelity, modesty, and unerring sureness in dealing with the things of sense, never conceive aught base or ignoble of themselves: but the multitude the contrary. Why, what am I?—A wretched human creature; with this miserable flesh of mine. Miserable indeed! but you have something better than that paltry flesh of yours. Why then cling to the one, and neglect the other?

X

Thou art but a poor soul laden with a lifeless body.

XI

The other day I had an iron lamp placed beside my household gods. I heard a noise at the door and on hastening down found my lamp carried off. I reflected that the culprit was in no very strange case. "To-morrow, my friend," I said, "you will find an earthenware lamp; for a man can only lose what he has."

XII

The reason why I lost my lamp was that the thief was superior to me in vigilance. He paid however this price for the lamp, that in exchange for it he consented to become a thief: in exchange for it, to become faithless.

XIII

But God hath introduced Man to be a spectator of Himself and of His works; and not a spectator only, but also an interpreter of them. Wherefore it is a shame for man to begin and to leave off where the brutes do. Rather he should begin there, and leave off where Nature leaves off in us: and that is at contemplation, and understanding, and a manner of life that is in harmony with herself.

See then that ye die not without being spectators of these things.

XIV

You journey to Olympia to see the work of Phidias; and each of you holds it a misfortune not to have beheld these things before you die. Whereas when there is no need even to take a journey, but you are on the spot, with the works before you, have you no care to contemplate and study these?

Will you not then perceive either who you are or unto what end you were born: or for what purpose the power of contemplation has been bestowed upon you?

"Well, but in life there are some things disagreeable and hard to bear."

And are there none at Olympia? Are you not scorched by the heat? Are you not cramped for room? Have you not to bathe with discomfort? Are you not drenched when it rains? Have you not to endure the clamour and shouting and such annoyances as these? Well, I suppose you set all this over against the splendour of the spectacle, and bear it patiently. What then? have you not received powers wherewith to endure all that comes to pass? have you not received greatness of heart, received courage, received fortitude? What care I, if I am great of heart, for aught that can come to pass? What shall cast me down or disturb me? What shall seem painful? Shall I not use the power to the end for which I received it, instead of moaning and wailing over what comes to pass?

XV

If what philosophers say of the kinship of God and Men be true, what remains for men to do but as Socrates did:—never, when asked one's country, to answer, "I am an Athenian or a Corinthian," but "I am a citizen of the world."

XVI

He that hath grasped the administration of the World, who hath learned that this Community, which consists of God and men, is the foremost and mightiest and most comprehensive of all:—that from God have descended the germs of life, not to my father only and father's father, but to all things that are born and grow upon the earth, and in an especial manner to those endowed with Reason (for those only are by their nature fitted to hold communion with God, being by means of Reason conjoined with Him)—why should not such an one call himself a citizen of the world? Why not a son of God? Why should he fear aught that comes to pass among men? Shall kinship with Cæsar, or any other of the great at Rome, be enough to hedge men around with safety and consideration, without a thought of apprehension: while to have God for our Maker, and Father, and Kinsman, shall not this set us free from sorrows and fears?

XVII

I do not think that an old fellow like me need have been sitting here to try and prevent your entertaining abject notions of yourselves, and talking of yourselves in an abject and ignoble way: but to prevent there being by chance among you any such young men as, after recognising their kindred to the Gods, and their bondage in these chains of the body and its manifold necessities, should desire to cast them off as burdens too grievous to be borne, and depart to their true kindred. This is the struggle in which your Master and Teacher, were he worthy of the name, should be engaged. You would come to me and say: "Epictetus, we can no longer endure being chained to this wretched body, giving it food and drink and rest and purification; aye, and for its sake forced to be subservient to this man and that. Are not these things indifferent and nothing to us? Is it not true that death is no evil? Are we not in a manner kinsmen of the Gods, and have we not come from them? Let us depart thither, whence we came: let us be freed from these chains that confine and press us down. Here are thieves and robbers and tribunals: and they that are called tyrants, who deem that they have after a fashion power over us, because of the miserable body and what appertains to it. Let us show them that they have power over none."

XVIII

And to this I reply:—

"Friends, wait for God. When He gives the signal, and releases you from this service, then depart to Him. But for the present, endure to dwell in the place wherein He hath assigned you your post. Short indeed is the time of your habitation therein, and easy to those that are thus minded. What tyrant, what robber, what tribunals have any terrors for those who thus esteem the body and all that belong to it as of no account? Stay; depart not rashly hence!"

XIX

Something like that is what should pass between a teacher and ingenuous youths. As it is, what does pass? The teacher is a lifeless body, and you are lifeless bodies yourselves. When you have had enough to eat to-day, you sit down and weep about to-morrow's food. Slave! if you have it, well and good; if not, you will depart: the door is open—why lament? What further room is there for tears? What further occasion for flattery? Why should one envy another? Why should you stand in awe of them that have much or are placed in power, especially if they be also strong and passionate? Why, what should they do to us? What they can do, we will not regard: what does concern us, that they cannot do. Who then shall still rule one that is thus minded?

XX

Seeing this then, and noting well the faculties which you have, you should say,—"Send now, O God, any trial that Thou wilt; lo, I have means and powers given me by Thee to acquit myself with honour through whatever comes to pass!"—No; but there you sit, trembling for fear certain things should come to pass, and moaning and groaning and lamenting over what does come to pass. And then you upbraid the Gods. Such meanness of spirit can have but one result—impiety.

Yet God has not only given us these faculties by means of which we may bear everything that comes to pass without being crushed or depressed thereby; but like a good King and Father, He has given us this without let or hindrance, placed wholly at our own disposition, without reserving to Himself any power of impediment or restraint. Though possessing all these things free and all your own, you do not use them! you do not perceive what it is you have received nor whence it comes, but sit moaning and groaning; some of you blind to the Giver, making no acknowledgment to your Benefactor; others basely giving themselves to complaints and accusations against God.

Yet what faculties and powers you possess for attaining courage and greatness of heart, I can easily show you; what you have for upbraiding and accusation, it is for you to show me!

XXI

How did Socrates bear himself in this regard? How else than as became one who was fully assured that he was the kinsman of the Gods?

XXII

If God had made that part of His own nature which He severed from Himself and gave to us, liable to be hindered or constrained either by Himself or any other, He would not have been God, nor would He have been taking care of us as He ought. . . . If you choose, you are free; if you choose, you need blame no man—accuse no man. All things will be at once according to your mind and according to the Mind of God.

XXIII

Petrifaction is of two sorts. There is petrifaction of the understanding; and also of the sense of shame. This happens when a man obstinately refuses to acknowledge plain truths, and persists in maintaining what is self-contradictory. Most of us dread mortification of the body, and would spare no pains to escape anything of that kind. But of mortification of the *soul* we are utterly heedless. With regard, indeed, to the soul, if a man is in such a state as to be incapable of following or understanding anything, I grant you we do think him in a bad way. But mortification of the sense of shame and modesty we go so far as to dub strength of mind!

XXIV

If we were as intent upon our own business as the old fellows at Rome are upon what interests them, we too might perhaps accomplish something. I know a man older than I am, now Superintendent of the Corn-market at Rome, and I remember when he passed through this place on his way back from exile, what an account he gave me of his former life, declaring that for the future, once home again, his only care should be to pass his remaining years in quiet and tranquillity. "For how few years have I left!" he cried. "That," I said, "you will not do; but the moment the scent of Rome is in your nostrils, you will forget it all; and if you can but gain admission to Court, you will be glad enough to elbow your way in, and thank God for it." "Epictetus," he replied, "if ever you find me setting as much as one foot within the Court, think what you will of me."

Well, as it was, what did he do? Ere ever he entered the city, he was met by a despatch from the Emperor. He took it, and forgot the whole of his resolutions. From that moment, he has been piling one thing upon another. I should like to be beside him to remind him of what he said when passing this way, and to add, How much better a prophet I am than you!

What then? do I say man is not made for an active life? Far from it! . . . But there is a great difference between other men's occupations and ours. . . . A glance at theirs will make it clear to you. All day long they do nothing but calculate, contrive, consult how to wring their profit out of food-stuffs, farm-plots and the like. . . . Whereas, I entreat you to learn what the administration of the World is, and what place a Being endowed with reason holds therein: to consider what you are yourself, and wherein your Good and Evil consists.

XXV

A man asked me to write to Rome on his behalf who, as most people thought, had met with misfortune; for having been before wealthy and distinguished, he had afterwards lost all and was living here. So I wrote about him in a humble style. He however on reading the letter returned it to me, with the words: "I asked for your help, not for your pity. No evil has happened unto me."

XXVI

True instruction is this:—to learn to wish that each thing should come to pass as it does. And how does it come to pass? As the Disposer has disposed it. Now He has disposed that there should be summer and winter, and plenty and dearth, and vice and virtue, and all such opposites, for the harmony of the whole.

XXVII

Have this thought ever present with thee, when thou losest any outward thing, what thou gainest in its stead; and if this be the more precious, say not, I have suffered loss.

XXVIII

Concerning the Gods, there are who deny the very existence of the Godhead; others say that it exists, but neither bestirs nor concerns itself nor has forethought for anything. A third party attribute to it existence and forethought, but only for great and heavenly matters, not for anything that is on earth. A fourth party admit things on earth as well as in heaven, but only in general, and not with respect to each individual. A fifth, of whom were Ulysses and Socrates, are those that cry:—

I move not without Thy knowledge!

XXIX

Considering all these things, the good and true man submits his judgment to Him that administers the Universe, even as good citizens to the law of the State. And he that is being instructed should come thus minded:—How may I in all things follow the Gods; and,

How may I rest satisfied with the Divine Administration; and, How may I become free? For he is free for whom all things come to pass according to his will, and whom none can hinder. What then, is freedom madness? God forbid. For madness and freedom exist not together.

"But I wish all that I desire to come to pass and in the manner that I desire."

—You are mad, you are beside yourself. Know you not that Freedom is a glorious thing and of great worth? But that what I desired at random I should wish at random to come to pass, so far from being noble, may well be exceeding base.

XXX

You must know that it is no easy thing for a principle to become a man's own, unless each day he maintain it and hear it maintained, as well as work it out in life.

XXXI

You are impatient and hard to please. If alone, you call it solitude: if in the company of men, you dub them conspirators and thieves, and find fault with your very parents, children, brothers and neighbours. Whereas when by yourself you should have called it Tranquillity and Freedom: and herein deemed yourself like unto the Gods. And when in the company of the many, you should not have called it a wearisome crowd and tumult, but an assembly and a tribunal; and thus accepted all with contentment.

XXXII

What then is the chastisement of those who accept it not? To be as they are. Is any discontented with being alone? let him be in solitude. Is any discontented with his parents? let him be a bad son, and lament. Is any discontented with his children? let him be a bad father.—"Throw him into prison!"—What prison?—Where he is already: for he is there against his will; and wherever a man is against his will, that to him is a prison. Thus Socrates was not in prison since he was there with his own consent.

XXXIII

Knowest thou what a speck thou art in comparison with the Universe?—That is, with respect to the body; since with respect to Reason, thou art not inferior to the Gods, nor less than they. For the greatness of Reason is not measured by length or height, but by the resolves of the mind. Place then thy happiness in that wherein thou art equal to the Gods.

XXXIV

Asked how a man might eat acceptably to the Gods, Epictetus replied:—If when he eats, he can be just, cheerful, equable, temperate, and orderly, can he not thus eat acceptably to the Gods? But when you call for warm water, and your slave does not answer, or when he answers brings it lukewarm, or is not even found to be in the house at all, then not to be vexed nor burst with anger, is not that acceptable to the Gods?

"But how can one endure such people?"

Slave, will you not endure your own brother, that has God to his forefather, even as a son sprung from the same stock, and of the same high descent as yourself? And if you are stationed in a high position, are you therefore forthwith to set up for a tyrant? Remember who you are, and whom you rule, that they are by nature your kinsmen, your brothers, the offspring of God.

"But I paid a price for them, not they for me."

Do you see whither you are looking—down to the earth, to the pit, to those despicable laws of the dead? But to the laws of the Gods you do not look.

XXXV

When we are invited to a banquet, we take what is set before us; and were one to call upon his host to set fish upon the table or sweet things, he would be deemed absurd. Yet in a word, we ask the Gods for what they do not give; and that, although they have given us so many things!

XXXVI

Asked how a man might convince himself that every single act of his was under the eye of God, Epictetus answered:—

"Do you not hold that all things are bound together in one?"

"I do."

"Well, and do you not hold that things on earth and things in heaven are continuous and in unison with each other?"

"I do," was the reply.

"Else how should the trees so regularly, as though by God's command, at His bidding flower; at His bidding send forth shoots, bear fruit and ripen it; at His bidding let it fall and shed their leaves, and folded up upon themselves lie in quietness and rest? How else, as the Moon waxes and wanes, as the Sun approaches and recedes, can it be that such vicissitude and alternation is seen in earthly things?

"If then all things that grow, nay, our own bodies, are thus bound up with the whole, is not this still truer of our souls? And if our souls are bound up and in contact with God, as being very parts and fragments plucked from Himself, shall He not feel every movement of theirs as though it were His own, and belonging to His own nature?"

XXXVII

"But," you say, "I cannot comprehend all this at once."

"Why, who told you that your powers were equal to God's?"

Yet God hath placed by the side of each a man's own Guardian Spirit,[4] who is charged to watch over him—a Guardian who sleeps not nor is deceived. For to what better or more watchful Guardian could He have committed each of us? So when you have shut the doors and made a darkness within, remember never to say that you are alone; for you are not alone, but God is within, and your Guardian Spirit, and what light do they need to behold what you do? To this God you also should have sworn allegiance, even as soldiers unto Cæsar. They, when their service is hired, swear to hold the life of Cæsar dearer than all else: and will you not swear your oath, that are deemed worthy of so many and great gifts? And will you not

[4] To the Stoics the Guardian Spirit was each man's Reason.

keep your oath when you have sworn it? And what oath will you swear? Never to disobey, never to arraign or murmur at aught that comes to you from His hand: never unwillingly to do or suffer aught that necessity lays upon you.

"Is this oath like theirs?"

They swear to hold no other dearer than Cæsar: you, to hold our true selves dearer than all else beside.

XXXVIII

"How shall my brother cease to be wroth with me?"

Bring him to me, and I will tell him. But to *thee* I have nothing to say about *his* anger.

XXXIX

When one took counsel of Epictetus, saying, "What I seek is this, how even though my brother be not reconciled to me, I may still remain as Nature would have me to be," he replied: "All great things are slow of growth; nay, this is true even of a grape or of a fig. If then you say to me now, I desire a fig, I shall answer, It needs time: wait till it first flower, then cast its blossom, then ripen. Whereas then the fruit of the fig-tree reaches not maturity suddenly nor yet in a single hour, do you nevertheless desire so quickly and easily to reap the fruit of the mind of man?—Nay, expect it not, even though I bade you!"

XL

Epaphroditus[5] had a shoemaker whom he sold as being good-for-nothing. This fellow, by some accident, was afterwards purchased by one of Cæsar's men, and became shoemaker to Cæsar. You should have seen what respect Epaphroditus paid him then. "How does the good Felicion? Kindly let me know!" And if any of us inquired, "What is Epaphroditus doing?" the answer was, "He is consulting about so and so with Felicion."—Had he not sold him as good-for-nothing? Who had in a trice converted him into a wiseacre?

This is what comes of holding of importance anything but the things that depend on the Will.

[5]A freedman of Nero, and at one time owner of Epictetus.

XLI

What you shun enduring yourself, attempt not to impose on others. You shun slavery—beware of enslaving others! If you can endure to do that, one would think you had been once upon a time a slave yourself. For Vice has nothing in common with virtue, nor Freedom with slavery.

XLII

Has a man been raised to the tribuneship? Every one that he meets congratulates him. One kisses him on the eyes, another on the neck, while the slaves kiss his hands. He goes home to find torches burning; he ascends to the Capitol to sacrifice.—Who ever sacrificed for having had right desires; for having conceived such inclinations as Nature would have him? In truth we thank the Gods for that wherein we place our happiness.

XLIII

A man was talking to me to-day about the priesthood of Augustus. I said to him, "Let the thing go, my good Sir; you will spend a great deal to no purpose."

"Well, but my name will be inserted in all documents and contracts."

"Will *you* be standing there to tell those that read them, That is my name written there? And even though you could now be there in every case, what will you do when you are dead?"

"At all events my name will remain."

"Inscribe it on a stone and it will remain just as well. And think, beyond Nicopolis what memory of you will there be?"

"But I shall have a golden wreath to wear."

"If you must have a wreath, get a wreath of roses and put it on; you will look more elegant!"

XLIV

Above all, remember that the door stands open. Be not more fearful than children; but as they, when they weary of the game, cry, "I will play no more," even so, when thou art in the like case, cry,

"I will play no more," and depart. But if thou stayest, make no lamentation.

XLV

Is there smoke in the room? If it be slight, I remain; if grievous, I quit it. For you must remember this and hold it fast, that the door stands open.

"You shall not dwell at Nicopolis!"

Well and good.

"Nor at Athens."

Then I will not dwell at Athens either.

"Nor at Rome."

Nor at Rome either.

"You shall dwell in Gyara!"[6]

Well: but to dwell in Gyara seems to me like a grievous smoke; I depart to a place where none can forbid me to dwell: *that* habitation is open unto all! As for the last garment of all, that is the poor body; beyond that, none can do aught unto me. This is why Demetrius[7] said to Nero: "You threaten me with death; it is Nature who threatens *you!*"

XLVI

The beginning of philosophy is to know the condition of one's own mind. If a man recognises that this is in a weakly state, he will not then want to apply it to questions of the greatest moment. As it is, men who are not fit to swallow even a morsel, buy whole treatises and try to devour them. Accordingly they either vomit them up again, or suffer from indigestion, whence come gripings, fluxions, and fevers. Whereas they should have stopped to consider their capacity.

XLVII

In theory it is easy to convince an ignorant person: in actual life, men not only object to offer themselves to be convinced, but hate the man who has convinced them. Whereas Socrates used to say that we should never lead a life not subjected to examination.

[6]An island in the Ægean, used as a place of banishment.

[7]A well-known Cynic philosopher.

XLVIII

This is the reason why Socrates, when reminded that he should prepare for his trial, answered: "Thinkest thou not that I have been preparing for it all my life?"

"In what way?"

"I have maintained that which in me lay."

"How so?"

"I have never, secretly or openly, done a wrong unto any."

XLIX

In what character dost thou now come forward?

As a witness summoned by God. "Come thou," saith God, "and testify for Me, for thou art worthy of being brought forward as a witness by Me. Is aught that is outside thy will either good or bad? Do I hurt any man? Have I placed the good of each in the power of any other than himself? What witness dost thou bear to God?"

"I am in evil state, Master, I am undone! None careth for me, none giveth me aught: all men blame, all speak evil of me."

Is this the witness thou wilt bear, and do dishonour to the calling wherewith He hath called thee, because He hath done thee so great honour, and deemed thee worthy of being summoned to bear witness in so great a cause?

L

Wouldst thou have men speak good of thee? speak good of them. And when thou hast learned to speak good of them, try to do good unto them, and thus thou wilt reap in return their speaking good of thee.

LI

When thou goest in to any of the great, remember that Another from above sees what is passing, and that thou shouldst please Him rather than man. He therefore asks thee:—

"In the Schools, what didst thou call exile, imprisonment, bonds, death and shame?"

"I called them things indifferent."

"What then dost thou call them now? Are they at all changed?"

"No."

"Is it then thou that art changed?"

"No."

"Say then, what are things indifferent?"

"Things that are not in our power."

"Say then, what follows?"

"That things which are not in our power are nothing to me."

"Say also what things you hold to be good."

"A will such as it ought to be, and a right use of the things of sense."

"And what is the end?"

"To follow Thee!"

LII

"That Socrates should ever have been so treated by the Athenians!"

Slave! why say "Socrates"? Speak of the thing as it is: That ever then the poor *body* of Socrates should have been dragged away and haled by main force to prison! That ever hemlock should have been given to the *body* of Socrates; that *that* should have breathed its life away!—Do you marvel at this? Do you hold this unjust? Is it for this that you accuse God? Had Socrates no compensation for this? Where then for him was the ideal Good? Whom shall we hearken to, you or him? And what says he?

"Anytus and Meletus[8] may put me to death: to injure me is beyond their power."

And again:—

"If such be the will of God, so let it be."

LIII

Nay, young man, for heaven's sake; but once thou hast heard these words, go home and say to thyself:—"It is not Epictetus that has told me these things: how indeed should he? No, it is some gracious God through him. Else it would never have entered his head to tell me them—he that is not used to speak to any one thus. Well, then, let us not lie under the wrath of God, but be obedient unto Him."—Nay, indeed; but if a raven by its croaking bears thee any sign, it is not the

[8] The accusers of Socrates. See Plato's *Apology*.

raven but God that sends the sign through the raven; and if He signifies anything to thee through human voice, will *He* not cause the man to say these words to thee, that thou mayest know the power of the Divine—how He sends a sign to some in one way and to others in another, and on the greatest and highest matters of all signifies His will through the noblest messenger?

What else does the poet mean:—

> I spake unto him erst Myself, and sent
> Hermes the shining One, to check and warn him,
> The husband not to slay, nor woo the wife!

LIV

In the same way my friend Heraclitus, who had a trifling suit about a petty farm at Rhodes, first showed the judges that his cause was just, and then at the finish cried, "I will not entreat you: nor do I care what sentence you pass. It is you who are on your trial, not I!"—And so he ended the case.[9]

LV

As for us, we behave like a herd of deer. When they flee from the huntsman's feathers[10] in affright, which way do they turn? What haven of safety do they make for? Why, they rush upon the nets! And thus they perish by confounding what they should fear with that wherein no danger lies. . . . Not death or pain is to be feared, but the *fear* of death or pain. Well said the poet therefore:—

> Death has no terror; only a Death of shame!

LVI

How is it then that certain external things are said to be natural, and others contrary to Nature?

Why, just as it might be said if we stood alone and apart from others. A foot, for instance, I will allow it is natural should be clean. But if you take it as a foot, and as a thing which does not stand by itself, it will beseem it (if need be) to walk in the mud, to tread on thorns, and sometimes even to be cut off, for the benefit of the whole

[9] Or, "And so he lost his case" (Long).
[10] Colored feathers fixed to ropes partly surrounding the cover.

body; else it is no longer a foot. In some such way we should conceive of ourselves also. What art thou?—A man.—Looked at as standing by thyself and separate, it is natural for thee in health and wealth long to live. But looked at as a *Man,* and only as a part of a Whole, it is for that Whole's sake that thou shouldst at one time fall sick, at another brave the perils of the sea, again, know the meaning of want and perhaps die an early death. Why then repine? Knowest thou not that as the foot is no more a foot if detached from the body, so thou in like case art no longer a Man? For what is a Man? A part of a City:—first, of the City of Gods and Men; next, of that which ranks nearest it, a miniature of the universal City. . . . In such a body, in such a world enveloping us, among lives like these, such things must happen to one or another. Thy part, then, being here, is to speak of these things as is meet, and to order them as befits the matter.

LVII

That was a good reply which Diogenes made to a man who asked him for letters of recommendation.—"That you are a man, he will know when he sees you;—whether a good or bad one, he will know if he has any skill in discerning the good and the bad. But if he has none, he will never know, though I write to him a thousand times." —It is as though a piece of silver money desired to be recommended to some one to be tested. If the man be a good judge of silver, he will know: the coin will tell its own tale.

LVIII

Even as the traveller asks his way of him that he meets, inclined in no wise to bear to the right rather than to the left (for he desires only the way leading whither he would go), so should we come unto God as to a guide; even as we use our eyes without admonishing them to show us some things rather than others, but content to receive the images of such things as they present unto us. But as it is we stand anxiously watching the victim, and with the voice of supplication call upon the augur:—"Master, have mercy on me: vouchsafe unto me a way of escape!" Slave, would you then have aught else than what is best? is there anything better than what is God's good pleasure?

Why, as far as in you lies, would you corrupt your Judge, and lead your Counsellor astray?

LIX

God is beneficent. But the Good also is beneficent. It should seem then that where the real nature of God is, there too is to be found the real nature of the Good. What then is the real nature of God?—Intelligence, Knowledge, Right Reason. Here then without more ado seek the real nature of the Good. For surely thou dost not seek it in a plant or in an animal that reasoneth not.

LX

Seek then the real nature of the Good in that without whose presence thou wilt not admit the Good to exist in aught else.—What then? Are not these other things also works of God?—They are; but not *preferred to honour,* nor are they portions of God. But thou art a thing preferred to honour: thou art thyself a fragment torn from God:—thou hast a portion of Him within thyself. How is it then that thou dost not know thy high descent—dost not know whence thou comest? When thou eatest, wilt thou not remember who thou art that eatest and whom thou feedest? In intercourse, in exercise, in discussion knowest thou not that it is a God whom thou feedest, a God whom thou exercisest, a God whom thou bearest about with thee, O miserable! and thou perceivest it not. Thinkest thou that I speak of a God of silver or gold, that is without thee? Nay, thou bearest Him within thee! all unconscious of polluting Him with thoughts impure and unclean deeds. Were an image of God present, thou wouldst not dare to act as thou dost, yet, when God Himself is present within thee, beholding and hearing all, thou dost not blush to think such thoughts and do such deeds, O thou that art insensible of thine own nature and liest under the wrath of God!

LXI

Why then are we afraid when we send a young man from the Schools into active life, lest he should indulge his appetites intemperately, lest he should debase himself by ragged clothing, or be puffed up by fine raiment? Knows he not the God within him; knows he not with whom he is starting on his way? Have we patience to hear him say to us, Would I had *thee* with me!—Hast thou not God where thou art, and having Him dost thou still seek for any other? Would He tell thee aught else than these things? Why, wert thou a statue of Phidias, an *Athena* or a *Zeus,* thou wouldst bethink thee both of thyself and thine artificer; and hadst thou any sense, thou wouldst strive to do no dishonour to thyself or him that fashioned thee, nor appear to beholders in unbefitting guise. But now, because God is thy Maker, is that why thou carest not of what sort thou shalt show thyself to be? Yet how different the artists and their workmanship! What human artist's work, for example, has in it the faculties that are displayed in fashioning it? Is it aught but marble, bronze, gold, or ivory? Nay, when the *Athena* of Phidias has put forth her hand and received therein a *Victory,* in that attitude she stands for evermore. But God's works move and breathe; they use and judge the things of sense. The workmanship of such an Artist, wilt thou dishonour Him? Aye, when he not only fashioned thee, but placed thee, like a ward, in the care and guardianship of thyself alone, wilt thou not only forget this, but also do dishonour to what is committed to thy care! If God had entrusted thee with an orphan, wouldst thou have thus neglected him? He hath delivered thee to thine own care, saying, I had none more faithful than myself: keep this man for me such as Nature hath made him—modest, faithful, high-minded, a stranger to fear, to passion, to perturbation. . . .

Such will I show myself to you all.—"What, exempt from sickness also: from age, from death?"—Nay, but accepting sickness, accepting death as becomes a God!

LXII

No labour, according to Diogenes, is good but that which aims at producing courage and strength of soul rather than of body.

LXIII

A guide, on finding a man who has lost his way, brings him back to the right path—he does not mock and jeer at him and then take himself off. You also must show the unlearned man the truth, and you will see that he will follow. But so long as you do not show it him, you should not mock, but rather feel your own incapacity.

LXIV

It was the first and most striking characteristic of Socrates never to become heated in discourse, never to utter an injurious or insulting word—on the contrary, he persistently bore insult from others and thus put an end to the fray. If you care to know the extent of his power in this direction, read Xenophon's *Banquet,* and you will see how many quarrels he put an end to. That is why the Poets are right in so highly commending this faculty:—

Quickly and wisely withal even bitter feuds would he settle.

Nevertheless the practice is not very safe at present, especially in Rome. One who adopts it, I need not say, ought not to carry it out in an obscure corner, but boldly accost, if occasion serve, some personage of rank or wealth.

"Can you tell me, sir, to whose care you entrust your horses?"

"I can."

"Is it to the first comer, who knows nothing about them?"

"Certainly not."

"Well, what of the man who takes care of your gold, your silver or your raiment?"

"He must be experienced also."

"And your body—have you ever considered about entrusting it to any one's care?"

"Of course I have."

"And no doubt to a person of experience as a trainer, a physician?"

"Surely."

"Are these things the best you possess, or have you anything more precious?"

"What can you mean?"

"I mean that which employs these; which weighs all things; which takes counsel and resolve."

"Oh, you mean the soul."

"You take me rightly; I do mean the soul. By Heaven, I hold that far more precious than all else I possess. Can you show me then what care you bestow on the soul? For it can scarcely be thought that a man of your wisdom and consideration in the city would suffer your most precious possession to go to ruin through carelessness and neglect."

"Certainly not."

"Well, do you take care of it yourself? Did any one teach you the right method, or did you discover it yourself?"

Now here comes in the danger: first, that the great man may answer, "Why, what is that to you, my good fellow? are you my master?" And then, if you persist in troubling him, may raise his hand to strike you. It is a practice of which I was myself a warm admirer until such experiences as these befell me.

LXV

When a youth was giving himself airs in the Theatre and saying, "I am wise, for I have conversed with many wise men," Epictetus replied, "I too have conversed with many rich men, yet I am not rich!"

LXVI

We see that a carpenter becomes a carpenter by learning certain things: that a pilot, by learning certain things, becomes a pilot. Possibly also in the present case the mere desire to be wise and good is not enough. It is necessary to learn certain things. This is then the object of our search. The Philosophers would have us first learn that there is a God, and that His Providence directs the Universe; further, that to hide from Him not only one's acts but even one's thoughts and intentions is impossible; secondly, what the nature of God is. Whatever that nature is discovered to be, the man who would please and obey Him must strive with all his might to be made like unto Him. If the Divine is faithful, he also must be faithful; if free, he also must be free; if beneficent, he also must be beneficent; if magnanimous, he also must be magnanimous. Thus as an imitator of God must he follow Him in every deed and word.

LXVII

If I show you, that you lack just what is most important and necessary to happiness, that hitherto your attention has been bestowed on everything rather than that which claims it most; and, to crown all, that you know neither what God nor Man is—neither what Good nor Evil is: why, that you are ignorant of everything else, perhaps you may bear to be told; but to hear that you know nothing of yourself, how could you submit to that? How could you stand your ground and suffer that to be proved? Clearly not at all. You instantly turn away in wrath. Yet what harm have I done you? Unless indeed the mirror harms the ill-favoured man by showing him to himself just as he is; unless the physician can be thought to insult his patient, when he tells him:—"Friend, do you suppose there is nothing wrong with you? why, you have a fever. Eat nothing to-day, and drink only water." Yet no one says, "What an insufferable insult!" Whereas, if you say to a man, "Your desires are inflamed, your instincts of rejection are weak and low, your aims are inconsistent, your impulses are not in harmony with Nature, your opinions are rash and false," he forthwith goes away and complains that you have insulted him.

LXVIII

Our way of life resembles a fair. The flocks and herds are passing along to be sold, and the greater part of the crowd to buy and sell. But there are some few who come only to look at the fair, to inquire how and why it is being held, upon what authority and with what object. So too, in this great Fair of life, some, like the cattle, trouble themselves about nothing but the fodder. Know all of you, who are busied about land, slaves and public posts, that these are nothing but fodder! Some few there are attending the Fair, who love to contemplate what the world is, what He that administers it. Can there be no Administrator? is it possible, that while neither city nor household could endure even for a moment without one to administer and see to its welfare, this Fabric, so fair, so vast, should be administered in order so harmonious, without a purpose and by blind chance? There is therefore an Administrator. What is His nature and how does He administer? And who are we that are His children and what work were we born to perform? Have we any close connection or relation with Him or not?

Such are the impressions of the few of whom I speak. And further, they apply themselves solely to considering and examining the great assembly before they depart. Well, they are derided by the multitude. So are the lookers-on by the traders: aye, and if the beasts had any sense, they would deride those who thought much of anything but fodder!

LXIX

I think I know now what I never knew before—the meaning of the common saying, *A fool you can neither bend nor break*. Pray heaven I may never have a *wise fool* for my friend! There is nothing more intractable.—"My resolve is fixed!"—Why, so madmen say too; but the more firmly they believe in their delusions, the more they stand in need of treatment.

LXX

—"Oh! when shall I see Athens and its Acropolis again?"—Miserable man! art thou not contented with the daily sights that meet thine eyes? canst thou behold aught greater or nobler than the Sun, Moon, and Stars; than the outspread Earth and Sea? If indeed thou apprehendest Him who administers the universe, if thou bearest Him about within thee, canst thou still hanker after mere fragments of stone and a fine rock? When thou art about to bid farewell to the Sun and Moon itself, wilt thou sit down and cry like a child? Why, what didst thou hear, what didst thou learn? why didst thou write thyself down a philosopher, when thou mightest have written what was the fact, namely, "I have made one or two *Compendiums,* I have read some works of Chrysippus, and I have not even touched the hem of Philosophy's robe"!

LXXI

Friend, lay hold with a desperate grasp, ere it is too late, on Freedom, on Tranquillity, on Greatness of soul! Lift up thy head, as one escaped from slavery; dare to look up to God, and say:—"Deal with me henceforth as Thou wilt; Thou and I are of one mind. I am Thine: I refuse nothing that seemeth good to Thee; lead on whither Thou wilt; clothe me in what garb Thou pleasest; wilt Thou have me a ruler or a subject—at home or in exile—poor or rich? All these things will I justify unto men for Thee. I will show the true nature of each. . . ."

Who would Hercules have been had he loitered at home? no Hercules, but Eurystheus. And in his wanderings through the world how many friends and comrades did he find? but nothing dearer to him than God. Wherefore he was believed to be God's son, as indeed he was. So then in obedience to Him, he went about delivering the earth from injustice and lawlessness.

But thou art not Hercules, thou sayest, and canst not deliver others from their iniquity—not even Theseus, to deliver the soil of Attica from its monsters? Purge away thine own, cast forth thence—from thine own mind, not robbers and monsters, but Fear, Desire, Envy, Malignity, Avarice, Effeminacy, Intemperance. And these may not be cast out, except by looking to God alone, by fixing thy affections on Him only, and by consecrating thyself to His commands. If thou choosest aught else, with sighs and groans thou wilt be forced to follow a Might greater than thine own, ever seeking Tranquillity without, and never able to attain unto her. For thou seekest her where she is not to be found; and where she is, there thou seekest her not!

LXXII

If a man would pursue Philosophy, his first task is to throw away conceit. For it is impossible for a man to begin to learn what he has a conceit that he already knows.

LXXIII

Give me but one young man, that has come to the School with this intention, who stands forth a champion of this cause, and says, "All else I renounce, content if I am but able to pass my life free from hindrance and trouble; to raise my head aloft and face all things as a free man; to look up to heaven as a friend of God, fearing nothing that may come to pass!" Point out such a one to me, that I may say, "Enter, young man, into possession of that which is thine own. For thy lot is to adorn Philosophy. Thine are these possessions; thine these books, these discourses!"

And when our champion has duly exercised himself in this part of the subject, I hope he will come back to me and say:—"What I desire is to be free from passion and from perturbation; as one who grudges no pains in the pursuit of piety and philosophy, what I desire is to know my duty to the Gods, my duty to my parents, to my brothers, to my country, to strangers."

"Enter then on the second part of the subject; it is thine also."

"But I have already mastered the second part; only I wished to stand firm and unshaken—as firm when asleep as when awake, as firm when elated with wine as in despondency and dejection."

"Friend, you are verily a God! you cherish great designs."

LXXIV

"The question at stake," said Epictetus, "is no common one; it is this:—*Are we in our senses, or are we not?*"

LXXV

If you have given way to anger, be sure that over and above the evil involved therein, you have strengthened the habit, and added fuel to the fire. If overcome by a temptation of the flesh, do not reckon it a single defeat, but that you have also strengthened your dissolute habits. Habits and faculties are necessarily affected by the corresponding acts. Those that were not there before, spring up: the rest gain in strength and extent. This is the account which Philosophers give of the origin of diseases of the mind:—Suppose you have once lusted after money: if reason sufficient to produce a sense of the evil be applied, then the lust is checked, and the mind at once regains its original authority; whereas if you have recourse to no remedy, you can no longer look for this return—on the contrary, the next time it is excited by the corresponding object, the flame of desire leaps up more quickly than before. By frequent repetition, the mind in the long run becomes callous; and thus this mental disease produces confirmed Avarice.

One who has had fever, even when it has left him, is not in the same condition of health as before, unless indeed his cure is complete. Something of the same sort is true also of diseases of the mind. Behind, there remains a legacy of traces and of blisters: and unless these are effectually erased, subsequent blows on the same spot will produce no longer mere blisters, but sores. If you do not wish to be prone to anger, do not feed the habit; give it nothing which may tend to its increase. At first, keep quiet and count the days when you were not angry: "I used to be angry every day, then every other day: next every two, next every three days!" and if you succeed in passing thirty days, sacrifice to the Gods in thanksgiving.

LXXVI

How then may this be attained?—Resolve, now if never before, to approve thyself to thyself; resolve to show thyself fair in God's sight; long to be pure with thine own pure self and God!

LXXVII

That is the true athlete, that trains himself to resist such outward impressions as these.

"Stay, wretched man! suffer not thyself to be carried away!" Great is the combat, divine the task! you are fighting for Kingship, for Liberty, for Happiness, for Tranquillity. Remember God: call upon Him to aid thee, like a comrade that stands beside thee in the fight.

LXXVIII

Who then is a Stoic—in the sense that we call that a statue of Phidias which is modelled after that master's art? Show me a man in this sense modelled after the doctrines that are ever upon his lips. Show me a man that is sick—and happy; in danger—and happy; on his death-bed—and happy; an exile—and happy; in evil report—and happy! Show me him, I ask again. So help me Heaven, I long to see *one* Stoic! Nay, if you cannot show me one fully modelled, let me at least see one in whom the process is at work—one whose bent is in that direction. Do me that favour! Grudge it not to an old man, to behold a sight that he has never yet beheld. Think you I wish to see the *Zeus* or *Athena* of Phidias, bedecked with gold and ivory?—Nay, show me, one of you, a human soul, desiring to be of one mind with God, no more to lay blame on God or man, to suffer nothing to disappoint, nothing to cross him, to yield neither to anger, envy, nor jealousy—in a word, why disguise the matter? one that from a man would fain become a God; one that while still imprisoned in this dead body makes fellowship with God his aim. Show me him!—Ah, you cannot! Then why mock yourselves and delude others? why stalk about tricked out in other men's attire, thieves and robbers that you are of names and things to which you can show no title!

LXXIX

If you have assumed a character beyond your strength, you have both played a poor figure in that, and neglected one that is within your powers.

LXXX

Fellow, you have come to blows at home with a slave: you have turned the household upside down, and thrown the neighbourhood into confusion; and do you come to me then with airs of assumed modesty—do you sit down like a sage and criticise my explanation of the readings, and whatever idle babble you say has come into my head? Have you come full of envy, and dejected because nothing is sent you from home; and while the discussion is going on, do you sit brooding on nothing but how your father or your brother are disposed towards you:—"What are they saying about me there? at this moment they imagine I am making progress and saying, He will return perfectly omniscient! I wish I could become omniscient before I return; but that would be very troublesome. No one sends me anything—the baths at Nicopolis are dirty; things are wretched at home and wretched here." And then they say, "Nobody is any the better for the School."—Who comes to the School with a sincere wish to learn: to submit his principles to correction and himself to *treatment?* Who, to gain a sense of his wants? Why then be surprised if you carry home from the School exactly what you bring into it?

LXXXI

"Epictetus, I have often come desiring to hear you speak, and you have never given me any answer; now if possible, I entreat you, say something to me."

"Is there, do you think," replied Epictetus, "an *art* of speaking as of other things, if it is to be done skilfully and with profit to the hearer?"

"Yes."

"And are all profited by what they hear, or only some among them? So that it seems there is an art of hearing as well as of speaking. . . . To make a statue needs skill: to view a statue aright needs skill also."

"Admitted."

"And I think all will allow that one who proposes to hear philosophers speak needs a considerable training in hearing. Is that not so? Then tell me on what subject you are able to *hear* me."

"Why, on good and evil."

"The good and evil of what? a horse, an ox?"

"No; of a man."

"Do we know then what Man is? what his nature is? what is the idea we have of him? And are our *ears* practised in any degree on the subject? Nay, do you understand what Nature is? can you follow me in any degree when I say that I shall have to use demonstration? Do you understand what Demonstration is? what True or False is? . . . must I *drive* you to Philosophy? . . . Show me what good I am to do by discoursing with you. Rouse my desire to do so. The sight of the pasture it loves stirs in a sheep the desire to feed: show it a stone or a bit of bread and it remains unmoved. Thus we also have certain natural desires, aye, and one that moves us to speak when we find a listener that is worth his salt: one that himself stirs the spirit. But if he sits by like a stone or a tuft of grass, how can he rouse a man's desire?"

"Then you will say nothing to me?"

"I can only tell you this: that one who knows not who he is and to what end he was born; what kind of world this is and with whom he is associated therein; one who cannot distinguish Good and Evil, Beauty and Foulness, . . . Truth and Falsehood, will never follow Reason in shaping his desires and impulses and repulsions, nor yet in assent, denial, or suspension of judgment; but will in one word go about deaf and blind, thinking himself to be somewhat, when he is in truth of no account. Is there anything new in all this? Is not this ignorance the cause of all the mistakes and mischances of men since the human race began? . . ."

"This is all I have to say to you, and even this against the grain. Why? Because you have not stirred my spirit. For what can I see in you to stir me, as a spirited horse will stir a judge of horses? Your body? That you maltreat. Your dress? That is luxurious. Your behaviour, your look?—Nothing whatever. When you want to hear a philosopher, do not say, 'You say nothing to me'; only show yourself worthy or fit to *hear,* and then you will see how you will move the speaker."

LXXXII

And now, when you see brothers apparently good friends and living in accord, do not immediately pronounce anything upon their friendship, though they should affirm it with an oath, though they should declare, "For us to live apart is a thing impossible!" For the heart of a bad man is faithless, unprincipled, inconstant: now overpowered by one impression, now by another. Ask not the usual questions, Were they born of the same parents, reared together, and under the same tutor; but ask this only, in what they place their real interest—whether in outward things or in the Will. If in outward things, call them not friends, any more than faithful, constant, brave or free: call them not even human beings, if you have any sense. . . . But should you hear that these men hold the Good to lie only in the *Will,* only in rightly dealing with the things of sense, take no more trouble to inquire whether they are father and son or brothers, or comrades of long standing; but, sure of this one thing, pronounce as boldly that they are friends as that they are faithful and just: for where else can Friendship be found than where Modesty is, where there is an interchange of things fair and honest, and of such only?

LXXXIII

No man can rob us of our Will—no man can lord it over that!

LXXXIV

When disease and death overtake me, I would fain be found engaged in the task of liberating mine own Will from the assaults of passion, from hindrance, from resentment, from slavery.

Thus would I fain be found employed, so that I may say to God, "Have I in aught transgressed Thy commands? Have I in aught perverted the faculties, the senses, the natural principles that Thou didst give me? Have I ever blamed Thee or found fault with Thine administration? When it was Thy good pleasure, I fell sick —and so did other men: but *my* will consented. Because it was Thy pleasure, I became poor: but *my* heart rejoiced. No power in the State was mine, because Thou wouldst not: such power I never desired! Hast Thou ever seen me of more doleful countenance on that account? Have I not ever drawn nigh unto Thee with cheerful look, waiting upon Thy commands, attentive to Thy signals? Wilt Thou that I now depart from the great Assembly of men? I go: I give Thee all thanks, that Thou hast deemed me worthy to take part with Thee in this Assembly: to behold Thy works, to comprehend this Thine administration."

Such I would were the subject of my thoughts, my pen, my study, when death overtakes me.

LXXXV

Seemeth it nothing to you, never to accuse, never to blame either God or Man? to wear ever the same countenance in going forth as in coming in? This was the secret of Socrates: yet he never said that he knew or taught anything. . . . Who amongst you makes this his aim? Were it indeed so, you would gladly endure sickness, hunger, aye, death itself.

LXXXVI

How are we constituted by Nature? To be free, to be noble, to be modest (for what other living thing is capable of blushing, or of feeling the impression of shame?) and to subordinate pleasure to the ends for which Nature designed us, as a handmaid and a minister, in order to call forth our activity; in order to keep us constant to the path prescribed by Nature.

LXXXVII

The husbandman deals with land; physicians and trainers with the body; the wise man with his own Mind.

LXXXVIII

Which of us does not admire what Lycurgus the Spartan did? A young citizen had put out his eye, and been handed over to him by the people to be punished at his own discretion. Lycurgus abstained from all vengeance, but on the contrary instructed and made a good man of him. Producing him in public in the theatre, he said to the astonished Spartans:—"I received this young man at your hands full of violence and wanton insolence; I restore him to you in his right mind and fit to serve his country."

LXXXIX

A money-changer may not reject Cæsar's coin, nor may the seller of herbs, but must when once the coin is shown, deliver what is sold for it, whether he will or no. So is it also with the Soul. Once the Good appears, it attracts towards itself; evil repels. But a clear and certain impression of the Good the Soul will never reject, any more than men do Cæsar's coin. On this hangs every impulse alike of Man and God.

XC

Asked what Common Sense was, Epictetus replied:—

As that may be called a Common Ear which distinguishes only sounds, while that which distinguishes musical notes is not common but produced by training; so there are certain things which men not entirely perverted see by the natural principles common to all. Such a constitution of the Mind is called Common Sense.

XCI

Canst thou judge men? . . . then make us imitators of thyself, as Socrates did. *Do this, do not do that, else will I cast thee into prison;* this is not governing men like reasonable creatures. Say rather, *As God hath ordained, so do; else thou wilt suffer chastisement and loss.* Askest thou what loss? None other than this: To have left undone what thou shouldst have done: to have lost the faithfulness, the reverence, the modesty that is in thee! Greater loss than this seek not to find!

XCII

"His son is dead."
What has happened?
"His son is dead."
Nothing more?
"Nothing."
"His ship is lost."
What has happened?
"His ship is lost."
"He has been haled to prison."
What has happened?
"He has been haled to prison."

But that any of these things are *misfortunes* to him, is an addition which every one makes of his own. But (you say) God is unjust in this.—Why? For having given thee endurance and greatness of soul? For having made such things to be no evils? For placing happiness within thy reach, even when enduring them? For opening unto thee a door, when things make not for thy good?—Depart, my friend, and find fault no more!

XCIII

You are sailing to Rome (you tell me) to obtain the post of Governor of Cnossus.[11] You are not content to stay at home with the honours you had before; you want something on a larger scale, and more conspicuous. But when did you ever undertake a voyage for the purpose of reviewing your own principles and getting rid of any of them that proved unsound? Whom did you ever visit for that object? What time did you ever set yourself for that? What age? Run over the times of your life—by yourself, if you are ashamed before me. Did you examine your principles when a boy? Did you not do everything just as you do now? Or when you were a stripling, attending the school of oratory and practising the art yourself, what did you ever imagine you lacked? And when you were a young man, entered upon public life, and were pleading causes and making a name, who any longer seemed equal to you?

[11] In Crete.

And at what moment would you have endured another examining your principles and proving that they were unsound? What then am I to say to you? "Help me in this matter!" you cry. Ah, for that I have no rule! And neither did you, if that was your object, come to me as a philosopher, but as you might have gone to a herb-seller or a cobbler.—"What do philosophers have rules for, then?"—Why, that whatever may betide, our ruling faculty may be as Nature would have it, and so remain. Think you this a small matter? Not so! but the greatest thing there is. Well, does it need but a short time? Can it be grasped by a passer-by?—grasp it, if you can!

Then you will say, "Yes, I met Epictetus!"

Aye, just as you might a statue or a monument. You *saw* me! and that is all. But a man who meets a man is one who learns the other's mind, and lets him see his in turn. Learn my mind—show me yours; and then go and say that you met me. Let us try each other; if I have any wrong principle, rid me of it; if *you* have, out with it. That is what meeting a philosopher means. Not so, you think; this is only a flying visit; while we are hiring the ship, we can see Epictetus too! Let us see what he has to say. Then on leaving you cry, "Out on Epictetus for a worthless fellow, provincial and barbarous of speech!" What else indeed did you come to judge of?

XCIV

Whether you will or no, you are poorer than I!

"What then do I lack?"

What you have not: Constancy of mind, such as Nature would have it to be: Tranquillity. Patron or no patron, what care I? but you do care. I am richer than you: I am not racked with anxiety as to what Cæsar may think of me; I flatter none on that account. This is what I have, instead of vessels of gold and silver! your vessels may be of gold, but your reason, your principles, your accepted views, your inclinations, your desires are of earthenware.

XCV

To you, all you have seems small: to me, all I have seems great. Your desire is insatiable, mine is satisfied. See children thrusting their hands into a narrow-necked jar, and striving to pull out the nuts and figs it contains: if they fill the hand, they cannot pull it out again, and then they fall to tears.—"Let go a few of them, and then you can draw out the rest!"—You, too, let your desire go! covet not many things, and you will obtain.

XCVI

Pittacus,[12] wronged by one whom he had it in his power to punish, let him go free, saying, *Forgiveness is better than revenge.* The one shows native gentleness, the other savagery.

XCVII

"My brother ought not to have treated me thus."

True: but *he* must see to that. However he may treat me, I must deal rightly by him. This is what lies with me, what none can hinder.

XCVIII

Nevertheless a man should also be prepared to be sufficient unto himself—to dwell with himself alone, even as God dwells with Himself alone, shares His repose with none, and considers the nature of His own administration, intent upon such thoughts as are meet unto Himself. So should we also be able to converse with ourselves, to need none else beside, to sigh for no distraction, to bend our thoughts upon the Divine Administration, and how we stand related to all else; to observe how human accidents touched us of old, and how they touch us now; what things they are that still have power to hurt us, and how they may be cured or removed; to perfect what needs perfecting as Reason would direct.

XCIX

If a man has frequent intercourse with others, either in the way of conversation, entertainment, or simple familiarity, he must either become like them, or change them to his own fashion. A live coal placed next a dead one will either kindle that or be quenched by it. Such being the risk, it is well to be cautious in admitting intimacies

[12] One of the Seven Wise Men of Greece. He ruled Mytilene in Lesbos in the seventh century B.C.

of this sort, remembering that one cannot rub shoulders with a soot-stained man without sharing the soot oneself. What will you do, supposing the talk turns on gladiators, or horses, or prize-fighters, or (what is worse) on *persons,* condemning this and that, approving the other? Or suppose a man sneers or jeers or shows a malignant temper? Has any among us the skill of the lute-player, who knows at the first touch which strings are out of tune and sets the instrument right: has any of you such a power as Socrates had, in all his intercourse with men, of winning them over to his own convictions? Nay, but *you* must needs be swayed hither and thither by the uninstructed. How comes it then that they prove so much stronger than you? Because they speak from the fulness of the heart—their low, corrupt views are their real convictions: whereas your fine sentiments are but from the lips, outwards; that is why they are so nerveless and dead. It turns one's stomach to listen to *your* exhortations, and hear of your miserable Virtue, that you prate of up and down. Thus it is that the Vulgar prove too strong for you. Everywhere strength, everywhere victory waits your conviction!

C

In general, any methods of discipline applied to the body which tend to modify its desires or repulsions, are good—for ascetic ends. But if done for display, they betray at once a man who keeps an eye on outward show; who has an ulterior purpose, and is looking for spectators to shout, "Oh what a great man!" This is why Apollonius so well said: "If you are bent upon a little private discipline, wait till you are choking with heat some day—then take a mouthful of cold water, and spit it out again, and tell no man!"

CI

Study how to give as one that is sick: that thou mayest hereafter give as one that is whole. Fast; drink water only; abstain altogether from desire, that thou mayest hereafter conform thy desire to Reason.

CII

Thou wouldst do good unto men? then show them by thine own example what kind of men philosophy can make, and cease from foolish trifling. Eating, do good to them that eat with thee; drinking, to them that drink with thee; yield unto all, give way, and bear with them. Thus shalt thou do them good: but vent not upon them thine own evil humour!

CIII

Even as bad actors cannot sing alone, but only in chorus: so some cannot walk alone.

Man, if thou art aught, strive to walk alone and hold converse with thyself, instead of skulking in the chorus! at length think; look around thee; bestir thyself, that thou mayest know who thou art!

CIV

You would fain be victor at the Olympic games, you say. Yes, but weigh the conditions, weigh the consequences; then and then only, lay to your hand—if it be for your profit. You must live by rule, submit to diet, abstain from dainty meats, exercise your body perforce at stated hours, in heat or in cold; drink no cold water, nor, it may be, wine. In a word, you must surrender yourself wholly to your trainer, as though to a physician.

Then in the hour of contest, you will have to delve the ground, it may chance dislocate an arm, sprain an ankle, gulp down abundance of yellow sand, be scourged with the whip—and with all this sometimes lose the victory. Count the cost—and then, if your desire still holds, try the wrestler's life. Else let me tell you that you will be behaving like a pack of children playing now at wrestlers, now at gladiators; presently falling to trumpeting and anon to stage-playing, when the fancy takes them for what they have seen. And you are even the same: wrestler, gladiator, philosopher, orator all by turns and none of them with your whole soul. Like an ape, you mimic what you see, to one thing constant never; the thing that is familiar charms no more. This is because you never undertook aught with due consideration, nor after strictly testing and viewing it from every side; no, your choice was thoughtless; the glow of your desire had waxed cold. . . .

Friend, bethink you first what it is that you would do, and then what your own nature is able to bear. Would you be a wrestler, consider your shoulders, your thighs, your loins—not all men are formed to the same end. Think you to be a philosopher while acting as you do? think you to go on thus eating, thus drinking, giving way in like manner to wrath and to displeasure? Nay, you must watch, you must labour; overcome certain desires; quit your familiar friends, submit to be despised by your slave, to be held in derision by them that meet you, to take the lower place in all things, in office, in positions of authority, in courts of law.

Weigh these things fully, and then, if you will, lay to your hand; if as the price of these things you would gain Freedom, Tranquillity, and passionless Serenity.

CV

He that hath no musical instruction is a child in Music; he that hath no letters is a child in Learning; he that is untaught is a child in Life.

CVI

Can any profit be derived from these men? Aye, from all.

"What, even from a reviler?"

Why, tell me what profit a wrestler gains from him who exercises him beforehand? The very greatest: he trains me in the practice of endurance, of controlling my temper, of gentle ways. You deny it. What, the man who lays hold of my neck, and disciplines loins and shoulders, does me good, . . . while he that trains me to keep my temper does me none? This is what it means, not knowing how to gain advantage from men! Is my neighbour bad? Bad to himself, but good to me: he brings my good temper, my gentleness into play. Is my father bad? Bad to himself, but good to me. This is the rod of Hermes; *touch what you will with it,* they say, *and it becomes gold.* Nay, but bring what you will and I will transmute it into Good. Bring sickness, bring death, bring poverty and reproach, bring trial for life—all these things through the rod of Hermes shall be turned to profit.

CVII

Till then these sound opinions have taken firm root in you, and you have gained a measure of strength for your security, I counsel you to be cautious in associating with the uninstructed. Else whatever impressions you receive upon the tablets of your mind in the School will day by day melt and disappear, like wax in the sun. Withdraw then somewhere far from the sun, while you have these waxen sentiments.

CVIII

We must approach this matter in a different way; it is great and mystical: it is no common thing; nor given to every man. Wisdom alone, it may be, will not suffice for the care of youth: a man needs also a certain measure of readiness—an aptitude for the office; aye, and certain bodily qualities; and above all, to be counselled of God Himself to undertake this post; even as He counselled Socrates to fill the post of one who confutes error, assigning to Diogenes[13] the royal office of high reproof, and to Zeno[14] that of positive instruction. Whereas *you* would fain set up for a physician provided with nothing but drugs! Where and how they should be applied you neither know nor care.

CIX

If what charms you is nothing but abstract principles, sit down and turn them over quietly in your mind: but never dub yourself a Philosopher, nor suffer others to call you so. Say rather: He is in error; for my desires, my impulses are unaltered. I give in my adhesion to what I did before; nor has my mode of dealing with the things of sense undergone any change.

CX

When a friend inclined to Cynic views asked Epictetus, what sort of person a true Cynic should be, requesting a general sketch of the system, he answered:—"We will consider that at leisure. At present I content myself with saying this much: If a man put his hand to so weighty a matter without God, the wrath of God abides upon him. That which he covets will but bring upon him public shame. Not even on finding himself in a well-ordered house does

[13] The well-known Cynic philosopher.
[14] Founder of the Stoic school of philosophy.

a man step forward and say to himself, I must be master here! Else the lord of that house takes notice of it, and, seeing him insolently giving orders, drags him forth and chastises him. So it is also in this great City, the World. Here also is there a Lord of the House, who orders all things:—

"Thou art the Sun! in thine orbit thou hast power to make the year and the seasons; to bid the fruits of the earth grow and increase, the winds arise and fall; thou canst in due measure cherish with thy warmth the frames of men; go make thy circuit, and thus minister unto all from the greatest to the least! . . .

"Thou canst lead a host against Troy; be Agamemnon!
"Thou canst meet Hector in single combat; be Achilles!

"But had Thersites stepped forward and claimed the chief command, he had been met with a refusal, or obtained it only to his own shame and confusion of face, before a cloud of witnesses."

CXI

Others may fence themselves with walls and houses, when they do such deeds as these, and wrap themselves in darkness—aye, they have many a device to hide themselves. Another may shut his door and station one before his chamber to say, if any comes, *He has gone forth! he is not at leisure!* But the true Cynic will have none of these things; instead of them, he must wrap himself in Modesty: else he will but bring himself to shame, naked and under the open sky. *That* is his house; that is his door; that is the slave that guards his chamber; that is his darkness!

CXII

Death? let it come when it will, whether it smite but a part or the whole: Fly, you tell me—fly! But whither shall I fly? Can any man cast me beyond the limits of the World? It may not be! And whithersoever I go, there shall I still find Sun, Moon, and Stars; there shall I find dreams, and omens, and converse with the Gods!

CXIII

Furthermore the true Cynic must know that he is sent as a Messenger from God to men, to show unto them that as touching good and evil they are in error; looking for these where they are not to be found, nor ever bethinking themselves where they are. And like Diogenes when brought before Philip after the battle of Chæronea, the Cynic must remember that he is a Spy. For a Spy he really is—to bring back word what things are on Man's side, and what against him. And when he has diligently observed all, he must come back with a true report, not terrified into announcing them to be foes that are no foes, nor otherwise perturbed or confounded by the things of sense.

CXIV

How can it be that one who hath nothing, neither raiment, nor house, nor home, nor bodily tendance, nor servant, nor city, should yet live tranquil and contented? Behold God hath sent you a man to show you in act and deed that it may be so. Behold me! I have neither city nor house nor possessions nor servants: the ground is my couch; I have no wife, no children, no shelter—nothing but earth and sky, and one poor cloak. And what lack I yet? am I not untouched by sorrow, by fear? am I not free? . . . when have I laid anything to the charge of God or Man? when have I accused any? hath any of you seen me with a sorrowful countenance? And in what wise treat I those of whom you stand in fear and awe? Is it not as slaves? Who when he seeth me doth not think that he beholdeth his Master and his King?

CXV

Give thyself more diligently to reflection: know thyself: take counsel with the Godhead: without God put thine hand unto nothing!

CXVI

"But to marry and to rear offspring," said the young man, "will the Cynic hold himself bound to undertake this as a chief duty?"

Grant me a republic of wise men, answered Epictetus, and perhaps none will lightly take the Cynic life upon him. For on whose account should he embrace that method of life? Suppose however that he does, there will then be nothing to hinder his marrying and rearing offspring. For his wife will be even such another as himself, and likewise her father; and in like manner will his children be brought up.

But in the present condition of things, which resembles an Army in battle array, ought not the Cynic to be free from all distraction and given wholly to the service of God, so that he can go in and out among men, neither fettered by the duties nor entangled by the relations of common life? For if he transgress them, he will forfeit the character of a good man and true; whereas if he observe them, there is an end of him as the Messenger, the Spy, the Herald of the Gods!

CXVII

Ask me if you choose if a Cynic shall engage in the administration of the State. O fool, seek you a nobler administration than that in which he is engaged? Ask you if a man shall come forward in the Athenian assembly and talk about revenue and supplies, when his business is to converse with all men, Athenians, Corinthians, and Romans alike, not about supplies, not about revenue, nor yet peace and war, but about Happiness and Misery, Prosperity and Adversity, Slavery and Freedom?

Ask you whether a man shall engage in the administration of the State who has engaged in such an Administration as this? Ask me too if he shall govern; and again I will answer, Fool, what greater government shall he hold than that he holds already?

CXVIII

Such a man needs also to have a certain habit of body. If he appear consumptive, thin and pale, his testimony has no longer the same authority. He must not only prove to the unlearned by showing them what his Soul is that it is possible to be a good man apart from all that *they* admire; but he must also show them, by his body, that a plain and simple manner of life under the open sky does no harm to the body either. "See, I am a proof of this! and my body also." As Diogenes used to do, who went about fresh of look and by the very appearance of his body drew men's eyes. But if a Cynic is an object of pity, he seems a mere beggar; all turn away, all are offended at him. Nor should he be slovenly of look, so as not to scare men from him in this way either; on the contrary, his very roughness should be clean and attractive.

CXIX

Kings and tyrants have armed guards wherewith to chastise certain persons, though they be themselves evil. But to the Cynic conscience gives this power—not arms and guards. When he knows that he has watched and laboured on behalf of mankind: that sleep hath found him pure, and left him purer still: that his thoughts have been the thought of a Friend of the Gods—of a servant, yet of one that hath a part in the government of the Supreme God: that the words are ever on his lips:—

Lead me, O God, and thou, O Destiny!

as well as these:—

If this be God's will, so let it be!

why should he not speak boldly unto his own brethren, unto his children—in a word, unto all that are akin to him!

CXX

Does a Philosopher *apply* to people to come and hear him? does he not rather, of his own nature, *attract* those that will be benefited by him—like the sun that warms, the food that sustains them? What Physician *applies* to men to come and be healed? (Though indeed I hear that the Physicians at Rome do nowadays apply for patients—in my time they were applied to.) I apply to you to come and hear that you are in evil case; that what deserves your attention most is the last thing to gain it; that you know not good from evil, and are in short a hapless wretch; a fine way to apply! though unless the words of the Philosopher affect you thus, speaker and speech are alike dead.

CXXI

A Philosopher's school is a Surgery: pain, not pleasure, you should have felt therein. For on entering none of you is whole. One has a shoulder out of joint, another an abscess: a third suffers from an issue, a fourth from pains in the head. And am I then to sit down and treat you to pretty sentiments and empty flourishes, so that you may applaud me and depart, with neither shoulder, nor head, nor issue, nor abscess a whit the better for your visit? Is it then for this that young men are to quit their homes, and leave parents, friends, kinsmen and substance to mouth out *Bravo* to your empty phrases!

CXXII

If any be unhappy, let him remember that he is unhappy by reason of himself alone. For God hath made all men to enjoy felicity and constancy of good.

CXXIII

Shall we never wean ourselves—shall we never heed the teachings of Philosophy (unless perchance they have been sounding in our ears like an enchanter's drone):—

This World is one great City, and one is the substance whereof it is fashioned: a certain period indeed there needs must be, while these give place to those; some must perish for others to succeed; some move and some abide: yet all is full of *friends*—first God, then Men, whom Nature hath bound by ties of kindred each to each.

CXXIV

Nor did the hero[15] weep and lament at leaving his children orphans. For he knew that no man is an orphan, but it is the Father that careth for all continually and for evermore. Not by mere report had he heard that the Supreme God is the Father of men: seeing that he called Him *Father* believing Him so to be, and in all that he did had ever his eyes fixed upon Him. Wherefore in whatsoever place he was, there it was given him to live happily.

CXXV

Know you not that the thing is a warfare? one man's duty is to mount guard, another must go out to reconnoitre, a third to battle; all cannot be in one place, nor would it even be expedient. But you, instead of executing your Commander's orders, complain if aught

[15] Hercules.

harsher than usual is enjoined; not understanding to what condition you are bringing the army, so far as in you lies. If all were to follow your example, none would dig a trench, none would cast a rampart around the camp, none would keep watch, or expose himself to danger; but all turn out useless for the service of war. . . . Thus it is here also. Every life is a warfare, and that long and various. You must fulfil a soldier's duty, and obey each order at your commander's nod: aye, if it be possible, divine what he would have done; for between that Commander and *this,* there is no comparison, either in might or in excellence.

CXXVI

Have you again forgotten? Know you not that a good man does nothing for appearance' sake, but for the sake of having done right? . . .

"Is there no reward then?"

Reward! do you seek any greater reward for a good man than doing what is right and just? Yet at the Great Games you look for nothing else; there the victor's crown you deem enough. Seems it to you so small a thing and worthless, to be a good man, and happy therein?

CXXVII

It befits thee not to be unhappy by reason of any, but rather to be happy by reason of all men, and especially by reason of God, who formed us to this end.

CXXVIII

What, did Diogenes love no man, he that was so gentle, so true a friend to men as cheerfully to endure such bodily hardships for the common weal of all mankind? But how loved he them? As behoved a minister of the Supreme God, alike caring for men and subject unto God.

CXXIX

I am by Nature made for my own good; not for my own evil.

CXXX

Remind thyself that he whom thou lovest is mortal—that what thou lovest is not thine own; it is given thee for the present, not irrevocably nor for ever, but even as a fig or a bunch of grapes at the appointed season of the year. . . .

"But these are words of evil omen." . . .

What, callest thou aught *of evil omen* save that which signifies some evil thing? *Cowardice* is a word of evil omen, if thou wilt, and meanness of spirit, and lamentation and mourning and shamelessness. . . .

But do not, I pray thee, call of evil omen a word that is significant of any natural thing:—as well call of evil omen the reaping of the corn; for it means the destruction of the ears, though not of the World!—as well say that the fall of the leaf is of evil omen; that the dried fig should take the place of the green; that raisins should be made from grapes. All these are changes from a former state into another; not destruction, but an ordered economy, a fixed administration. Such is leaving home, a change of small account; such is Death, a greater change, from what now is, not to what is not, but to what is not *now*.

"Shall I then no longer be?"

Not so; thou wilt be; but something different, of which the World now hath need. For thou too wert born not when thou chosest, but when the World had need of thee.

CXXXI

Wherefore a good man and true, bearing in mind who he is and whence he came and from whom he sprang, cares only how he may fill his post with due discipline and obedience to God.

Wilt thou that I continue to live? Then will I live, as one that is free and noble, as Thou wouldst have me. For Thou hast made me free from hindrance in what appertaineth unto me. But hast Thou no further need of me? I thank Thee! Up to this hour have I stayed for Thy sake and none other's: and now in obedience to Thee I depart.

"How dost thou depart?"

Again I say, as Thou wouldst have me; as one that is free, as Thy servant, as one whose ear is open unto what Thou dost enjoin, what Thou dost forbid.

CXXXII

Whatsoever place or post Thou assignest me, *sooner will I die a thousand deaths,* as Socrates said, *than desert it.* And where wilt Thou have me to be? At Rome or Athens? At Thebes or on a desert island? Only remember me there! Shouldst Thou send me where man cannot live as Nature would have him, I will depart, not in disobedience to Thee, but as though Thou wert sounding the signal for my retreat: I am not deserting Thee—far be that from me! I only perceive that thou needest me no longer.

CXXXIII

If you are in Gyaros, do not let your mind dwell upon life at Rome, and all the pleasures it offered to you when living there, and all that would attend your return. Rather be intent on this—how he that lives in Gyaros may live in Gyaros like a man of spirit. And if you are at Rome, do not let your mind dwell upon the life at Athens, but study only how to live at Rome.

Finally, in the room of all other pleasures put this—the pleasure which springs from conscious obedience to God.

CXXXIV

To a good man there is no evil, either in life or death. And if God supply not food, has He not, as a wise Commander, sounded the signal for retreat and nothing more? I obey, I follow—speaking good of my Commander, and praising His acts. For at His good pleasure I came; and I depart when it pleases Him; and while I was yet alive that was my work, to sing praises unto God!

CXXXV

Reflect that the chief source of all evils to Man, and of baseness and cowardice, is not death, but the *fear* of death.

Against this fear then, I pray you, harden yourself; to this let all your reasonings, your exercises, your reading tend. Then shall you know that thus alone are men set free.

CXXXVI

He is free who lives as he wishes to live; to whom none can do violence, none hinder or compel; whose impulses are unimpeded, whose desires attain their purpose, who falls not into what he would avoid. Who then would live in error?—None. Who would live deceived and prone to fall, unjust, intemperate, in abject whining at his lot?—None. Then doth no wicked man live as he would, and therefore neither is he free.

CXXXVII

Thus do the more cautious of travellers act. The road is said to be beset by robbers. The traveller will not venture alone, but awaits the companionship on the road of an ambassador, a quæstor or a proconsul. To him he attaches himself and thus passes by in safety. So doth the wise man in the world. Many are the companies of robbers and tyrants, many the storms, the straits, the losses of all a man holds dearest. Whither shall he fly for refuge—how shall he pass by unassailed? What companion on the road shall he await for protection? Such and such a wealthy man, of consular rank? And how shall I be profited, if he is stripped and falls to lamentation and weeping? And how if my fellow-traveller himself turns upon me and robs me? What am I to do? I will become a friend of Cæsar's! in his train none will do me wrong! In the first place—O the indignities I must endure to win distinction! O the multitude of hands there will be to rob me! And if I succeed, Cæsar too is but a mortal. While should it come to pass that I offend him, whither shall I flee from his presence? To the wilderness? And may not fever await me there? What then is to be done? Cannot a fellow-traveller be found that is honest and loyal, strong and secure against surprise? Thus doth the wise man reason, considering that if he would pass through in safety, he must attach himself unto God.

CXXXVIII

"How understandest thou *attach himself to God?"*

That what God wills, he should will also; that what God wills not, neither should he will.

"How then may this come to pass?"

By considering the movements of God, and His administration.

CXXXIX

And dost thou that hast received all from another's hands, repine and blame the Giver, if He takes anything from thee? Why, who art thou, and to what end comest thou here? was it not He that brought thee into the world; was it not He that made the Light manifest unto thee, that gave thee fellow-workers, and senses, and the power to reason? And how brought He thee into the world? Was it not as one born to die; as one bound to live out his earthly life in some small tabernacle of flesh; to behold His administration, and for a little while to share with Him in the mighty march of this great Festival Procession? Now therefore that thou hast beheld, while it was permitted thee, the Solemn Feast and Assembly, wilt thou not cheerfully depart, when He summons thee forth, with adoration and thanksgiving for what thou hast seen and heard?—"Nay, but I would fain have stayed longer at the Festival."—Ah, so would the mystics fain have the rites prolonged; so perchance would the crowd at the Great Games fain behold more wrestlers still. But the Solemn Assembly is over! Come forth, depart with thanksgiving and modesty—give place to others that must come into being even as thyself.

CXL

Why art thou thus insatiable? why thus unreasonable? why encumber the world?—"Aye, but I fain would have my wife and children with me too."—What, are they then *thine,* and not His that gave them—His that made thee? Give up then that which is not thine own: yield it to One who is better than thou. "Nay, but why did He bring one into the world on these conditions?"—If it suits thee not, depart! He hath no need of a spectator who finds fault with his lot! Them that will take part in the Feast he needeth—that will lift their voices with the rest, that men may applaud the more, and exalt the Great Assembly in hymns and songs of praise. But the wretched and the fearful He will not be displeased to see absent from it: for when they were present, they did not behave as at a Feast, nor fulfil their proper office; but moaned as though in pain, and found fault with their fate, their fortune and their companions; insensible to what had fallen to their lot, insensible to the powers they had received for a very different purpose—the powers of Magnanimity, Nobility of Heart, of Fortitude, of Freedom!

CXLI

Art *thou* then free? a man may say. So help me heaven, I long and pray for freedom! But I cannot look my masters boldly in the face; I still value the poor body; I still set much store on its preservation whole and sound.

But I can point thee out a free man, that thou mayest be no more in search of an example. Diogenes was free. How so? Not because he was of free parentage (for that, indeed, was not the case), but because he was himself free. He had cast away every handle whereby slavery might lay hold upon him, nor was it possible for any to approach and take hold of him to enslave him. All things sat loose upon him—all things were to him attached by but slender ties. Hadst thou seized upon his possessions, he would rather have let them go than have followed thee for them—aye, had it been even a limb, or mayhap his whole body; and in like manner, relatives, friends, and country. For he knew whence they came—from whose hands and on what terms he had received them. His true forefathers, the Gods, his true Country, he never would have abandoned; nor would he have yielded to any man in obedience and submission to the one nor in cheerfully dying for the other. For he was ever mindful that everything that comes to pass has its source and origin *there;* being indeed brought about for the weal of that his true Country, and directed by Him in whose governance it is.

CXLII

Ponder on this—on these convictions, on these words: fix thine eyes on these examples, if thou wouldst be free, if thou hast thine heart set upon the matter according to its worth. And what marvel if thou purchase so great a thing at so great and high a price? For the sake of this that men deem liberty, some hang themselves, others cast themselves down from the rock; aye, time has been when whole cities came utterly to an end: while for the sake of the Freedom that is true, and sure, and unassailable, dost thou grudge to God what He gave, when He claims it? Wilt thou not study, as Plato saith, to endure, not death alone, but torture, exile, stripes—in a word, to render up all that is not thine own? Else thou wilt be a slave amid slaves, wert thou ten thousand times a consul; aye, not a whit the less, though thou climb the Palace steps. And thou shalt know how true is the saying of Cleanthes, that though the words of philosophy may run counter to the opinions of the world, yet have they reason on their side.

CXLIII

Asked how a man should best grieve his enemy, Epictetus replied, "By setting himself to live the noblest life himself."

CXLIV

I am free, I am a friend of God, ready to render Him willing obedience. Of all else I may set store by nothing—neither by mine own body, nor possessions, nor office, nor good report, nor, in a word, aught else beside. For it is not His Will, that I should so set store by these things. Had it been His pleasure, He would have placed my Good therein. But now He hath not done so: therefore I cannot transgress one jot of His commands. In everything hold fast to that which is thy Good—but to all else (as far as is given thee) within the measure of Reason only, contented with this alone. Else thou wilt meet with failure, ill success, let and hindrance. These are the Laws ordained of God—these are His Edicts; these a man should expound and interpret; to these submit himself, not to the laws of Masurius and Cassius.[16]

[16] Famous Roman jurists.

CXLV

Remember that not the love of power and wealth sets us under the heel of others, but even the love of tranquillity, of leisure, of change of scene—of learning in general, it matters not what the outward thing may be—to set store by it is to place thyself in subjection to another. Where is the difference then between desiring to be a Senator, and desiring not to be one: between thirsting for office and thirsting to be quit of it? Where is the difference between crying, *Woe is me, I know not what to do, bound hand and foot as I am to my books so that I cannot stir!* and crying, *Woe is me, I have not time to read!* As though a book were not as much an outward thing and independent of the will, as office and power and the receptions of the great.

Or what reason hast thou (tell me) for desiring to read? For if thou aim at nothing beyond the mere delight of it, or gaining some scrap of knowledge, thou art but a poor, spiritless knave. But if thou desirest to study to its proper end, what else is this than a life that flows on tranquil and serene? And if thy reading secures thee not serenity, what profits it?—"Nay, but it doth secure it," quoth he, "and that is why I repine at being deprived of it."—And what serenity is this that lies at the mercy of every passer-by? I say not at the mercy of the Emperor or Emperor's favourite, but such as trembles at a raven's croak and piper's din, a fever's touch or a thousand things of like sort! Whereas the life serene has no more certain mark than this, that it ever moves with constant unimpeded flow.

CXLVI

If thou hast put malice and evil speaking from thee, altogether, or in some degree: if thou hast put away from thee rashness, foulness of tongue, intemperance, sluggishness: if thou art not moved by what once moved thee, or in like manner as thou once wert moved—then thou mayst celebrate a daily festival, to-day because thou hast done well in this matter, to-morrow in that. How much greater cause is here for offering sacrifice, than if a man should become Consul or Prefect?

CXLVII

These things hast thou from thyself and from the Gods: only remember who it is that giveth them—to whom and for what purpose they were given. Feeding thy soul on thoughts like these, dost thou debate in what place happiness awaits thee? in what place thou shalt do God's pleasure? Are not the Gods nigh unto all places alike; see they not alike what everywhere comes to pass?

CXLVIII

To each man God hath granted this inward freedom. These are the principles that in a house create love, in a city concord, among nations peace, teaching a man gratitude towards God and cheerful confidence, wherever he may be, in dealing with outward things that he knows are neither his nor worth striving after.

CXLIX

If you seek Truth, you will not seek to gain a victory by every possible means; and when you have found Truth, you need not fear being defeated.

CL

What foolish talk is this? how can I any longer lay claim to right principles, if I am not content with being what I am, but am all aflutter about what I am supposed to be?

CLI

God hath made all things in the world, nay, the world itself, free from hindrance and perfect, and its parts for the use of the whole. No other creature is capable of comprehending His administration thereof; but the reasonable being Man possesses faculties for the consideration of all these things—not only that he is himself a part, but what part he is, and how it is meet that the parts should give place to the whole. Nor is this all. Being naturally constituted noble, magnanimous, and free, he sees that the things which surround him are of two kinds. Some are free from hindrance and in the power of the will. Others are subject to hindrance, and depend on the will of other men. If then he place his own good, his own best interest, only in that which is free from hindrance and in his power, he will be free, tranquil, happy, unharmed, noble-hearted, and pious; giving thanks for all things unto God, finding fault with nothing that comes to pass, laying no charge against anything. Whereas if he place his good in outward things, depending not on the will, he must perforce be subject to hindrance and restraint, the slave of those that have power over the things he desires and fears; he must perforce be impious, as deeming himself injured at the hands of God; he must be unjust, as ever prone to claim more than his due; he must perforce be of a mean and abject spirit.

CLII

Whom then shall I yet fear? the lords of the Bedchamber, lest they should shut me out? If they find me desirous of entering in, let them shut me out, if they will.

"Then why comest thou to the door?"

Because I think it meet and right, so long as the Play lasts, to take part therein.

"In what sense art thou then shut out?"

Because, unless I am admitted, it is not my *will* to enter: on the contrary, my will is simply that which comes to pass. For I esteem what God wills better than what I will. To Him will I cleave as His minister and attendant; having the same movements, the same desires, in a word the same Will as He. There is no such thing as being shut out for me, but only for them that would force their way in.

CLIII

But what says Socrates?—"One man finds pleasure in improving his land, another his horses. My pleasure lies in seeing that I myself grow better day by day."

CLIV

The dress is suited to the craft; the craftsman takes his name from the craft, not from the dress. For this reason Euphrates was right in saying, "I long endeavoured to conceal my following the philosophic life; and this profited me much. In the first place, I knew that what I did aright, I did not for the sake of lookers-on, but for my own. I ate aright—unto myself; I kept the even tenor of my walk, my glance composed and serene—all unto myself and unto God. Then as I fought alone, I was alone in peril. If I did anything amiss or shameful, the cause of Philosophy was not in me endangered; nor did I wrong the multitude by transgressing as a professed philosopher. Wherefore those that knew not my purpose marvelled how it came about, that whilst all my life and conversation was passed with philosophers without exception, I was yet none myself. And what harm that the philosopher should be known by his acts, instead of by mere outward signs and symbols?"

CLV

First study to conceal what thou art; seek wisdom a little while unto thyself. Thus grows the fruit; first, the seed must be buried in the earth for a little space; there it must be hid and slowly grow, that it may reach maturity. But if it produce the ear before the jointed stalk, it is imperfect—a thing from the garden of Adonis.[17] Such a sorry growth art thou; thou hast blossomed too soon: the winter cold will wither thee away!

CLVI

First of all, condemn the life thou art now leading: but when thou hast condemned it, do not despair of thyself—be not like them of mean spirit, who once they have yielded, abandon themselves entirely and as it were allow the torrent to sweep them away. No; learn what the wrestling masters do. Has the boy fallen? "Rise," they say, "wrestle again, till thy strength come to thee." Even thus should it be with thee. For know that there is nothing more tractable than the human soul. It needs but to *will,* and the thing is done; the soul is set upon the right path: as on the contrary it needs but to nod over the task, and all is lost. For ruin and recovery alike are from within.

CLVII

It is the critical moment that shows the man. So when the crisis is upon you, remember that God, like a trainer of wrestlers, has

[17] Potted plants of forced growth carried in the processions in honor of Adonis.

matched you with a rough and stalwart antagonist.—"To what end?" you ask. That you may prove the victor at the Great Games. Yet without toil and sweat this may not be!

CLVIII

If thou wouldst make progress, be content to seem foolish and void of understanding with respect to outward things. Care not to be thought to know anything. If any should make account of thee, distrust thyself.

CLIX

Remember that in life thou shouldst order thy conduct as at a banquet. Has any dish that is being served reached thee? Stretch forth thy hand and help thyself modestly. Doth it pass thee by? Seek not to detain it. Has it not yet come? Send not forth thy desire to meet it, but wait until it reaches thee. Deal thus with children, thus with wife; thus with office, thus with wealth—and one day thou wilt be meet to share the Banquets of the Gods. But if thou dost not so much as touch that which is placed before thee, but despisest it, then shalt thou not only share the Banquets of the Gods, but their Empire also.

CLX

Remember that thou art an actor in a play, and of such sort as the Author chooses, whether long or short. If it be his good pleasure to assign thee the part of a beggar, a ruler, or a simple citizen, thine it is to play it fitly. For thy business is to act the part assigned thee, well: to choose it, is another's.

CLXI

Keep death and exile daily before thine eyes, with all else that men deem terrible, but more especially Death. Then wilt thou never think a mean thought, nor covet anything beyond measure.

CLXII

As a mark is not set up in order to be missed, so neither is such a thing as natural evil produced in the World.

CLXIII

Piety towards the Gods, be sure, consists chiefly in thinking rightly concerning them—that they *are,* and that they govern the Universe with goodness and justice; and that thou thyself art appointed to obey them, and to submit under all circumstances that arise; acquiescing cheerfully in whatever may happen, sure that it is brought to pass and accomplished by the most Perfect Understanding. Thus thou wilt never find fault with the Gods, nor charge them with neglecting thee.

CLXIV

Lose no time in setting before you a certain stamp of character and behaviour to observe both when by yourself and in company with others. Let silence be your general rule; or say only what is necessary and in few words. We shall, however, when occasion demands, enter into discourse sparingly, avoiding such common topics as gladiators, horse-races, athletes; and the perpetual talk about food and drink. Above all avoid speaking of *persons,* either in the way of praise or blame, or comparison.

If you can, win over the conversation of your company to what it should be by your own. But if you should find yourself cut off without escape among strangers and aliens, be silent.

CLXV

Laughter should not be much, nor frequent, nor unrestrained.

CLXVI

Refuse altogether to take an oath if you can, if not, as far as may be.

CLXVII

Banquets of the unlearned and of them that are without, avoid. But if you have occasion to take part in them, let not your attention be relaxed for a moment, lest you slip after all into evil ways. For you may rest assured that be a man ever so pure himself, he cannot escape defilement if his associates are impure.

CLXVIII

Take what relates to the body as far as the bare use warrants—as meat, drink, raiment, house and servants. But all that makes for show and luxury reject.

CLXIX

If you are told that such an one speaks ill of you, make no defence against what was said, but answer, He surely knew not my other faults, else he would not have mentioned these only!

CLXX

When you visit any of those in power, bethink yourself that you will not find him in: that you may not be admitted: that the door may be shut in your face: that he may not concern himself about you. If with all this, it is your duty to go, bear what happens, and never say to yourself, It was not worth the trouble! For that would smack of the foolish and unlearned who suffer outward things to touch them.

CLXXI

In company avoid frequent and undue talk about your own actions and dangers. However pleasant it may be to you to enlarge upon the risks you have run, others may not find such pleasure in listening to your adventures. Avoid provoking laughter also: it is a habit from which one easily slides into the ways of the foolish, and apt to diminish the respect which your neighbours feel for you. To border on coarse talk is also dangerous. On such occasions, if a convenient opportunity offer, rebuke the speaker. If not, at least by relapsing into silence, colouring, and looking annoyed, show that you are displeased with the subject.

CLXXII

When you have decided that a thing ought to be done, and are doing it, never shun being *seen* doing it, even though the multitude should be likely to judge the matter amiss. For if you are not acting rightly, shun the act itself; if rightly, however, why fear misplaced censure?

CLXXIII

It stamps a man of mean capacity to spend much time on the things of the body, as to be long over bodily exercises, long over eating, long over drinking, long over other bodily functions. Rather should these things take the second place, while all your care is directed tc the understanding.

CLXXIV

Everything has two handles, one by which it may be borne, the other by which it may not. If your brother sin against you lay not hold of it by the handle of his injustice, for by that it may not be borne: but rather by this, that he is your brother, the comrade of your youth; and thus you will lay hold on it so that it may be borne.

CLXXV

Never call yourself a Philosopher nor talk much among the unlearned about Principles, but do that which follows from them. Thus at a banquet, do not discuss how people ought to eat; but eat as you ought. Remember that Socrates thus entirely avoided ostentation. Men would come to him desiring to be recommended to philosophers, and he would conduct them thither himself—so well did he bear being overlooked. Accordingly if any talk concerning principles should arise among the unlearned, be you for the most part silent. For you run great risk of spewing up what you have ill digested. And when a man tells you that you know nothing and you are not nettled at it, then you may be sure that you have begun the work.

CLXXVI

When you have brought yourself to supply the needs of the body at small cost, do not pique yourself on that, nor if you drink only water, keep saying on each occasion, *I drink water!* And if you ever want to practise endurance and toil, do so unto yourself and not unto others—do not embrace statues![18]

[18]As Diogenes is said to have done in winter.

CLXXVII

When a man prides himself on being able to understand and interpret the writings of Chrysippus,[19] say to yourself:—

If Chrysippus had not written obscurely, this fellow would have had nothing to be proud of. But what is it that *I* desire? To understand Nature, and to follow her! Accordingly I ask who is the Interpreter. On hearing that it is Chrysippus, I go to him. But it seems I do not understand what he wrote. So I seek one to interpret that. So far there is nothing to pride myself upon. But when I have found my interpreter, what remains is to put in practice his instructions. This itself is the only thing to be proud of. But if I admire the interpretation and that alone, what else have I turned out but a mere commentator instead of a lover of wisdom?—except indeed that I happen to be interpreting Chrysippus instead of Homer. So when any one says to me, *Prithee, read me Chrysippus,* I am more inclined to blush, when I cannot show my deeds to be in harmony and accordance with his sayings.

CLXXVIII

At feasts, remember that you are entertaining two guests, body and soul. What you give to the body, you presently lose; what you give to the soul, you keep for ever.

CLXXIX

At meals see to it that those who serve be not more in number than those who are served. It is absurd for a crowd of persons to be dancing attendance on half a dozen chairs.

CLXXX

It is best to share with your attendants what is going forward, both in the labour of preparation and in the enjoyment of the feast itself. If such a thing be difficult at the time, recollect that you who are not weary are being served by those that are; you who are eating and drinking by those who do neither; you who are talking by those who are silent; you who are at ease by those who are under con-

[19] The so-called "Second Founder" of the Stoics.

straint. Thus no sudden wrath will betray you into unreasonable conduct, nor will you behave harshly by irritating another.

CLXXXI

When Xanthippe was chiding Socrates for making scanty preparation for entertaining his friends, he answered:—"If they are friends of ours, they will not care for that; if they are not, we shall care nothing for them!"

CLXXXII

Asked, *Who is the rich man?* Epictetus replied, *"He who is content."*

CLXXXIII

Favorinus[20] tells us how Epictetus would also say that there were two faults far graver and fouler than any others—inability to bear, and inability to forbear, when we neither patiently bear the blows that must be borne, nor abstain from the things and the pleasures we ought to abstain from. "So," he went on, "if a man will only have these two words at heart, and heed them carefully by ruling and watching over himself, he will for the most part fall into no sin, and his life will be tranquil and serene." He meant the words Ἀνέχου καὶ ἀπέχου—"BEAR AND FORBEAR."

CLXXXIV

On all occasions these thoughts should be at hand:—

Lead me, O God, and Thou, O Destiny,[21]
Be what it may the goal appointed me,
Bravely I'll follow; nay, and if I would not,
I'd prove a coward, yet must follow still!

Again:

Who to Necessity doth bow aright,
Is learn'd in wisdom and the things of God.

Once more:—

Crito, if this be God's will, so let it be. As for me, Anytus and Meletus can indeed put me to death, but injure me, never!

[20] A Roman orator and sophist.

[21] These verses are by Cleanthes, the successor of Zeno as leader of the Stoics, and author of the Hymn printed in Appendix B.

CLXXXV

We shall then be like Socrates, when we can indite hymns of praise to the Gods in prison.

CLXXXVI

It is hard to combine and unite these two qualities, the carefulness of one who is affected by circumstances, and the intrepidity of one who heeds them not. But it is not impossible: else were happiness also impossible. We should act as we do in seafaring.

"What can I do?"—Choose the master, the crew, the day, the opportunity. Then comes a sudden storm. What matters it to me? my part has been fully done. The matter is in the hands of another—the Master of the ship. The ship is foundering. What then have I to do? I do the only thing that remains to me—to be drowned without fear, without a cry, without upbraiding God, but knowing that what has been born must likewise perish. For I am not Eternity, but a human being—a part of the whole, as an hour is part of the day. I must come like the hour, and like the hour must pass!

CLXXXVII

And now we are sending you to Rome to spy out the land; but none send a coward as such a spy, that, if he hear but a noise and see a shadow moving anywhere, loses his wits and comes flying to say, *The enemy are upon us!*

So if *you* go now, and come and tell us: "Everything at Rome is terrible: Death is terrible, Exile is terrible, Slander is terrible, Want is terrible; fly, comrades! the enemy are upon us!" we shall reply, Get you gone, and prophesy to yourself! we have but erred in sending such a spy as you. Diogenes, who was sent as a spy long before you, brought us back another report than this. He says that Death is no evil; for it need not even bring shame with it. He says that Fame is but the empty noise of madmen. And what report did this spy bring us of Pain, what of Pleasure, what of Want? That to be clothed in sackcloth is better than any purple robe; that sleeping on the bare ground is the softest couch; and in proof of each assertion he points to his own courage, constancy, and freedom; to his own healthy and muscular frame. "There is no enemy near," he cries, "all is perfect peace!"

CLXXXVIII

If a man has this peace—not the peace proclaimed by Cæsar (how indeed should *he* have it to proclaim?), nay, but the peace proclaimed by God through reason, will not that suffice him when alone, when he beholds and reflects:—Now can no evil happen unto me; for me there is no robber, for me no earthquake; all things are full of peace, full of tranquillity; neither highway nor city nor gathering of men, neither neighbour nor comrade can do me hurt. Another supplies my food, whose care it is; another my raiment; another hath given me perceptions of sense and primary conceptions. And when He supplies my necessities no more, it is that He is sounding the retreat, that He hath opened the door, and is saying to thee, Come!—Whither? To nought that thou needest fear, but to the friendly kindred elements whence thou didst spring. Whatsoever of fire is in thee, unto fire shall return; whatsoever of earth, unto earth; of spirit, unto spirit; of water, unto water. There is no Hades, no fabled rivers of Sighs, of Lamentation, or of Fire: but all things are full of Beings spiritual and divine. With thoughts like these, beholding the Sun, Moon, and Stars, enjoying earth and sea, a man is neither helpless nor alone!

CLXXXIX

What wouldst thou be found doing when overtaken by Death? If I might choose, I would be found doing some deed of true humanity, of wide import, beneficent and noble. But if I may not be found engaged in aught so lofty, let me hope at least for this—what none may hinder, what is surely in my power—that I may be found raising up in myself that which had fallen; learning to deal more wisely with the things of sense; working out my own tranquillity, and thus rendering that which is its due to every relation of life. . . .

If death surprise me thus employed, it is enough if I can stretch forth my hands to God and say, "The faculties which I received at Thy hands for apprehending this thine Administration, I have not neglected. As far as in me lay, I have done Thee no dishonour. Behold how I have used the senses, the primary conceptions which

Thou gavest me. Have I ever laid anything to Thy charge? Have I ever murmured at aught that came to pass, or wished it otherwise? Have I in anything transgressed the relations of life? For that Thou didst beget me, I thank Thee for that Thou hast given: for the time during which I have used the things that were Thine, it suffices me. Take them back and place them wherever Thou wilt! They were all Thine, and Thou gavest them me."—If a man depart thus minded, is it not enough? What life is fairer or more noble, what end happier than his?

(APPENDIX A)

FRAGMENTS

ATTRIBUTED TO EPICTETUS

I

A LIFE entangled with Fortune is like a torrent. It is turbulent and muddy; hard to pass and masterful of mood: noisy and of brief continuance.

II

The soul that companies with Virtue is like an ever-flowing source. It is a pure, clear, and wholesome draught; sweet, rich, and generous of its store; that injures not, neither destroys.

III

It is a shame that one who sweetens his drink with the gifts of the bee, should embitter God's gift Reason with vice.

IV

Crows pick out the eyes of the dead, when the dead have no longer need of them; but flatterers mar the soul of the living, and *her* eyes they blind.

V

Keep neither a blunt knife nor an ill-disciplined looseness of tongue.

VI

Nature hath given men one tongue but two ears, that we may hear from others twice as much as we speak.

VII

Do not give sentence in another tribunal till you have been yourself judged in the tribunal of Justice.

VIII

It is shameful for a Judge to be judged by others.

IX

Give me by all means the shorter and nobler life, instead of one that is longer but of less account!

X

Freedom is the name of virtue: Slavery, of vice. . . . None is a slave whose acts are free.

XI

Of pleasures, those which occur most rarely give the most delight.

XII

Exceed due measure, and the most delightful things become the least delightful.

XIII

The anger of an ape—the threat of a flatterer:—these deserve equal regard.

XIV

Chastise thy passions that they avenge not themselves upon thee.

XV

No man is free who is not master of himself.

XVI

A ship should not ride on a single anchor, nor life on a single hope.

XVII

Fortify thyself with contentment: that is an impregnable stronghold.

XVIII

No man who is a lover of money, of pleasure, of glory, is likewise a lover of Men; but only he that is a lover of whatsoever things are fair and good.

XIX

Think of God more often than thou breathest.

XX

Choose the life that is noblest, for custom can make it sweet to thee.

XXI

Let thy speech of God be renewed day by day, aye, rather than thy meat and drink.

XXII

Even as the Sun doth not wait for prayers and incantations to rise, but shines forth and is welcomed by all: so thou also wait not for clapping of hands and shouts and praise to do thy duty; nay, do good of thine own accord, and thou wilt be loved like the Sun.

XXIII

Let no man think that he is loved by any who loveth none.

XXIV

If thou rememberest that God standeth by to behold and visit all that thou doest; whether in the body or in the soul, thou surely wilt not err in any prayer or deed; and thou shalt have God to dwell with thee.

NOTE.—Schweighäuser's great edition collects 181 fragments attributed to Epictetus, of which but a few are certainly genuine. Some (as xxi., xxiv., above) bear the stamp of Pythagorean origin; others, though changed in form, may well be based upon Epictetean sayings. Most have been preserved in the Anthology of John of Stobi (Stobæus), a Byzantine collector, of whom scarcely anything is known but that he probably wrote towards the end of the fifth century, and made his vast body of extracts from more than five hundred authors for his son's use. The best examination of the authenticity of the Fragments is *Quæstiones Epicteteæ,* by R. Asmus, 1888. The above selection includes some of doubtful origin but intrinsic interest.—*Crossley.*

(APPENDIX B)

THE HYMN OF CLEANTHES

Chiefest glory of deathless Gods, Almighty for ever,
Sovereign of Nature that rulest by law, what Name shall we give Thee?—
Blessed be Thou! for on Thee should call all things that are mortal.
For that we are Thine offspring; nay, all that in myriad motion
Lives for its day on the earth bears one impress—Thy likeness—upon it.
Wherefore my song is of Thee, and I hymn Thy power for ever.

Lo, the vast orb of the Worlds, round the Earth evermore as it rolleth,
Feels Thee its Ruler and Guide, and owns Thy lordship rejoicing.
Aye, for Thy conquering hands have a servant of living fire—
Sharp is the bolt!—where it falls, Nature shrinks at the shock and doth shudder.
Thus Thou directest the Word universal that pulses through all things,
Mingling its life with Lights that are great and Lights that are lesser,
E'en as beseemeth its birth, High King through ages unending.

Nought is done that is done without Thee in the earth or the waters
Or in the heights of heaven, save the deed of the fool and the sinner.
Thou canst make rough things smooth; at Thy Voice, lo, jarring disorder
Moveth to music, and Love is born where hatred abounded.
Thus hast Thou fitted alike things good and things evil together,
That over all might reign one Reason, supreme and eternal;
Though thereunto the hearts of the wicked be hardened and heedless—

Woe unto them!—for while ever their hands are grasping at good things,
Blind are their eyes, yea, stopped are their ears to God's Law universal,
Calling through wise obedience to live the life that is noble.
This they mark not, but heedless of right, turn each to his own way,
Here, a heart fired with ambition, in strife and straining unhallowed;
There, thrusting honour aside, fast set upon getting and gaining;
Others again given over to lusts and dissolute softness,
Working never God's Law, but that which warreth upon it.

Nay, but, O Giver of all things good, whose home is the dark cloud,
Thou that wieldest Heaven's bolt, save men from their ignorance grievous;
Scatter its night from their souls, and grant them to come to that Wisdom
Wherewithal, sistered with Justice, Thou rulest and governest all things;
That we, honoured by Thee, may requite Thee with worship and honour,
Evermore praising thy works, as is meet for men that shall perish;
Seeing that none, be he mortal or God, hath privilege nobler
Than without stint, without stay, to extol Thy Law universal.

INDEX FOR REFERENCE

Schweigh. = Epicteteæ Philosophiæ Monumenta, Schweighäuser, Lips., 1799.

Schenkl = Epicteti Dissertationes, H. Schenkl, Ed. Minor, Lips. (Teubner), 1898.

Asmus = Quæstiones Epicteteæ, R. Asmus, Friburg, 1888.

I. Arrian, *Discourses* i. 16, 15–19
II. *ib.* ii. 23, 36–39
III. *ib.* iv. 4, 26
IV. *ib.* iv. 12, 11–12
V. *ib.* iii. 23, 29
VI. *ib.* i. 7, 10
VII. *ib.* iv. 6, 20
VIII. *ib.* i. 2, 11–18
IX. *ib.* i. 3, 1–6
X. Fragment, quoted by M. Antoninus, iv. 41; Schweigh. clxxvi.
XI. Arrian, *Disc.* i. 18, 15
XII. *ib.* i. 29, 21
XIII. *ib.* i. 6, 19–22
XIV. *ib.* i. 6, 23–29
XV. *ib.* i. 9, 1
XVI. *ib.* i. 9, 4–7
XVII. *ib.* i. 9, 10–15
XVIII. *ib.* i. 9, 16–17
XIX. *ib.* i. 9, 18–22
XX. *ib.* i. 6, 37–43
XXI. *ib.* i. 9, 22
XXII. *ib.* i. 17, 27–28
XXIII. *ib.* i. 5, 3–5
XXIV. *ib.* i. 10, 1–10 (abbreviated)
XXV. *ib.* i. 9, 27–28
XXVI. *ib.* i. 12, 15–16
XXVII. *ib.* iv. 3, 1
XXVIII. *ib.* i. 12, 1–3
XXIX. *ib.* i. 12, 7–12
XXX. Fragment (from "Memoirs of Epict."); Schweigh. lxxii.; Schenkl, 16
XXXI. Arrian, *Disc.* i. 12, 20–21
XXXII. *ib.* i. 12, 22–23
XXXIII. *ib.* i. 12, 26–27
XXXIV. *ib.* i. 13
XXXV. Fragment (Stobæus); Schweigh. xv.; Schenkl, 17
XXXVI. Arrian, *Disc.* i. 14, 1–6
XXXVII. *ib.* i. 14, 12–17
XXXVIII. *ib.* i. 15, 5
XXXIX. *ib.* i. 15, 6–8
XL. *ib.* i. 19, 19–23
XLI. Fragment, Schweigh. xlii.; Schenkl, *Gn. Epict. Stob.* 36
XLII. Arrian, *Disc.* i. 19, 24–25
XLIII. *ib.* i. 19, 26–29
XLIV. *ib.* i. 24, 20
XLV. *ib.* i. 25, 18–22
XLVI. *ib.* i. 26, 15–16
XLVII. *ib.* i. 26, 17–18
XLVIII. *ib.* ii. 2, 8–9
XLIX. *ib.* i. 29, 46–49
L. Fragment (Stobæus); Schweigh. vii.
LI. Arrian, *Disc.* i. 30, 1–4
LII. *ib.* i. 29, 16–18
LIII. *ib.* iii. 1, 36–38
LIV. *ib.* ii. 2, 17
LV. *ib.* ii. 1, 8 and 13
LVI. *ib.* ii. 5, 24–29
LVII. *ib.* ii. 3, 1–2
LVIII. *ib.* ii. 7, 10–14
LIX. *ib.* ii. 8, 1–3
LX. *ib.* ii. 8, 9–14
LXI. *ib.* ii. 8, 15–23 and 27–28
LXII. Fragment (Stobæus); Schweigh. lvii.
LXIII. *ib.* ii. 12, 3–4
LXIV. *ib.* ii. 12, 14–25
LXV. Fragment; Schweigh. clxx. (v. Asmus, p. 20)
LXVI. Arrian, *Disc.* ii. 14, 10–13
LXVII. *ib.* ii. 14, 19–22
LXVIII. *ib.* ii. 14, 23–29
LXIX. *ib.* ii. 15, 13–14
LXX. *ib.* ii. 16, 32–34
LXXI. *ib.* ii. 16, 41–47
LXXII. *ib.* ii. 17, 1
LXXIII. *ib.* ii. 17, 29–33
LXXIV. Fragment (M. Antoninus); Schweigh. clxxviii.; Schenkl, 28
LXXV. Arrian, *Disc.* ii. 18, 5–12
LXXVI. *ib.* ii. 18, 19
LXXVII. *ib.* ii. 18, 27–29
LXXVIII. *ib.* ii. 19, 23–28

INDEX FOR REFERENCE TO APPENDIX A

THE MEDITATIONS OF MARCUS AURELIUS

TRANSLATED BY

GEORGE LONG, M.A.

INTRODUCTORY NOTE

Marcus Annius Verus was born in Rome, A.D. 121, and assumed the name of Marcus Aurelius Antoninus, by which he is known to history, on his adoption by the Emperor T. Aurelius Antoninus. He succeeded to the imperial throne in 161, and ruled till his death in 180. His reign, though marked by justice and moderation at home, was troubled by constant warfare on the frontiers of the Empire, and Aurelius spent much of his later years in the uncongenial task of commanding armies that no longer proved irresistible against the barbarian hordes.

M. Aurelius was educated by the orator Fronto, but turned aside from rhetoric to the study of the Stoic philosophy, of which he was the last distinguished representative. The "Meditations," which he wrote in Greek, are among the most noteworthy expressions of this system, and exhibit it favorably on its practical side. His own precepts he carried out with singular consistency; and both in his public and his private life he was in the highest degree conscientious. He and his predecessor are noted as the only Roman emperors who can be said to have ruled with a single eye to the welfare of their subjects.

During his reign Rome was visited by a severe pestilence, and this, with reverses suffered by his armies, threw the populace into a panic, and led them to demand the sacrifice of the Christians, whom they regarded as having brought down the anger of the gods. Aurelius seems to have shared the panic; and his record is stained by his sanction of a cruel persecution. This incident in the career of the last, and one of the loftiest, of the pagan moralists may be regarded as symbolic of the dying effort of heathenism to check the advancing tide of Christianity.

The "Meditations" picture with faithfulness the mind and character of this noblest of the Emperors. Simple in style and sincere in tone, they record for all time the height reached by pagan aspiration in its effort to solve the problem of conduct; and the essential agreement of his practice with his teaching proved that "Even in a palace life may be led well."

THE MEDITATIONS OF MARCUS AURELIUS ANTONINUS

I

FROM my grandfather Verus [I learned] good morals and the government of my temper.

2. From the reputation and remembrance of my father, modesty and a manly character.

3. From my mother, piety and beneficence, and abstinence, not only from evil deeds, but even from evil thoughts; and further simplicity in my way of living, far removed from the habits of the rich.

4. From my great-grandfather, not to have frequented public schools, and to have had good teachers at home, and to know that on such things a man should spend liberally.

5. From my governor, to be neither of the green nor of the blue party at the games in the Circus, nor a partizan either of the Parmularius or the Scutarius at the gladiators' fights; from him too I learned endurance of labour, and to want little, and to work with my own hands, and not to meddle with other people's affairs, and not to be ready to listen to slander.

6. From Diognetus, not to busy myself about trifling things, and not to give credit to what was said by miracle-workers and jugglers about incantations and the driving away of dæmons and such things; and not to breed quails [for fighting], nor to give myself up passionately to such things; and to endure freedom of speech; and to have become intimate with philosophy; and to have been a hearer, first of Bacchius, then of Tandasis and Marcianus; and to have written dialogues in my youth; and to have desired a plank bed and skin, and whatever else of the kind belongs to the Grecian discipline.

7. From Rusticus I received the impression that my character required improvement and discipline; and from him I learned not to be led astray to sophistic emulation, nor to writing on speculative

matters, nor to delivering little hortatory orations, nor to showing myself off as a man who practises much discipline, or does benevolent acts in order to make a display; and to abstain from rhetoric, and poetry, and fine writing; and not to walk about in the house in my outdoor dress, nor to do other things of the kind; and to write my letters with simplicity, like the letter which Rusticus wrote from Sinuessa to my mother; and with respect to those who have offended me by words, or done me wrong, to be easily disposed to be pacified and reconciled, as soon as they have shown a readiness to be reconciled; and to read carefully, and not to be satisfied with a superficial understanding of a book; nor hastily to give my assent to those who talk overmuch; and I am indebted to him for being acquainted with the discourses of Epictetus, which he communicated to me out of his own collection.

8. From Apollonius I learned freedom of will and undeviating steadiness of purpose; and to look to nothing else, not even for a moment, except to reason; and to be always the same, in sharp pains, on the occasion of the loss of a child, and in long illness; and to see clearly in a living example that the same man can be both most resolute and yielding, and not peevish in giving his instruction; and to have had before my eyes a man who clearly considered his experience and his skill in expounding philosophical principles as the smallest of his merits; and from him I learned how to receive from friends what are esteemed favours, without being either humbled by them or letting them pass unnoticed.

9. From Sextus, a benevolent disposition, and the example of a family governed in a fatherly manner, and the idea of living conformably to nature; and gravity without affectation, and to look carefully after the interests of friends, and to tolerate ignorant persons, and those who form opinions without consideration: he had the power of readily accommodating himself to all, so that intercourse with him was more agreeable than any flattery; and at the same time he was most highly venerated by those who associated with him; and he had the faculty both of discovering and ordering, in an intelligent and methodical way, the principles necessary for life; and he never showed anger or any other passion, but was entirely free from passion, and also most affectionate; and he could express approbation

without noisy display, and he possessed much knowledge without ostentation.

10. From Alexander, the grammarian, to refrain from fault-finding, and not in a reproachful way to chide those who uttered any barbarous or solecistic or strange-sounding expression; but dexterously to introduce the very expression which ought to have been used, and in the way of answer or giving confirmation, or joining in an inquiry about the thing itself, not about the word, or by some other fit suggestion.

11. From Fronto I learned to observe what envy and duplicity and hypocrisy are in a tyrant, and that generally those among us who are called Patricians are rather deficient in paternal affection.

12. From Alexander the Platonic, not frequently nor without necessity to say to any one, or to write in a letter, that I have no leisure; nor continually to excuse the neglect of duties required by our relation to those with whom we live, by alleging urgent occupations.

13. From Catulus, not to be indifferent when a friend finds fault, even if he should find fault without reason, but to try to restore him to his usual disposition; and to be ready to speak well of teachers, as it is reported of Domitius and Athenodotus; and to love my children truly.

14. From my brother Severus, to love my kin, and to love truth, and to love justice; and through him I learned to know Thrasea, Helvidius, Cato, Dion, Brutus; and from him I received the idea of a polity in which there is the same law for all, a polity administered with regard to equal rights and equal freedom of speech, and the idea of a kingly government which respects most of all the freedom of the governed; I learned from him also consistency and undeviating steadiness in my regard for philosophy, and a disposition to do good, and to give to others readily, and to cherish good hopes, and to believe that I am loved by my friends; and in him I observed no concealment of his opinions with respect to those whom he condemned, and that his friends had no need to conjecture what he wished or did not wish, but it was quite plain.

15. From Maximus I learned self-government, and not to be led aside by anything; and cheerfulness in all circumstances, as well as in illness; and a just admixture in the moral character of sweetness

and dignity, and to do what was set before me without complaining. I observed that everybody believed that he thought as he spoke, and that in all that he did he never had any bad intention; and he never showed amazement and surprise, and was never in a hurry, and never put off doing a thing, nor was perplexed nor dejected, nor did he ever laugh to disguise his vexation, nor, on the other hand, was he ever passionate or suspicious. He was accustomed to do acts of beneficence and was ready to forgive, and was free from all falsehood; and he presented the appearance of a man who could not be diverted from right rather than of a man who had been improved. I observed, too, that no man could ever think that he was despised by Maximus, or ever venture to think himself a better man. He had also the art of being humorous in an agreeable way.

16. In my father I observed mildness of temper, and unchangeable resolution in the things which he had determined after due deliberation; and no vainglory in those things which men call honours; and a love of labour and perseverance; and a readiness to listen to those who had anything to propose for the common weal; and undeviating firmness in giving to every man according to his deserts; and a knowledge derived from experience of the occasions for vigorous action and for remission. And I observed that he had overcome all passion for joys; and he considered himself no more than any other citizen, and he released his friends from all obligation to sup with him or to attend him of a necessity when he went abroad, and those who failed to accompany him by reason of any urgent circumstances, always found him the same. I observed, too, his habit of careful inquiry in all matters of deliberation, and his persistency, and that he never stopped his investigation through being satisfied with appearances which first present themselves; and that his disposition was to keep his friends, and not to be soon tired of them, nor yet to be extravagant in his affection; and to be satisfied on all occasions, and cheerful; and to foresee things a long way off, and to provide for the smallest without display; and to check immediately popular applause and flattery, and to be ever watchful over the things which were necessary for the administration of the empire, and to be a good manager of the expenditure, and patiently to endure the blame which he got for such conduct; and he was neither superstitious with

respect to the gods, nor did he court men by gifts or by trying to please them, or by flattering the populace; but he showed sobriety in all things and firmness, and never any mean thoughts or action, nor love of novelty. And the things which conduce in any way to the commodity of life, and of which fortune gives an abundant supply, he used without arrogance and without excusing himself; so that when he had them, he enjoyed them without affectation, and when he had them not he did not want them. No one could ever say of him that he was either a sophist or a [home-bred] flippant slave or a pedant; but every one acknowledged him to be a man ripe, perfect, above flattery, able to manage his own and other men's affairs. Besides this, he honoured those who were true philosophers, and he did not reproach those who pretended to be philosophers, nor yet was he easily led by them. He was also easy in conversation, and he made himself agreeable without any offensive affectation. He took a reasonable care of his body's health, not as one who was greatly attached to life, nor out of regard to personal appearance, nor yet in a careless way, but so that, through his own attention, he very seldom stood in need of the physician's art or of medicine or external applications. He was most ready to give way without envy to those who possessed any particular faculty, such as that of eloquence or knowledge of the law or of morals, or of anything else; and he gave them his help, that each might enjoy reputation according to his deserts; and he always acted conformably to the institutions of his country, without showing any affectation of doing so. Further, he was not fond of change, nor unsteady, but he loved to stay in the same places, and to employ himself about the same things; and after his paroxysms of headache he came immediately fresh and vigorous to his usual occupations. His secrets were not many, but very few and very rare, and these only about public matters; and he showed prudence and economy in the exhibition of the public spectacles and the construction of public buildings, his donations to the people, and in such things, for he was a man who looked to what ought to be done, not to the reputation which is got by a man's acts. He did not take the bath at unseasonable hours; he was not fond of building houses, nor curious about what he eat, nor about the texture and colour of his clothes, nor about the beauty of his slaves. His dress came from Lorium, his villa on the coast, and from Lanuvium generally. We know how he behaved to the toll-collector at Tusculum who asked his pardon; and such was all his behaviour. There was in him nothing harsh, nor implacable, nor violent, nor, as one may say, anything carried to the sweating point; but he examined all things severally as if he had abundance of time, and without confusion, in an orderly way, vigorously and consistently. And that might be applied to him which is recorded of Socrates, that he was able both to abstain from, and to enjoy, those things which many are too weak to abstain from, and cannot enjoy without excess. But to be strong enough both to bear the one and to be sober in the other is the mark of a man who has a perfect and invincible soul, such as he showed in the illness of Maximus.

17. To the gods I am indebted for having good grandfathers, good parents, a good sister, good teachers, good associates, good kinsmen and friends, nearly everything good. Further, I owe it to the gods that I was not hurried into any offence against any of them, though I had a disposition which, if opportunity had offered, might have led me to do something of this kind; but, through their favour, there never was such a concurrence of circumstances as put me to the trial. Further, I am thankful to the gods that I was not longer brought up with my grandfather's concubine, and that I preserved the flower of my youth, and that I did not make proof of my virility before the proper season, but even deferred the time; that I was subjected to a ruler and a father who was able to take away all pride from me, and to bring me to the knowledge that it is possible for a man to live in a palace without wanting either guards or embroidered dresses, or torches and statues, and suchlike show; but it is in such a man's power to bring himself very near to the fashion of a private person, without being for this reason either meaner in thought, or more remiss in action, with respect to the things which must be done for the public interest in a manner that befits a ruler. I thank the gods for giving me such a brother, who was able by his moral character to rouse me to vigilance over myself, and who, at the same time, pleased me by his respect and affection; that my children have not been stupid nor deformed in body; that I did not make more proficiency in rhetoric, poetry, and the other studies, in which I

should perhaps have been completely engaged, if I had seen that I was making progress in them; that I made haste to place those who brought me up in the station of honour which they seemed to desire without putting them off with hope of my doing it some time after, because they were then still young; that I knew Apollonius, Rusticus, Maximus; that I received clear and frequent impressions about living according to nature, and what kind of a life that is, so that, so far as depended on the gods, and their gifts and help, and inspirations, nothing hindered me from forthwith living according to nature, though I still fall short of it through my own fault, and though not observing the admonitions of the gods, and, I may almost say, their direct instructions; that my body has held out so long in such a kind of life; that I never touched either Benedicta or Theodotus, and that, after having fallen into amatory passions, I was cured; and, though I was often out of humour with Rusticus, I never did anything of which I had occasion to repent; that, though it was my mother's fate to die young, she spent the last years of her life with me; that, whenever I wished to help any man in his need, or on any other occasion, I was never told that I had not the means of doing it; and that to myself the same necessity never happened, to receive anything from another; that I have such a wife, so obedient, and so affectionate, and so simple; that I had abundance of good masters for my children; and that remedies have been shown to me by dreams, both others, and against blood-spitting and giddiness; . . . and that, when I had an inclination to philosophy, I did not fall into the hands of any sophist, and that I did not waste my time on writers [of histories], or in the resolution of syllogisms, or occupy myself about the investigation of appearances in the heavens; for all these things require the help of the gods and fortune.

Among the Quadi at the Granua.

II

BEGIN the morning by saying to thyself, I shall meet with the busybody, the ungrateful, arrogant, deceitful, envious, unsocial. All these things happen to them by reason of their ignorance of what is good and evil. But I who have seen the nature of the good that it is beautiful and of the bad that it is ugly, and the nature of him who does wrong, that it is akin to me, not [only] of the same blood or seed, but that it participates in [the same] intelligence and [the same] portion of the divinity, I can neither be injured by any of them, for no one can fix on me what is ugly, nor can I be angry with my kinsman, nor hate him. For we are made for co-operation, like feet, like hands, like eyelids, like the rows of the upper and lower teeth. To act against one another then is contrary to nature; and it is acting against one another to be vexed and to turn away.

2. Whatever this is that I am, it is a little flesh and breath, and the ruling part. Throw away thy books; no longer distract thyself: it is not allowed; but as if thou wast now dying, despise the flesh, it is blood and bones and a network, a contexture of nerves, veins and arteries. See the breath also, what kind of a thing it is; air, and not always the same, but every moment sent out and again sucked in. The third then is the ruling part: consider thus: Thou art an old man; no longer let this be a slave, no longer be pulled by the strings like a puppet to unsocial movements, no longer be either dissatisfied with thy present lot, or shrink from the future.

3. All that is from the gods is full of providence. That which is from fortune is not separated from nature or without an interweaving and involution with the things which are ordered by Providence. From thence all things flow; and there is besides necessity, and that which is for the advantage of the whole universe, of which thou art a part. But that is good for every part of nature which the nature of the whole brings, and what serves to maintain this nature. Now the universe is preserved, as by the changes of the elements, so by the changes of things compounded of the elements. Let these principles be enough for thee; let them always be fixed opinions. But cast away the thirst after books, that thou mayest not die murmuring, but cheerfully, truly, and from thy heart thankful to the gods.

4. Remember how long thou hast been putting off these things, and how often thou hast received an opportunity from the gods, and yet dost not use it. Thou must now at last perceive of what universe thou art a part, and of what administrator of the universe thy existence is an efflux, and that a limit of time is fixed for thee, which if thou dost not use for clearing away the clouds from thy mind, it will go and thou wilt go, and it will never return.

5. Every moment think steadily as a Roman and a man to do what thou hast in hand with perfect and simple dignity, and feeling of affection, and freedom, and justice; and to give thyself relief from all other thoughts. And thou wilt give thyself relief, if thou doest every act of thy life as if it were the last, laying aside all carelessness and passionate aversion from the commands of reason, and all hypocrisy, and self-love, and discontent with the portion which has been given to thee. Thou seest how few the things are, the which if a man lays hold of, he is able to live a life which flows in quiet, and is like the existence of the gods; for the gods on their part will require nothing more from him who observes these things.

6. Do wrong to thyself, do wrong to thyself, my soul; but thou wilt no longer have the opportunity of honouring thyself. Every man's life is sufficient. But thine is nearly finished, though thy soul reverences not itself, but places thy felicity in the souls of others.

7. Do the things external which fall upon thee distract thee? Give thyself time to learn something new and good, and cease to be whirled around. But then thou must also avoid being carried about the other way. For those too are triflers who have wearied themselves in life by their activity, and yet have no object to which to direct every movement, and, in a word, all their thoughts.

8. Through not observing what is in the mind of another a man has seldom been seen to be unhappy; but those who do not observe the movements of their own minds must of necessity be unhappy.

9. This thou must always bear in mind, what is the nature of the whole, and what is my nature, and how this is related to that, and what kind of a part it is of what kind of a whole; and that there is no one who hinders thee from always doing and saying the things which are according to the nature of which thou art a part.

10. Theophrastus, in his comparison of bad acts—such a comparison as one would make in accordance with the common notions of mankind—says, like a true philosopher, that the offences which are committed through desire are more blamable than those which are committed through anger. For he who is excited by anger seems to turn away from reason with a certain pain and unconscious contraction; but he who offends through desire, being overpowered by pleasure, seems to be in a manner more intemperate and more womanish

in his offences. Rightly then, and in a way worthy of philosophy, he said that the offence which is committed with pleasure is more blamable than that which is committed with pain; and on the whole the one is more like a person who has been first wronged and through pain is compelled to be angry; but the other is moved by his own impulse to do wrong, being carried toward doing something by desire.

11. Since it is possible that thou mayest depart from life this very moment, regulate every act and thought accordingly. But to go away from among men, if there are gods, is not a thing to be afraid of, for the gods will not involve thee in evil; but if indeed they do not exist, or if they have no concern about human affairs, what is it to me to live in a universe devoid of gods or devoid of providence? But in truth they do exist, and they do care for human things, and they have put all the means in man's power to enable him not to fall into real evils. And as to the rest, if there was anything evil, they would have provided for this also, that it should be altogether in a man's power not to fall into it. Now, that which does not make a man worse, how can it make a man's life worse? But neither through ignorance, nor having the knowledge, but not the power to guard against or correct these things, is it possible that the nature of the universe has overlooked them; nor is it possible that it has made so great a mistake, either through want of power or want of skill, that good and evil should happen indiscriminately to the good and the bad. But death certainly, and life, honour and dishonour, pain and pleasure, all these things equally happen to good men and bad, being things which make us neither better nor worse. Therefore they are neither good nor evil.

12. How quickly all these things disappear, in the universe the bodies themselves, but in time the remembrance of them; what is the nature of all sensible things, and particularly those which attract with the bait of pleasure or terrify by pain, or are noised about by vapoury fame; how worthless, and contemptible, and sordid, and perishable, and dead they are—all this it is the part of the intellectual faculty to observe. To observe, too, who these are whose opinions and voices give reputation; what death is, and the fact that, if a man looks at it in itself, and by the abstractive power of reflection resolves

into their parts all the things which present themselves to the imagination in it, he will then consider it to be nothing else than an operation of nature; and if any one is afraid of an operation of nature he is a child. This, however, is not only an operation of nature, but it is also a thing which conduces to the purposes of nature. To observe, too, how man comes near to the Deity, and by what part of him, and when this part of man is so disposed (vi. 28).

13. Nothing is more wretched than a man who traverses everything in a round, and pries into things beneath the earth, as the poet says, and seeks by conjecture what is in the minds of his neighbours, without perceiving that it is sufficient to attend to the dæmon within him, and to reverence it sincerely. And reverence of the dæmon consists in keeping it pure from passion and thoughtlessness, and dissatisfaction with what comes from gods and men. For the things from the gods merit veneration for their excellence; and the things from men should be dear to us by reason of kinship; and sometimes even, in a manner, they move our pity by reason of men's ignorance of good and bad; this defect being not less than that which deprives us of the power of distinguishing things that are white and black.

14. Though thou shouldest be going to live three thousand years, and as many times ten thousand years, still remember that no man loses any other life than this which he now lives, nor lives any other than this which he now loses. The longest and shortest are thus brought to the same. For the present is the same to all, though that which perishes is not the same; and so that which is lost appears to be a mere moment. For a man cannot lose either the past or the future: for what a man has not, how can any one take this from him? These two things then thou must bear in mind: the one, that all things from eternity are of like forms and come round in a circle, and that it makes no difference whether a man shall see the same things during a hundred years or two hundred, or an infinite time; and the second, that the longest liver and he who will die soonest lose just the same. For the present is the only thing of which a man can be deprived, if it is true that this is the only thing which he has, and that a man cannot lose a thing if he has it not.

15. Remember that all is opinion. For what was said by the Cynic

Monimus is manifest: and manifest too is the use of what was said, if a man receives what may be got out of it as far as it is true.

16. The soul of man does violence to itself, first of all when it becomes an abscess and, as it were, a tumour on the universe, so far as it can. For to be vexed at anything which happens is a separation of ourselves from nature, in some part of which the natures of all other things are contained. In the next place, the soul does violence to itself when it turns away from any man, or even moves towards him with the intention of injuring, such as are the souls of those who are angry. In the third place, the soul does violence to itself when it is overpowered by pleasure or by pain. Fourthly, when it plays a part, and does or says anything insincerely and untruly. Fifthly, when it allows any act of its own and any movement to be without an aim, and does anything thoughtlessly and without considering what it is, it being right that even the smallest things be done with reference to an end; and the end of rational animals is to follow the reason and the law of the most ancient city and polity.

17. Of human life the time is a point, and the substance is in a flux, and the perception dull, and the composition of the whole body subject to putrefaction, and the soul of a whirl, and fortune hard to divine, and fame a thing devoid of judgment. And, to say all in a word, everything which belongs to the body is a stream, and what belongs to the soul is a dream and vapour, and life is a warfare and a stranger's sojourn, and after-fame is oblivion. What, then, is that which is able to conduct a man? One thing, and only one—philosophy. But this consists in keeping the dæmon within a man free from violence and unharmed, superior to pains and pleasures, doing nothing without a purpose, nor yet falsely and with hypocrisy, not feeling the need of another man's doing or not doing anything; and besides, accepting all that happens, and all that is allotted, as coming from thence, wherever it is, from whence he himself came; and, finally, waiting for death with a cheerful mind, as being nothing else than a dissolution of the elements of which every living being is compounded. But if there is no harm to the elements themselves in each continually changing into another, why should a man have any apprehension about the change and dissolution of all the elements? For

it is according to nature, and nothing is evil which is according to nature.

This in Carnuntum.

III

WE ought to consider not only that our life is daily wasting away and a smaller part of it is left, but another thing also must be taken into the account, that if a man should live longer it is quite uncertain whether the understanding will still continue sufficient for the comprehension of things, and retain the power of contemplation which strives to acquire the knowledge of the divine and the human. For if he shall begin to fall into dotage, perspiration and nutrition and imagination and appetite, and whatever else there is of the kind, will not fail; but the power of making use of ourselves, and filling up the measure of our duty, and clearly separating all appearances, and considering whether a man should now depart from life, and whatever else of the kind absolutely requires a disciplined reason, all this is already extinguished. We must make haste then, not only because we are daily nearer to death, but also because the conception of things and the understanding of them cease first.

2. We ought to observe also that even the things which follow after the things which are produced according to nature contain something pleasing and attractive. For instance, when bread is baked some parts are split at the surface, and these parts which thus open, and have a certain fashion contrary to the purpose of the baker's art, are beautiful in a manner, and in a peculiar way excite a desire for eating. And again, figs, when they are quite ripe, gape open, and in the ripe olives the very circumstance of their being near to rottenness adds a peculiar beauty to the fruit. And the ears of corn bending down, and the lion's eyebrows, and the foam which flows from the mouth of wild boars, and many other things—though they are far from being beautiful, if a man should examine them severally—still, because they are consequent upon the things which are formed by nature, help to adorn them, and they please the mind; so that if a man should have a feeling and deeper insight with respect to the things which are

produced in the universe, there is hardly one of those which follow by way of consequence which will not seem to him to be in a manner disposed so as to give pleasure. And so he will see even the real gaping jaws of wild beasts with no less pleasure than those which painters and sculptors show by imitation; and in an old woman and an old man he will be able to see a certain maturity and comeliness; and the attractive loveliness of young persons he will be able to look on with chaste eyes; and many such things will present themselves, not pleasing to every man, but to him only who has become truly familiar with nature and her works.

3. Hippocrates after curing many diseases himself fell sick and died. The Chaldæi foretold the deaths of many, and then fate caught them too. Alexander, and Pompeius, and Caius Cæsar, after so often completely destroying whole cities, and in battle cutting to pieces many ten thousands of cavalry and infantry, themselves too at last departed from life. Heraclitus, after so many speculations on the conflagration of the universe, was filled with water internally and died smeared all over with mud. And lice destroyed Democritus; and other lice killed Socrates. What means all this? Thou hast embarked, thou hast made the voyage, thou art come to shore; get out. If indeed to another life, there is no want of gods, not even there. But if to a state without sensation, thou wilt cease to be held by pains and pleasures, and to be a slave to the vessel which is as much inferior as that which serves it is superior; for the one is intelligence and deity; the other is earth and corruption.

4. Do not waste the remainder of thy life in thoughts about others, when thou dost not refer thy thoughts to some object of common utility. For thou losest the opportunity of doing something else when thou hast such thoughts as these, What is such a person doing, and why, and what is he saying, and what is he thinking of, and what is he contriving, and whatever else of the kind makes us wander away from the observation of our own ruling power. We ought then to check in the series of our thoughts everything that is without a purpose and useless, but most of all the overcurious feeling and the malignant; and a man should use himself to think of those things only about which if one should suddenly ask, What hast thou now in thy thoughts? with perfect openness thou mightest immediately

answer, This or That; so that from thy words it should be plain that everything in thee is simple and benevolent, and such as befits a social animal, one that cares not for thoughts about pleasure or sensual enjoyments at all, nor has any rivalry or envy and suspicion, or anything else for which thou wouldst blush if thou shouldst say that thou hadst it in thy mind. For the man who is such and no longer delays being among the number of the best, is like a priest and minister of the gods, using too the [deity] which is planted within him, which makes the man uncontaminated by pleasure, unharmed by any pain, untouched by any insult, feeling no wrong, a fighter in the noblest fight, one who cannot be overpowered by any passion, dyed deep with justice, accepting with all his soul everything which happens and is assigned to him as his portion; and not often, nor yet without great necessity and for the general interest, imagining what another says, or does, or thinks. For it is only what belongs to himself that he makes the matter for his activity; and he constantly thinks of that which is allotted to himself out of the sum total of things, and he makes his own acts fair, and he is persuaded that his own portion is good. For the lot which is assigned to each man is carried along with him and carries him along with it. And he remembers also that every rational animal is his kinsman, and that to care for all men is according to man's nature; and a man should hold on to the opinion not of all but of those only who confessedly live according to nature. But as to those who live not so, he always bears in mind what kind of men they are both at home and from home, both by night and by day, and what they are, and with what men they live an impure life. Accordingly, he does not value at all the praise which comes from such men, since they are not even satisfied with themselves.

5. Labour not unwillingly, nor without regard to the common interest, nor without due consideration, nor with distraction; nor let studied ornament set off thy thoughts, and be not either a man of many words, or busy about too many things. And further, let the deity which is in thee be the guardian of a living being, manly and of ripe age, and engaged in matter political, and a Roman, and a ruler, who has taken his post like a man waiting for the signal which summons him from life, and ready to go, having need neither of oath nor of any man's testimony. Be cheerful also, and seek not

external help nor the tranquillity which others give. A man then must stand erect, not be kept erect by others.

6. If thou findest in human life anything better than justice, truth, temperance, fortitude, and, in a word, anything better than thy own mind's self-satisfaction in the things which it enables thee to do according to right reason, and in the condition that is assigned to thee without thy own choice; if, I say, thou seest anything better than this, turn to it with all thy soul, and enjoy that which thou hast found to be the best. But if nothing appears to be better than the deity which is planted in thee, which has subjected to itself all thy appetites, and carefully examines all the impressions, and, as Socrates said, has detached itself from the persuasions of sense, and has submitted itself to the gods, and cares for mankind; if thou findest everything else smaller and of less value than this, give place to nothing else, for if thou dost once diverge and incline to it, thou wilt no longer without distraction be able to give the preference to that good thing which is thy proper possession and thy own; for it is not right that anything of any other kind, such as praise from the many, or power, or enjoyment of pleasure, should come into competition with that which is rationally and politically [or, practically] good. All these things, even though they may seem to adapt themselves [to the better things] in a small degree, obtain the superiority all at once, and carry us away. But do thou, I say, simply and freely choose the better, and hold to it.—But that which is useful is the better.—Well then, if it is only useful to thee as a rational being, keep to it; but if it is only useful to thee as an animal, say so, and maintain thy judgment without arrogance; only take care that thou makest the inquiry by a sure method.

7. Never value anything as profitable to thyself which shall compel thee to break thy promise, to lose thy self-respect, to hate any man, to suspect, to curse, to act the hypocrite, to desire anything which needs walls and curtains: for he who has preferred to everything else his own intelligence and dæmon and the worship of its excellence, acts no tragic part, does not groan, will not need either solitude or much company; and, what is chief of all, he will live without either pursuing or flying from [death]; but whether for a longer or a shorter time he shall have the soul inclosed in the body, he cares not at all; for even if he must depart immediately, he will go as readily as if he

were going to do anything else which can be done with decency and order; taking care of this only all through life, that his thoughts turn not away from anything which belongs to an intelligent animal and a member of a civil community.

8. In the mind of one who is chastened and purified thou wilt find no corrupt matter, nor impurity, nor any sore skinned over. Nor is his life incomplete when fate overtakes him, as one may say of an actor who leaves the stage before ending and finishing the play. Besides, there is in him nothing servile, nor affected, nor too closely bound [to other things], nor yet detached [from other things], nothing worthy of blame, nothing which seeks a hiding-place.

9. Reverence the faculty which produces opinion. On this faculty it entirely depends whether there shall exist in thy ruling part any opinion inconsistent with nature and the constitution of the rational animal. And this faculty promises freedom from hasty judgment, and friendship towards men, and obedience to the gods.

10. Throwing away then all things, hold to these only which are few; and besides bear in mind that every man lives only this present time, which is an indivisible point, and that all the rest of his life is either past or it is uncertain. Short then is the time which every man lives, and small the nook of the earth where he lives; and short too the longest posthumous fame, and even this only continued by a succession of poor human beings, who will very soon die, and who know not even themselves, much less him who died long ago.

11. To the aids which have been mentioned let this one still be added:—Make for thyself a definition or description of the thing which is presented to thee, so as to see distinctly what kind of a thing it is in its substance, in its nudity, in its complete entirety, and tell thyself its proper name, and the names of the things of which it has been compounded, and into which it will be resolved. For nothing is so productive of elevation of mind as to be able to examine methodically and truly every object which is presented to thee in life, and always to look at things so as to see at the same time what kind of universe this is, and what kind of use everything performs in it, and what value everything has with reference to the whole, and what with reference to man, who is a citizen of the highest city, of which all other cities are like families; what each thing is, and of what it

is composed, and how long it is the nature of this thing to endure which now makes an impression on me, and what virtue I have need of with respect to it, such as gentleness, manliness, truth, fidelity, simplicity, contentment, and the rest. Wherefore, on every occasion a man should say: This comes from God; and this is according to the apportionment and spinning of the thread of destiny, and suchlike coincidence and chance; and this is from one of the same stock and a kinsman and partner, one who knows not however what is according to his nature. But I know; for this reason I behave towards him according to the natural law of fellowship with benevolence and justice. At the same time however in things indifferent I attempt to ascertain the value of each.

12. If thou workest at that which is before thee, following right reason seriously, vigorously, calmly, without allowing anything else to distract thee, but keeping thy divine part pure, as if thou shouldst be bound to give it back immediately; if thou holdest to this, expecting nothing, fearing nothing, but satisfied with thy present activity according to nature, and with heroic truth in every word and sound which thou utterest, thou wilt live happy. And there is no man who is able to prevent this.

13. As physicians have always their instruments and knives ready for cases which suddenly require their skill, so do thou have principles ready for the understanding of things divine and human, and doing everything, even the smallest, with a recollection of the bond which unites the divine and human to one another. For neither wilt thou do anything well which pertains to man without at the same time having a reference to things divine; nor the contrary.

14. No longer wander at hazard; for neither wilt thou read thy own memoirs, nor the acts of the ancient Romans and Hellenes, and the selections from books which thou wast reserving for thy old age. Hasten then to the end which thou hast before thee, and, throwing away idle hopes, come to thy own aid, if thou carest at all for thyself, while it is in thy power.

15. They know not how many things are signified by the words stealing, sowing, buying, keeping quiet, seeing what ought to be done; for this is not effected by the eyes, but by another kind of vision.

16. Body, soul, intelligence: to the body belong sensations, to the soul appetites, to the intelligence principles. To receive the impressions of forms by means of appearances belongs even to animals; to be pulled by the strings of desire belongs both to wild beasts and to men who have made themselves into women, and to a Phalaris and a Nero: and to have the intelligence that guides to the things which appear suitable belongs also to those who do not believe in the gods, and who betray their country, and do their impure deeds when they have shut the doors. If then everything else is common to all that I have mentioned, there remains that which is peculiar to the good man, to be pleased and content with what happens, and with the thread which is spun for him; and not to defile the divinity which is planted in his breast, nor disturb it by a crowd of images, but to preserve it tranquil, following it obediently as a god, neither saying anything contrary to the truth, nor doing anything contrary to justice. And if all men refuse to believe that he lives a simple, modest, and contented life, he is neither angry with any of them, nor does he deviate from the way which leads to the end of life, to which a man ought to come pure, tranquil, ready to depart, and without any compulsion perfectly reconciled to his lot.

IV

THAT which rules within, when it is according to nature, is so affected with respect to the events which happen, that it always easily adapts itself to that which is possible and is presented to it. For it requires no definite material, but it moves towards its purpose, under certain conditions however; and it makes a material for itself out of that which opposes it, as fire lays hold of what falls into it, by which a small light would have been extinguished: but when the fire is strong, it soon appropriates to itself the matter which is heaped on it, and consumes it, and rises higher by means of this very material.

2. Let no act be done without a purpose, nor otherwise than according to the perfect principles of art.

3. Men seek retreats for themselves, houses in the country, seashores, and mountains; and thou too art wont to desire such things

very much. But this is altogether a mark of the most common sort of men, for it is in thy power whenever thou shalt choose to retire into thyself. For nowhere, either with more quiet or more freedom from trouble, does a man retire than into his own soul, particularly when he has within him such thoughts that by looking into them he is immediately in perfect tranquillity; and I affirm that tranquillity is nothing else than the good ordering of the mind. Constantly then give to thyself this retreat, and renew thyself; and let thy principles be brief and fundamental, which, as soon as thou shalt recur to them, will be sufficient to cleanse the soul completely, and to send thee back free from all discontent with the things to which thou returnest. For with what art thou discontented? With the badness of men? Recall to thy mind this conclusion, that rational animals exist for one another, and that to endure is a part of justice, and that men do wrong involuntarily; and consider how many already, after mutual enmity, suspicion, hatred, and fighting, have been stretched dead, reduced to ashes; and be quiet at last.—But perhaps thou art dissatisfied with that which is assigned to thee out of the universe.—Recall to thy recollection this alternative; either there is providence or atoms [fortuitous concurrence of things]; or remember the arguments by which it has been proved that the world is a kind of political community [and be quiet at last].—But perhaps corporeal things will still fasten upon thee.—Consider then further that the mind mingles not with the breath, whether moving gently or violently, when it has once drawn itself apart and discovered its own power, and think also of all that thou hast heard and assented to about pain and pleasure [and be quiet at last].—But perhaps the desire of the thing called fame will torment thee.—See how soon everything is forgotten, and look at the chaos of infinite time on each side of [the present], and the emptiness of applause, and the changeableness and want of judgment in those who pretend to give praise, and the narrowness of the space within which it is circumscribed [and be quiet at last]. For the whole earth is a point, and how small a nook in it is this thy dwelling, and how few are there in it, and what kind of people are they who will praise thee.

This then remains: Remember to retire into this little territory of thy own, and, above all, do not distract or strain thyself, but be free, and look at things as a man, as a human being, as a citizen, as a mortal. But among the things readiest to thy hand to which thou shalt turn, let there be these, which are two. One is that things do not touch the soul, for they are external and remain immovable; but our perturbations come only from the opinion which is within. The other is that all these things, which thou seest, change immediately and will no longer be; and constantly bear in mind how many of these changes thou hast already witnessed. The universe is transformation: life is opinion.

4. If our intellectual part is common, the reason also, in respect of which we are rational beings, is common: if this is so, common also is the reason which commands us what to do, and what not to do; if this is so, there is a common law also; if this is so, we are fellow-citizens; if this is so, we are members of some political community; if this is so, the world is in a manner a state. For of what other common political community will any one say that the whole human race are members? And from thence, from this common political community comes also our very intellectual faculty and reasoning faculty and our capacity for law; or whence do they come? For as my earthly part is a portion given to me from certain earth, and that which is watery from another element, and that which is hot and fiery from some peculiar source (for nothing comes out of that which is nothing, as nothing also returns to non-existence), so also the intellectual part comes from some source.

5. Death is such as generation is, a mystery of nature; a composition out of the same elements, and a decomposition into the same; and altogether not a thing of which any man should be ashamed, for it is not contrary to [the nature of] a reasonable animal, and not contrary to the reason of our constitution.

6. It is natural that these things should be done by such persons, it is a matter of necessity; and if a man will not have it so, he will not allow the fig-tree to have juice. But by all means bear this in mind, that within a very short time both thou and he will be dead; and soon not even your names will be left behind.

7. Take away thy opinion, and then there is taken away the complaint, "I have been harmed." Take away the complaint, "I have been harmed," and the harm is taken away.

8. That which does not make a man worse than he was, also does not make his life worse, nor does it harm him either from without or from within.

9. The nature of that which is [universally] useful has been compelled to do this.

10. Consider that everything which happens, happens justly, and if thou observest carefully, thou wilt find it to be so. I do not say only with respect to the continuity of the series of things, but with respect to what is just, and as if it were done by one who assigns to each thing its value. Observe then as thou hast begun; and whatever thou doest, do it in conjunction with this, the being good, and in the sense in which a man is properly understood to be good. Keep to this in every action.

11. Do not have such an opinion of things as he has who does thee wrong, or such as he wishes thee to have, but look at them as they are in truth.

12. A man should always have these two rules in readiness; the one, to do only whatever the reason of the ruling and legislating faculty may suggest for the use of men; the other, to change thy opinion, if there is any one at hand who sets thee right and moves thee from any opinion. But this change of opinion must proceed only from a certain persuasion, as of what is just or of common advantage, and the like, not because it appears pleasant or brings reputation.

13. Hast thou reason? I have.—Why then dost not thou use it? For if this does its own work, what else dost thou wish?

14. Thou hast existed as a part. Thou shalt disappear in that which produced thee; but rather thou shalt be received back into its seminal principle by transmutation.

15. Many grains of frankincense on the same altar: one falls before, another falls after; but it makes no difference.

16. Within ten days thou wilt seem a god to those to whom thou art now a beast and an ape, if thou wilt return to thy principles and the worship of reason.

17. Do not act as if thou wert going to live ten thousand years. Death hangs over thee. While thou livest, while it is in thy power, be good.

18. How much trouble he avoids who does not look to see what

his neighbour says or does or thinks, but only to what he does himself, that it may be just and pure; or, as Agathon says, look not round at the depraved morals of others, but run straight along the line without deviating from it.

19. He who has a vehement desire for posthumous fame does not consider that every one of those who remember him will himself also die very soon; then again also they who have succeeded them, until the whole remembrance shall have been extinguished as it is transmitted through men who foolishly admire and perish. But suppose that those who will remember are even immortal, and that the remembrance will be immortal, what then is this to thee? And I say not, what is it to the dead? but, what is it to the living? What is praise, except indeed so far as it has a certain utility? For thou now rejectest unseasonably the gift of nature, clinging to something else. . . .

20. Everything which is in any way beautiful is beautiful in itself, and terminates in itself, not having praise as part of itself. Neither worse then nor better is a thing made by being praised. I affirm this also of the things which are called beautiful by the vulgar; for example, material things and works of art. That which is really beautiful has no need of anything; not more than law, not more than truth, not more than benevolence or modesty. Which of these things is beautiful because it is praised, or spoiled by being blamed? Is such a thing as an emerald made worse than it was, if it is not praised? or gold, ivory, purple, a lyre, a little knife, a flower, a shrub?

21. If souls continue to exist, how does the air contain them from eternity?—But how does the earth contain the bodies of those who have been buried from time so remote? For as here the mutation of these bodies after a certain continuance, whatever it may be, and their dissolution make room for other dead bodies; so the souls which are removed into the air after subsisting for some time are transmuted and diffused, and assume a fiery nature by being received into the seminal intelligence of the universe, and in this way make room for the fresh souls which come to dwell there. And this is the answer which a man might give on the hypothesis of souls continuing to exist. But we must not only think of the number of

bodies which are thus buried, but also of the number of animals which are daily eaten by us and the other animals. For what a number is consumed, and thus in a manner buried in the bodies of those who feed on them! And nevertheless this earth receives them by reason of the changes [of these bodies] into blood, and the transformations into the aërial or the fiery element.

What is the investigation into the truth in this matter? The division into that which is material and that which is the cause of form [the formal] (vii. 29).

22. Do not be whirled about, but in every movement have respect to justice, and on the occasion of every impression maintain the faculty of comprehension [or understanding].

23. Everything harmonizes with me which is harmonious to thee, O Universe. Nothing for me is too early nor too late, which is in due time for thee. Everything is fruit to me which thy seasons bring, O Nature: from thee are all things, in thee are all things, to thee all things return. The poet says, Dear city of Cecrops; and wilt not thou say, Dear city of Zeus?

24. Occupy thyself with few things, says the philosopher, if thou wouldst be tranquil.—But consider if it would not be better to say, Do what is necessary, and whatever the reason of the animal which is naturally social requires, and as it requires. For this brings not only the tranquillity which comes from doing well, but also that which comes from doing few things. For the greatest part of what we say and do being unnecessary, if a man takes this away, he will have more leisure and less uneasiness. Accordingly on every occasion a man should ask himself, Is this one of the unnecessary things? Now a man should take away not only unnecessary acts but also unnecessary thoughts, for thus superfluous acts will not follow after.

25. Try how the life of the good man suits thee, the life of him who is satisfied with his portion out of the whole, and satisfied with his own just acts and benevolent disposition.

26. Hast thou seen those things? Look also at these. Do not disturb thyself. Make thyself all simplicity. Does any one do wrong? It is to himself that he does the wrong. Has anything happened to thee? Well, out of the universe from the beginning everything

which happens has been apportioned and spun out to thee. In a word, thy life is short. Thou must turn to profit the present by the aid of reason and justice. Be sober in thy relaxation.

27. Either it is a well arranged universe or a chaos huddled together, but still a universe. But can a certain order subsist in thee, and disorder in the All? And this, too, when all things are so separated and diffused and sympathetic.

28. A black character, a womanish character, a stubborn character, bestial, childish, animal, stupid, counterfeit, scurrilous, fraudulent, tyrannical.

29. If he is a stranger to the universe who does not know what is in it, no less is he a stranger who does not know what is going on in it. He is a runaway, who flies from social reason; he is blind, who shuts the eyes of the understanding; he is poor, who has need of another, and has not from himself all things which are useful for life. He is an abscess on the universe, who withdraws and separates himself from the reason of our common nature through being displeased with the things which happen, for the same nature produces this, and has produced thee too; he is a piece rent asunder from the state, who tears his own soul from that of reasonable animals, which is one.

30. The one is a philosopher without a tunic, and the other without a book: here is another half naked: Bread I have not, he says, and I abide by reason. And I do not get the means of living out of my learning, and I abide [by my reason].

31. Love the art, poor as it may be, which thou hast learned, and be content with it; and pass through the rest of life like one who has intrusted to the gods with his whole soul all that he has, making thyself neither the tyrant nor the slave of any man.

32. Consider, for example, the times of Vespasian. Thou wilt see all these things, people marrying, bringing up children, sick, dying, warring, feasting, trafficking, cultivating the ground, flattering, obstinately arrogant, suspecting, plotting, wishing for some to die, grumbling about the present, loving, heaping up treasure, desiring consulship, kingly power. Well, then, that life of these people no longer exists at all. Again, remove to the times of Trajan. Again, all is the same. Their life, too, is gone. In like manner view also

the other epochs of time and of whole nations, and see how many after great efforts soon fell and were resolved into the elements. But chiefly thou shouldst think of those whom thou hast thyself known distracting themselves about idle things, neglecting to do what was in accordance with their proper constitution, and to hold firmly to this and to be content with it. And herein it is necessary to remember that the attention given to everything has its proper value and proportion. For thus thou wilt not be dissatisfied, if thou appliest thyself to smaller matters no further than is fit.

33. The words which were formerly familiar are now antiquated; so also the names of those who were famed of old, are now in a manner antiquated: Camillus, Cæso, Volesus, Leonnatus, and a little after also Scipio and Cato, then Augustus, then also Hadrianus and Antoninus. For all things soon pass away and become a mere tale, and complete oblivion soon buries them. And I say this of those who have shone in a wondrous way. For the rest, as soon as they have breathed out their breath, they are gone, and no man speaks of them. And, to conclude the matter, what is even an eternal remembrance? A mere nothing. What, then, is that about which we ought to employ our serious pains? This one thing, thoughts just, and acts social, and words which never lie, and a disposition which gladly accepts all that happens, as necessary, as usual, as flowing from a principle and source of the same kind.

34. Willingly give thyself up to Clotho [one of the fates], allowing her to spin thy thread into whatever things she pleases.

35. Everything is only for a day, both that which remembers and that which is remembered.

36. Observe constantly that all things take place by change, and accustom thyself to consider that the nature of the Universe loves nothing so much as to change the things which are and to make new things like them. For everything that exists is in a manner the seed of that which will be. But thou art thinking only of seeds which are cast into the earth or into a womb: but this is a very vulgar notion.

37. Thou wilt soon die, and thou art not yet simple, nor free from perturbations, nor without suspicion of being hurt by external things, nor kindly disposed towards all; nor dost thou yet place wisdom only in acting justly.

38. Examine men's ruling principles, even those of the wise, what kind of things they avoid, and what kind they pursue.

39. What is evil to thee does not subsist in the ruling principle of another; nor yet in any turning and mutation of thy corporeal covering. Where is it then? It is in that part of thee in which subsists the power of forming opinions about evils. Let this power then not form [such] opinions, and all is well. And if that which is nearest to it, the poor body, is cut, burnt, filled with matter and rottenness, nevertheless let the part which forms opinions about these things be quiet, that is, let it judge that nothing is either bad or good which can happen equally to the bad man and the good. For that which happens equally to him who lives contrary to nature and to him who lives according to nature, is neither according to nature nor contrary to nature.

40. Constantly regard the universe as one living being, having one substance and one soul; and observe how all things have reference to one perception, the perception of this one living being; and how all things act with one movement; and how all things are the co-operating causes of all things which exist; observe too the continuous spinning of the thread and the contexture of the web.

41. Thou art a little soul bearing about a corpse, as Epictetus used to say (I. c. 19).

42. It is no evil for things to undergo change, and no good for things to subsist in consequence of change.

43. Time is like a river made up of the events which happen, and a violent stream; for as soon as a thing has been seen, it is carried away, and another comes in its place, and this will be carried away too.

44. Everything which happens is as familiar and well known as the rose in spring and the fruit in summer; for such is disease, and death, and calumny, and treachery, and whatever else delights fools or vexes them.

45. In the series of things those which follow are always aptly fitted to those which have gone before; for this series is not like a mere enumeration of disjointed things, which has only a necessary sequence, but it is a rational connection: and as all existing things are arranged together harmoniously, so the things which come into

existence exhibit no mere succession, but a certain wonderful relationship (vi. 38; vii. 9; vii. 75, note).

46. Always remember the saying of Heraclitus, that the death of earth is to become water, and the death of water is to become air, and the death of air is to become fire, and reversely. And think too of him who forgets whither the way leads, and that men quarrel with that with which they are most constantly in communion, the reason which governs the universe; and the things which they daily meet with seem to them strange: and consider that we ought not to act and speak as if we were asleep, for even in sleep we seem to act and speak; and that we ought not, like children who learn from their parents, simply to act and speak as we have been taught.

47. If any god told thee that thou shalt die to-morrow, or certainly on the day after to-morrow, thou wouldst not care much whether it was on the third day or on the morrow, unless thou wast in the highest degree mean-spirited—for how small is the difference?—so think it no great thing to die after as many years as thou canst name rather than to-morrow.

48. Think continually how many physicians are dead after often contracting their eyebrows over the sick; and how many astrologers after predicting with great pretensions the deaths of others; and how many philosophers after endless discourses on death or immortality; how many heroes after killing thousands; and how many tyrants who have used their power over men's lives with terrible insolence as if they were immortal; and how many cities are entirely dead, so to speak, Helice and Pompeii and Herculaneum, and others innumerable. Add to the reckoning all whom thou hast known, one after another. One man after burying another has been laid out dead, and another buries him; and all this in a short time. To conclude, always observe how ephemeral and worthless human things are, and what was yesterday a little mucus, to-morrow will be a mummy or ashes. Pass then through this little space of time conformably to nature, and end thy journey in content, just as an olive falls off when it is ripe, blessing nature who produced it, and thanking the tree on which it grew.

49. Be like the promontory against which the waves continually break, but it stands firm and tames the fury of the water around it.

Unhappy am I, because this has happened to me.—Not so, but Happy am I, though this has happened to me, because I continue free from pain, neither crushed by the present nor fearing the future. For such a thing as this might have happened to every man; but every man would not have continued free from pain on such an occasion. Why, then, is that rather a misfortune than this a good fortune? And dost thou in all cases call that a man's misfortune, which is not a deviation from man's nature? And does a thing seem to thee to be a deviation from man's nature, when it is not contrary to the will of man's nature? Well, thou knowest the will of nature. Will then this which has happened prevent thee from being just, magnanimous, temperate, prudent, secure against inconsiderate opinions and falsehood; will it prevent thee from having modesty, freedom, and everything else, by the presence of which man's nature obtains all that is its own? Remember, too, on every occasion which leads thee to vexation to apply this principle: not that this is a misfortune, but that to bear it nobly is good fortune.

50. It is a vulgar but still a useful help towards contempt of death, to pass in review those who have tenaciously stuck to life. What more then have they gained than those who have died early? Certainly they lie in their tombs somewhere at last, Cadicianus, Fabius, Julianus, Lepidus, or any one else like them, who have carried out many to be buried, and then were carried out themselves. Altogether the interval is small [between birth and death]; and consider with how much trouble, and in company with what sort of people, and in what a feeble body this interval is laboriously passed. Do not then consider life a thing of any value. For look to the immensity of time behind thee, and to the time which is before thee, another boundless space. In this infinity then what is the difference between him who lives three days and him who lives three generations?

51. Always run to the short way; and the short way is the natural: accordingly say and do everything in conformity with the soundest reason. For such a purpose frees a man from trouble, and warfare, and all artifice and ostentatious display.

V

IN THE morning when thou risest unwillingly, let this thought be present—I am rising to the work of a human being. Why then am I dissatisfied if I am going to do the things for which I exist and for which I was brought into the world? Or have I been made for this, to lie in the bedclothes and keep myself warm?—But this is more pleasant.—Dost thou exist then to take thy pleasure, and not at all for action or exertion? Dost thou not see the little plants, the little birds, the ants, the spiders, the bees working together to put in order their several parts of the universe? And art thou unwilling to do the work of a human being, and dost thou not make haste to do that which is according to thy nature?—But it is necessary to take rest also.—It is necessary: however nature has fixed bounds to this too: she has fixed bounds both to eating and drinking, and yet thou goest beyond these bounds, beyond what is sufficient; yet in thy acts it is not so, but thou stoppest short of what thou canst do. So thou lovest not thyself, for if thou didst, thou wouldst love thy nature and her will. But those who love their several arts exhaust themselves in working at them unwashed and without food; but thou valuest thy own nature less than the turner values the turning art, or the dancer the dancing art, or the lover of money values his money, or the vainglorious man his little glory. And such men, when they have a violent affection to a thing, choose neither to eat nor to sleep rather than to perfect the things which they care for. But are the acts which concern society more vile in thy eyes and less worthy of thy labour?

2. How easy it is to repel and to wipe away every impression which is troublesome or unsuitable, and immediately to be in all tranquillity.

3. Judge every word and deed which are according to nature to be fit for thee; and be not diverted by the blame which follows from any people, nor by their words, but if a thing is good to be done or said, do not consider it unworthy of thee. For those persons have their peculiar leading principle and follow their peculiar movement; which things do not thou regard, but go straight on, following thy own nature and the common nature; and the way of both is one.

4. I go through the things which happen according to nature until I shall fall and rest, breathing out my breath into that element out of which I daily draw it in, and falling upon that earth out of which my father collected the seed, and my mother the blood, and my nurse the milk; out of which during so many years I have been supplied with food and drink; which bears me when I tread on it and abuse it for so many purposes.

5. Thou sayest, men cannot admire the sharpness of thy wits.—Be it so; but there are many other things of which thou canst not say, I am not formed for them by nature. Show those qualities then which are altogether in thy power: sincerity, gravity, endurance of labour, aversion to pleasure, contentment with thy portion and with few things, benevolence, frankness, no love of superfluity, freedom from trifling magnanimity. Dost thou not see how many qualities thou art immediately able to exhibit, in which there is no excuse of natural incapacity and unfitness, and yet thou still remainest voluntarily below the mark? or art thou compelled through being defectively furnished by nature to murmur, and to be stingy, and to flatter, and to find fault with thy poor body, and to try to please men, and to make great display, and to be restless in thy mind? No, by the gods: but thou mightest have been delivered from these things long ago. Only if in truth thou canst be charged with being rather slow and dull of comprehension, thou must exert thyself about this also, not neglecting it nor yet taking pleasure in thy dullness.

6. One man, when he has done a service to another, is ready to set it down to his account as a favour conferred. Another is not ready to do this, but still in his own mind he thinks of the man as his debtor, and he knows what he has done. A third in a manner does not even know what he has done, but he is like a vine which has produced grapes, and seeks for nothing more after it has once produced its proper fruit. As a horse when he has run, a dog when he has tracked the game, a bee when it has made the honey, so a man when he has done a good act, does not call out for others to come and see, but he goes on to another act, as a vine goes on to produce again the grapes in season.—Must a man then be one of these, who in a manner act thus without observing it?—Yes.—But this very thing is necessary, the observation of what a man is doing; for it may be

said, it is characteristic of the social animal to perceive that he is working in a social manner, and indeed to wish that his social partner also should perceive it.—It is true what thou sayest, but thou dost not rightly understand what is now said; and for this reason thou wilt become one of those of whom I spoke before, for even they are misled by a certain show of reason. But if thou wilt choose to understand the meaning of what is said, do not fear that for this reason thou wilt omit any social act.

7. A prayer of the Athenians: Rain, rain, O dear Zeus, down on the plowed fields of the Athenians and on the plains.—In truth we ought not to pray at all, or we ought to pray in this simple and noble fashion.

8. Just as we must understand when it is said, That Æsculapius prescribed to this man horse-exercise, or bathing in cold water, or going without shoes, so we must understand it when it is said, That the nature of the universe prescribed to this man disease or mutilation or loss or anything else of the kind. For in the first case prescribed means something like this: he prescribed this for this man as a thing adapted to procure health; and in the second case it means, That which happens to [or suits] every man is fixed in a manner for him suitably to his destiny. For this is what we mean when we say that things are suitable to us, as the workmen say of squared stones in walls or the pyramids, that they are suitable, when they fit them to one another in some kind of connection. For there is altogether one fitness [harmony]. And as the universe is made up out of all bodies to be such a body as it is, so out of all existing causes necessity [destiny] is made up to be such a cause as it is. And even those who are completely ignorant understand what I mean, for they say, It [necessity, destiny] brought this to such a person.—This then was brought and this was prescribed to him. Let us then receive these things, as well as those which Æsculapius prescribes. Many, as a matter of course, even among his prescriptions, are disagreeable, but we accept them in the hope of health. Let the perfecting and accomplishment of the things, which the common nature judges to be good, be judged by thee to be of the same kind as thy health. And so accept everything which happens,

even if it seem disagreeable, because it leads to this, to the health of the universe and to the prosperity and felicity of Zeus [the universe]. For he would not have brought on any man what he has brought, if it were not useful for the whole. Neither does the nature of anything, whatever it may be, cause anything which is not suitable to that which is directed by it. For two reasons, then, it is right to be content with that which happens to thee; the one, because it was done for thee and prescribed for thee, and in a manner had reference to thee, originally from the most ancient causes spun with thy destiny; and the other, because even that which comes severally to every man is to the power which administers the universe a cause of felicity and perfection, nay even of its very continuance. For the integrity of the whole is mutilated, if thou cuttest off anything whatever from the conjunction and the continuity either of the parts or of the causes. And thou dost cut off, as far as it is in thy power, when thou art dissatisfied, and in a manner triest to put anything out of the way.

9. Be not disgusted, nor discouraged, nor dissatisfied, if thou dost not succeed in doing everything according to right principles; but when thou hast failed, return back again, and be content if the greater part of what thou doest is consistent with man's nature, and love this to which thou returnest; and do not return to philosophy as if she were a master, but act like those who have sore eyes and apply a bit of sponge and egg, or as another applies a plaster, or drenching with water. For thus thou wilt not fail to obey reason and thou wilt repose in it. And remember that philosophy requires only the things which thy nature requires; but thou wouldst have something else which is not according to nature. It may be objected, Why, what is more agreeable than this [which I am doing]? But is not this the very reason why pleasure deceives us? And consider if magnanimity, freedom, simplicity, equanimity, piety are not more agreeable. For what is more agreeable than wisdom itself, when thou thinkest of the security and the happy course of all things which depend on the faculty of understanding and knowledge?

10. Things are in such a kind of envelopment that they have seemed to philosophers, not a few nor those common philosophers,

altogether unintelligible; nay even to the Stoics themselves they seem difficult to understand. And all our assent is changeable; for where is the man who never changes? Carry thy thoughts then to the objects themselves, and consider how short-lived they are and worthless, and that they may be in the possession of a filthy wretch or a whore or a robber. Then turn to the morals of those who live with thee, and it is hardly possible to endure even the most agreeable of them, to say nothing of a man being hardly able to endure himself. In such darkness, then, and dirt, and in so constant a flux, both of substance and of time, and of motion, and of things moved, what there is worth being highly prized, or even an object of serious pursuit, I cannot imagine. But on the contrary it is a man's duty to comfort himself, and to wait for the natural dissolution and not to be vexed at the delay, but to rest in these principles only: the one, that nothing will happen to me which is not conformable to the nature of the universe; and the other, that it is in my power never to act contrary to my god and dæmon: for there is no man who will compel me to this.

11. About what am I now employing my own soul? On every occasion I must ask myself this question, and inquire, what have I now in this part of me which they call the ruling principle? and whose soul have I now? that of a child, or of a young man, or of a feeble woman, or of a tyrant, or of a domestic animal, or of a wild beast?

12. What kind of things those are which appear good to the many, we may learn even from this. For if any man should conceive certain things as being really good, such as prudence, temperance, justice, fortitude, he would not after having first conceived these endure to listen to anything which should not be in harmony with what is really good. But if a man has first conceived as good the things which appear to the many to be good, he will listen and readily receive as very applicable that which was said by the comic writer. Thus even the many perceive the difference. For were it not so, this saying would not offend and would not be rejected [in the first case], while we receive it when it is said of wealth, and of the means which further luxury and fame, as said fitly and wittily. Go on then and ask if we should value and think those things to be good, to which

after their first conception in the mind the words of the comic writer might be aptly applied—that he who has them, through pure abundance has not a place to ease himself in.

13. I am composed of the formal and the material; and neither of them will perish into non-existence, as neither of them came into existence out of non-existence. Every part of me then will be reduced by change into some part of the universe, and that again will change into another part of the universe, and so on forever. And by consequence of such a change I too exist, and those who begot me, and so on forever in the other direction. For nothing hinders us from saying so, even if the universe is administered according to definite periods [of revolution].

14. Reason and the reasoning art [philosophy] are powers which are sufficient for themselves and for their own works. They move then from a first principle which is their own, and they make their way to the end which is proposed to them; and this is the reason why such acts are named Catorthóseis or right acts, which word signifies that they proceed by the right road.

15. None of these things ought to be called a man's which do not belong to a man, as man. They are not required of a man, nor does man's nature promise them, nor are they the means of man's nature attaining its end. Neither then does the end of man lie in these things, nor yet that which aids to the accomplishment of this end, and that which aids toward this end is that which is good. Besides, if any of these things did belong to man, it would not be right for a man to despise them and to set himself against them; nor would a man be worthy of praise who showed that he did not want these things, nor would he who stinted himself in any of them be good, if indeed these things were good. But now the more of these things a man deprives himself of, or of other things like them, or even when he is deprived of any of them, the more patiently he endures the loss, just in the same degree he is a better man.

16. Such as are thy habitual thoughts, such also will be the character of thy mind; for the soul is dyed by the thoughts. Dye it then with a continuous series of such thoughts as these: for instance, that where a man can live, there he can also live well. But he must live in a palace—well then, he can also live well in a palace. And again,

consider that for whatever purpose each thing has been constituted, for this it has been constituted, and toward this it is carried; and its end is in that toward which it is carried; and where the end is, there also is the advantage and the good of each thing. Now the good for the reasonable animal is society; for that we are made for society has been shown above. Is it not plain that the inferior exist for the sake of the superior? but the things which have life are superior to those which have not life, and of those which have life the superior are those which have reason.

17. To seek what is impossible is madness: and it is impossible that the bad should not do something of this kind.

18. Nothing happens to any man which he is not formed by nature to bear. The same things happen to another, and either because he does not see that they have happened or because he would show a great spirit he is firm and remains unharmed. It is a shame then that ignorance and conceit should be stronger than wisdom.

19. Things themselves touch not the soul, not in the least degree; nor have they admission to the soul, nor can they turn or move the soul: but the soul turns and moves itself alone, and whatever judgments it may think proper to make, such it makes for itself the things which present themselves to it.

20. In one respect man is the nearest thing to me, so far as I must do good to men and endure them. But so far as some men make themselves obstacles to my proper acts, man becomes to me one of the things which are indifferent, no less than the sun or wind or a wild beast. Now it is true that these may impede my action, but they are no impediments to my affects and disposition, which have the power of acting conditionally and changing: for the mind converts and changes every hindrance to its activity into an aid; and so that which is a hindrance is made a furtherance to an act; and that which is an obstacle on the road helps us on this road.

21. Reverence that which is best in the universe; and this is that which makes use of all things and directs all things. And in like manner also reverence that which is best in thyself; and this is of the same kind as that. For in thyself also, that which makes use of everything else, is this, and thy life is directed by this.

22. That which does no harm to the state, does no harm to the

citizen. In the case of every appearance of harm apply this rule: if the state is not harmed by this, neither am I harmed. But if the state is harmed, thou must not be angry with him who does harm to the state. Show him where his error is.

23. Often think of the rapidity with which things pass by and disappear, both the things which are and the things which are produced. For substance is like a river in a continual flow, and the activities of things are in constant change, and the causes work in infinite varieties; and there is hardly anything which stands still. And consider this which is near to thee, this boundless abyss of the past and of the future in which all things disappear. How then is he not a fool who is puffed up with such things or plagued about them or makes himself miserable? for they vex him only for a time, and a short time.

24. Think of the universal substance, of which thou hast a very small portion; and of universal time, of which a short and indivisible interval has been assigned to thee; and of that which is fixed by destiny, and how small a part of it thou art.

25. Does another do me wrong? Let him look to it. He has his own disposition, his own activity. I now have what the universal nature wills me to have; and I do what my nature now wills me to do.

26. Let the part of thy soul which leads and governs be undisturbed by the movements in the flesh, whether of pleasure or of pain; and let it not unite with them, but let it circumscribe itself and limit those affects to their parts. But when these affects rise up to the mind by virtue of that other sympathy that naturally exists in a body which is all one, then thou must not strive to resist the sensation, for it is natural: but let not the ruling part of itself add to the sensation the opinion that it is either good or bad.

27. Live with the gods. And he does live with the gods who constantly shows to them that his own soul is satisfied with that which is assigned to him, and that it does all that the dæmon wishes, which Zeus hath given to every man for his guardian and guide, a portion of himself. And this is every man's understanding and reason.

28. Art thou angry with him whose arm-pits stink? art thou angry with him whose mouth smells foul? What good will this

anger do thee? He has such a mouth, he has such arm-pits: it is necessary that such an emanation must come from such things—but the man has reason, it will be said, and he is able, if he takes pains, to discover wherein he offends—I wish thee well of thy discovery. Well then, and thou hast reason: by thy rational faculty stir up his rational faculty; show him his error, admonish him. For if he listens, thou wilt cure him, and there is no need of anger. [Neither tragic actor nor whore.[1]]

29. As thou intendest to live when thou are gone out, . . . so it is in thy power to live here. But if men do not permit thee, then get away out of life, yet so as if thou wert suffering no harm. The house is smoky, and I quit it. Why dost thou think that this is any trouble? But so long as nothing of the kind drives me out, I remain, am free, and no man shall hinder me from doing what I choose; and I choose to do what is according to the nature of the rational and social animal.

30. The intelligence of the universe is social. Accordingly it has made the inferior things for the sake of the superior, and it has fitted the superior to one another. Thou seest how it has subordinated, co-ordinated and assigned to everything its proper portion, and has brought together into concord with one another the things which are the best.

31. How hast thou behaved hitherto to the gods, thy parents, brethren, children, teachers, to those who looked after thy infancy, to thy friends, kinsfolk, to thy slaves? Consider if thou hast hitherto behaved to all in such a way that this may be said of thee:

Never has wronged a man in deed or word.

And call to recollection both how many things thou hast passed through, and how many things thou hast been able to endure: and that the history of thy life is now complete, and thy service is ended: and how many beautiful things thou hast seen: and how many pleasures and pains thou hast despised; and how many things called honourable thou hast spurned; and to how many ill-minded folks thou hast shown a kind disposition.

32. Why do unskilled and ignorant souls disturb him who has skill and knowledge? What soul then has skill and knowledge?

[1]This sentence is imperfect or corrupt, or both.

That which knows beginning and end, and knows the reason which pervades all substance and through all time by fixed periods [revolutions] administers the universe.

33. Soon, very soon, thou wilt be ashes, or a skeleton, and either a name or not even a name; but name is sound and echo, and the things which are much valued in life are empty and rotten and trifling, and [like] little dogs biting one another, and little children quarrelling, laughing, and then straightway weeping. But fidelity and modesty and justice and truth are fled

> Up to Olympus from the wide-spread earth.
> *Hesiod, Works, etc.*, v. 197.

What then is there which still detains thee here? if the objects of sense are easily changed and never stand still, and the organs of perception are dull and easily receive false impressions; and the poor soul itself is an exhalation from blood. But to have good repute amid such a world as this is an empty thing. Why then dost thou not wait in tranquillity for thy end, whether it is extinction or removal to another state? And until that time comes, what is sufficient? Why, what else than to venerate the gods and bless them, and to do good to men, and to practise tolerance and self-restraint; but as to everything which is beyond the limits of the poor flesh and breath, to remember that this is neither thine nor in thy power.

34. Thou canst pass thy life in an equable flow of happiness, if thou canst go by the right way, and think and act in the right way. These two things are common both to the soul of God and to the soul of man, and to the soul of every rational being, not to be hindered by another; and to hold good to consist in the disposition to justice and the practice of it, and in this to let thy desire find its termination.

35. If this is neither my own badness, nor an effect of my own badness, and the common weal is not injured, why am I troubled about it? and what is the harm to the common weal?

36. Do not be carried along inconsiderately by the appearance of things, but give help [to all] according to thy ability and their fitness; and if they should have sustained loss in matters which are indifferent, do not imagine this to be a damage. For it is a bad

habit. But as the old man, when he went away, asked back his foster-child's top, remembering that it was a top, so do thou in this case also.

When thou art calling out on the Rostra, hast thou forgotten, man, what these things are? Yes; but they are objects of great concern to these people—wilt thou too then be made a fool for these things? I was once a fortunate man, but I lost it, I know not how. But fortunate means that a man has assigned to himself a good fortune; and a good fortune is good disposition of the soul, good emotions, good actions.

VI

THE substance of the universe is obedient and compliant; and the reason which governs it has in itself no cause for doing evil, for it has no malice, nor does it do evil to anything, nor is anything harmed by it. But all things are made and perfected according to this reason.

2. Let it make no difference to thee whether thou art cold or warm, if thou art doing thy duty; and whether thou art drowsy or satisfied with sleep; and whether ill-spoken of or praised; and whether dying or doing something else. For it is one of the acts of this life, this act by which we die; it is sufficient then in this act also to do well what we have in hand (vi. 22, 28).

3. Look within. Let neither the peculiar quality of anything nor its value escape thee.

4. All existing things soon change, and they will either be reduced to vapour, if indeed all substance is one, or they will be dispersed.

5. The reason which governs knows what its own disposition is, and what it does, and on what material it works.

6. The best way of avenging thyself is not to become like [the wrong-doer].

7. Take pleasure in one thing and rest in it, in passing from one social act to another social act, thinking of God.

8. The ruling principle is that which rouses and turns itself, and while it makes itself such as it is and such as it wills to be, it also makes everything which happens appear to itself to be such as it wills.

9. In conformity to the nature of the universe every single thing is accomplished, for certainly it is not in conformity to any other nature that each thing is accomplished, either a nature which externally comprehends this, or a nature which is comprehended within this nature, or a nature external and independent of this (xi. 1; vi. 40; viii. 50).

10. The universe is either a confusion, and a mutual involution of things, and a dispersion; or it is unity and order and providence. If then it is the former, why do I desire to tarry in a fortuitous combination of things and such a disorder? and why do I care about anything else than how I shall at last become earth? and why am I disturbed, for the dispersion of my elements will happen whatever I do. But if the other supposition is true, I venerate, and I am firm, and I trust in him who governs (iv. 27).

11. When thou hast been compelled by circumstances to be disturbed in a manner, quickly return to thyself and do not continue out of tune longer than the compulsion lasts; for thou wilt have more mastery over the harmony by continually recurring to it.

12. If thou hadst a step-mother and a mother at the same time, thou wouldst be dutiful to thy step-mother, but still thou wouldst constantly return to thy mother. Let the court and philosophy now be to thee step-mother and mother; return to philosophy frequently and repose in her, through whom what thou meetest with in the court appears to thee tolerable, and thou appearest tolerable in the court.

13. When we have meat before us and such eatables, we receive the impression, that this is the dead body of a fish, and this is the dead body of a bird or of a pig; and again, that this Falernian is only a little grape juice, and this purple robe some sheep's wool dyed with the blood of a shell-fish: such then are these impressions, and they reach the things themselves and penetrate them, and so we see what kind of things they are. Just in the same way ought we to act all through life, and where there are things which appear most worthy of our approbation, we ought to lay them bare and look at their worthlessness, and strip them of all the words by which they are exalted. For outward show is a wonderful perverter of the reason, and when thou art most sure that thou art employed about things

worth thy pains, it is then that it cheats thee most. Consider then what Crates says of Xenocrates himself.

14. Most of the things which the multitude admire are referred to objects of the most general kind, those which are held together by cohesion or natural organization, such as stones, wood, fig-trees, vines, olives. But those which are admired by men who are a little more reasonable are referred to the things which are held together by a living principle, as flocks, herds. Those which are admired by men who are still more instructed are the things which are held together by a rational soul, not however a universal soul, but rational so far as it is a soul skilled in some art, or expert in some other way, or simply rational so far as it possesses a number of slaves. But he who values a rational soul, a soul universal and fitted for political life, regards nothing else except this; and above all things he keeps his soul in a condition and in an activity conformable to reason and social life, and he co-operates to this end with those who are of the same kind as himself.

15. Some things are hurrying into existence, and others are hurrying out of it; and of that which is coming into existence part is already extinguished. Motions and changes are continually renewing the world, just as the uninterrupted course of time is always renewing the infinite duration of ages. In this flowing stream then, on which there is no abiding, what is there of the things which hurry by on which a man would set a high price? It would be just as if a man should fall in love with one of the sparrows which fly by, but it has already passed out of sight. Something of this kind is the very life of every man, like the exhalation of the blood and the respiration of the air. For such as it is to have once drawn in the air and to have given it back, which we do every moment, just the same is it with the whole respiratory power, which thou didst receive at thy birth yesterday and the day before, to give it back to the element from which thou didst first draw it.

16. Neither is transpiration, as in plants, a thing to be valued, nor respiration, as in domesticated animals and wild beasts, nor the receiving of impressions by the appearances of things, nor being moved by desires as puppets by strings, nor assembling in herds,

nor being nourished by food; for this is just like the act of separating and parting with the useless part of our food. What then is worth being valued? To be received with clapping of hands? No. Neither must we value the clapping of tongues, for the praise which comes from the many is a clapping of tongues. Suppose then that thou hast given up this worthless thing called fame, what remains that is worth valuing? This, in my opinion, to move thyself and to restrain thyself in conformity to thy proper constitution, to which end both all employments and arts lead. For every art aims at this, that the thing which has been made should be adapted to the work for which it has been made; and both the vine-planter who looks after the vine, and the horse-breaker, and he who trains the dog, seek this end. But the education and the teaching of youth aim at something. In this then is the value of the education and the teaching. And if this is well, thou wilt not seek anything else. Wilt thou not cease to value many other things too? Then thou wilt be neither free, nor sufficient for thy own happiness, nor without passion. For of necessity thou must be envious, jealous, and suspicious of those who can take away those things, and plot against those who have that which is valued by thee. Of necessity a man must be altogether in a state of perturbation who wants any of these things; and besides, he must often find fault with the gods. But to reverence and honour thy own mind will make thee content with thyself, and in harmony with society, and in agreement with the gods, that is, praising all that they give and have ordered.

17. Above, below, all around are the movements of the elements. But the motion of virtue is in none of these: it is something more divine, and advancing by a way hardly observed it goes happily on its road.

18. How strangely men act. They will not praise those who are living at the same time and living with themselves; but to be themselves praised by posterity, by those whom they have never seen or ever will see, this they set much value on. But this is very much the same as if thou shouldst be grieved because those who have lived before thee did not praise thee.

19. If a thing is difficult to be accomplished by thyself, do not

think that it is impossible for man; but if anything is possible for man and conformable to his nature, think that this can be attained by thyself too.

20. In the gymnastic exercises suppose that a man has torn thee with his nails, and by dashing against thy head has inflicted a wound. Well, we neither show any signs of vexation, nor are we offended, nor do we suspect him afterward as a treacherous fellow; and yet we are on our guard against him, not however as an enemy, nor yet with suspicion, but we quietly get out of his way. Something like this let thy behaviour be in all the other parts of life; let us overlook many things in those who are like antagonists in the gymnasium. For it is in our power, as I said, to get out of the way, and to have no suspicion nor hatred.

21. If any man is able to convince me and show me that I do not think or act right, I will gladly change; for I seek the truth by which no man was ever injured. But he is injured who abides in his error and ignorance.

22. I do my duty: other things trouble me not; for they are either things without life, or things without reason, or things that have rambled and know not the way.

23. As to the animals which have no reason, and generally all things and objects, do thou, since thou hast reason and they have none, make use of them with a generous and liberal spirit. But toward human beings, as they have reason, behave in a social spirit. And on all occasions call on the gods, and do not perplex thyself about the length of time in which thou shalt do this; for even three hours so spent are sufficient.

24. Alexander the Macedonian and his groom by death were brought to the same state; for either they were received among the same seminal principles of the universe, or they were alike dispersed among the atoms.

25. Consider how many things in the same indivisible time take place in each of us, things which concern the body and things which concern the soul; and so thou wilt not wonder if many more things, or rather all things which come into existence in that which is the one and all, which we call Cosmos, exist in it at the same time.

26. If any man should propose to thee the question, how the

name Antoninus is written, wouldst thou with a straining of the voice utter each letter? What then if they grow angry, wilt thou be angry too? Wilt thou not go on with composure and number every letter? Just so then in this life also remember that every duty is made up of certain parts. These it is thy duty to observe and without being disturbed or showing anger toward those who are angry with thee to go on thy way and finish that which is set before thee.

27. How cruel it is not to allow men to strive after the things which appear to them to be suitable to their nature and profitable! And yet in a manner thou dost not allow them to do this, when thou art vexed because they do wrong. For they are certainly moved toward things because they suppose them to be suitable to their nature and profitable to them. But it is not so. Teach them then, and show them without being angry.

28. Death is a cessation of the impressions through the senses, and of the pulling of the strings which move the appetites, and of the discursive movements of the thoughts, and of the service to the flesh (ii. 12).

29. It is a shame for the soul to be first to give way in this life, when thy body does not give way.

30. Take care that thou art not made into a Cæsar, that thou art not dyed with this dye; for such things happen. Keep thyself then simple, good, pure, serious, free from affectation, a friend of justice, a worshiper of the gods, kind, affectionate, strenuous in all proper acts. Strive to continue to be such as philosophy wished to make thee. Reverence the gods, and help men. Short is life. There is only one fruit of this terrene life, a pious disposition and social acts. Do everything as a disciple of Antoninus. Remember his constancy in every act which was conformable to reason, and his evenness in all things, and his piety, and the serenity of his countenance, and his sweetness, and his disregard of empty fame, and his efforts to understand things; and how he would never let anything pass without having first most carefully examined it and clearly understood it; and how he bore with those who blamed him unjustly without blaming them in return; how he did nothing in a hurry; and how he listened not to calumnies, and how exact an examiner of manners and actions he was; and not given to reproach people, nor timid, nor suspicious,

nor a sophist; and with how little he was satisfied, such as lodging, bed, dress, food, servants; and how laborious and patient; and how he was able on account of his sparing diet to hold out to the evening, not even requiring to relieve himself by any evacuations except at the usual hour; and his firmness and uniformity in his friendships; and how he tolerated freedom of speech in those who opposed his opinions; and the pleasure that he had when any man showed him anything better; and how religious he was without superstition. Imitate all this that thou mayest have as good a conscience, when thy last hour comes, as he had (i. 16).

31. Return to thy sober senses and call thyself back; and when thou hast roused thyself from sleep and hast perceived that they were only dreams which troubled thee, now in thy waking hours look at these [the things about thee] as thou didst look at those [the dreams].

32. I consist of a little body and a soul. Now to this little body all things are indifferent, for it is not able to perceive differences. But to the understanding those things only are indifferent, which are not the works of its own activity. But whatever things are the works of its own activity, all these are in its power. And of these however only those which are done with reference to the present; for as to the future and the past activities of the mind, even these are for the present indifferent.

33. Neither the labour which the hand does nor that of the foot is contrary to nature, so long as the foot does the foot's work and the hand the hand's. So then neither to a man as a man is his labour contrary to nature, so long as it does the things of a man. But if the labour is not contrary to his nature, neither is it an evil to him.

34. How many pleasures have been enjoyed by robbers, patricides, tyrants.

35. Dost thou not see how the handicraftsmen accommodate themselves up to a certain point to those who are not skilled in their craft—nevertheless they cling to the reason [the principles] of their art and do not endure to depart from it? Is it not strange if the architect and the physician shall have more respect to the reason [the principles] of their own arts than man to his own reason, which is common to him and the gods?

36. Asia, Europe are corners of the universe; all the sea a drop in the universe; Athos a little clod of the universe; all the present time is a point in eternity. All things are little, changeable, perishable. All things come from thence, from that universal ruling power either directly proceeding or by way of sequence. And accordingly the lion's gaping jaws, and that which is poisonous, and every harmful thing, as a thorn, as mud, are after-products of the grand and beautiful. Do not then imagine that they are of another kind from that which thou dost venerate, but form a just opinion of the source of all (vii. 75).

37. He who has seen present things has seen all, both everything which has taken place from all eternity and everything which will be for time without end; for all things are of one kin and of one form.

38. Frequently consider the connection of all things in the universe and their relation to one another. For in a manner all things are implicated with one another, and all in this way are friendly to one another; for one thing comes in order after another, and this is by virtue of the active movement and mutual conspiration and the unity of the substance (ix. 1).

39. Adapt thyself to the things with which thy lot has been cast; and the men among whom thou hast received thy portion, love them, but do it truly [sincerely].

40. Every instrument, tool, vessel, if it does that for which it has been made, is well, and yet he who made it is not there. But in the things which are held together by nature there is within and there abides in them the power which made them; wherefore the more is it fit to reverence this power, and to think that, if thou dost live and act according to its will, everything in thee is in conformity to intelligence. And thus also in the universe the things which belong to it are in conformity to intelligence.

41. Whatever of the things which are not within thy power thou shalt suppose to be good for thee or evil, it must of necessity be that, if such a bad thing befall thee or the loss of such a good thing, thou wilt blame the gods, and hate men too, those who are the cause of the misfortune or the loss, or those who are suspected of being likely to be the cause; and indeed we do much injustice, because we make a difference between these things [because we do not regard these

things as indifferent]. But if we judge only those things which are in our power to be good or bad, there remains no reason either for finding fault with God or standing in a hostile attitude to man.

42. We are all working together to one end, some with knowledge and design, and others without knowing what they do; as men also when they are asleep, of whom it is Heraclitus, I think, who says that they are labourers and co-operators in the things which take place in the universe. But men co-operate after different fashions: and even those co-operate abundantly, who find fault with what happens and those who try to oppose it and to hinder it; for the universe had need even of such men as these. It remains then for thee to understand among what kind of workmen thou placest thyself; for he who rules all things will certainly make a right use of thee, and he will receive thee among some part of the co-operators and of those whose labours conduce to one end. But be not thou such a part as the mean and ridiculous verse in the play, which Chrysippus speaks of.

43. Does the sun undertake to do the work of the rain, or Æsculapius the work of the Fruit-bearer [the earth]? And how is it with respect to each of the stars, are they not different, and yet they work together to the same end?

44. If the gods have determined about me and about the things which must happen to me, they have determined well, for it is not easy even to imagine a deity without forethought; and as to doing me harm, why should they have any desire towards that? for what advantage would result to them from this or to the whole, which is the special object of their providence? But if they have not determined about me individually, they have certainly determined about the whole at least, and the things which happen by way of sequence in this general arrangement I ought to accept with pleasure and to be content with them. But if they determine about nothing—which it is wicked to believe, or if we do believe it, let us neither sacrifice nor pray nor swear by them, nor do anything else which we do as if the gods were present and lived with us—but if however the gods determine about none of the things which concern us, I am able to determine about myself, and I can inquire about that which is useful; and that is useful to every man which is conformable to his own

constitution and nature. But my nature is rational and social; and my city and country, so far as I am Antoninus, is Rome, but so far as I am a man, it is the world. The things then which are useful to these cities are alone useful to me.

45. Whatever happens to every man, this is for the interest of the universal: this might be sufficient. But further thou wilt observe this also as a general truth, if thou dost observe, that whatever is profitable to any man is profitable also to other men. But let the word profitable be taken here in the common sense as said of things of the middle kind [neither good nor bad].

46. As it happens to thee in the amphitheatre and such places, that the continual sight of the same things and the uniformity make the spectacle wearisome, so it is in the whole of life; for all things above, below, are the same and from the same. How long then?

47. Think continually that all kinds of men and of all kinds of pursuits and of all nations are dead, so that thy thoughts come down even to Philistion and Phœbus and Origanion. Now turn thy thoughts to the other kinds [of men]. To that place then we must remove, where there are so many great orators, and so many noble philosophers, Heraclitus, Pythagoras, Socrates; so many heroes of former days, and so many generals after them, and tyrants; besides these, Eudoxus, Hipparchus, Archimedes, and other men of acute natural talents, great minds, lovers of labour, versatile, confident, mockers even of the perishable and ephemeral life of man, as Menippus and such as are like him. As to all these consider that they have long been in the dust. What harm then is this to them; and what to those whose names are altogether unknown? One thing here is worth a great deal, to pass thy life in truth and justice, with a benevolent disposition even to liars and unjust men.

48. When thou wishest to delight thyself, think of the virtues of those who live with thee; for instance, the activity of one, and the modesty of another, and the liberality of a third, and some other good quality of a fourth. For nothing delights so much as the examples of the virtues, when they are exhibited in the morals of those who live with us and present themselves in abundance, as far as is possible. Wherefore we must keep them before us.

49. Thou art not dissatisfied, I suppose, because thou weighest

only so many litræ and not three hundred. Be not dissatisfied then that thou must live only so many years and not more; for as thou art satisfied with the amount of substance which has been assigned to thee, so be content with the time.

50. Let us try to persuade them [men]. But act even against their will, when the principles of justice lead that way. If, however, any man by using force stands in thy way, betake thyself to contentment and tranquillity, and at the same time employ the hindrance toward the exercise of some other virtue; and remember that thy attempt was with a reservation [conditionally], that thou didst not desire to do impossibilities. What then didst thou desire? Some such effort as this. But thou attainest thy object, if the things to which thou wast moved are [not] accomplished.

51. He who loves fame considers another man's activity to be his own good; and he who loves pleasure, his own sensations; but he who has understanding, considers his own acts to be his own good.

52. It is in our power to have no opinion about a thing, and not to be disturbed in our soul, for things themselves have no natural power to form our judgments.

53. Accustom thyself to attend carefully to what is said by another, and as much as it is possible, be in the speaker's mind.

54. That which is not good for the swarm, neither is it good for the bee.

55. If sailors abused the helmsman or the sick the doctor, would they listen to anybody else; or how could the helmsman secure the safety of those in the ship or the doctor the health of those whom he attends?

56. How many together with whom I came into the world are already gone out of it.

57. To the jaundiced honey tastes bitter, and to those bitten by mad dogs water causes fear; and to little children the ball is a fine thing. Why then am I angry? Dost thou think that a false opinion has less power than the bile in the jaundiced or the poison in him who is bitten by a mad dog?

58. No man will hinder thee from living according to the reason of thy own nature: nothing will happen to thee contrary to the reason of the universal nature.

59. What kind of people are those whom men wish to please, and for what objects, and by what kind of acts? How soon will time cover all things, and how many it has covered already.

VII

WHAT is badness? It is that which thou hast often seen. And on the occasion of everything which happens keep this in mind, that it is that which thou hast often seen. Everywhere up and down thou wilt find the same things, with which the old histories are filled, those of the middle ages and those of our own day; with which cities and houses are filled now. There is nothing new; all things are both familiar and short-lived.

2. How can our principles become dead, unless the impressions [thoughts] which correspond to them are extinguished? But it is in thy power continuously to fan these thoughts into a flame. I can have that opinion about anything, which I ought to have. If I can, why am I disturbed? The things which are external to my mind have no relation at all to my mind. Let this be the state of thy affects, and thou standest erect. To recover thy life is in thy power. Look at things again as thou didst use to look at them; for in this consists the recovery of thy life.

3. The idle business of show, plays on the stage, flocks of sheep, herds, exercises with spears, a bone to cast to little dogs, a bit of bread into fish-ponds, labourings of ants and burden-carrying, runnings about of frightened little mice, puppets pulled by strings—[all alike]. It is thy duty then in the midst of such things to show good humour and not a proud air; to understand, however, that every man is worth just so much as the things are worth about which he busies himself.

4. In discourse thou must attend to what is said, and in every movement thou must observe what is doing. And in the one thou shouldst see immediately to what end it refers, but in the other watch carefully what is the thing signified.

5. Is my understanding sufficient for this or not? If it is sufficient I use it for the work as an instrument given by the universal nature. But if it is not sufficient, then either I retire from the work and give

way to him who is able to do it better, unless there be some reason why I ought not to do so; or I do it as well as I can, taking to help me the man who with the aid of my ruling principle can do what is now fit and useful for the general good. For whatsoever either by myself or with another I can do, ought to be directed to this only, to that which is useful and well suited to society.

6. How many after being celebrated by fame have been given up to oblivion; and how many who have celebrated the fame of others have long been dead.

7. Be not ashamed to be helped; for it is thy business to do thy duty like a soldier in the assault on a town. How then, if being lame thou canst not mount up on the battlements alone, but with the help of another it is possible?

8. Let not future things disturb thee, for thou wilt come to them, if it shall be necessary, having with thee the same reason which now thou usest for present things.

9. All things are implicated with one another, and the bond is holy; and there is hardly anything unconnected with any other thing. For things have been co-ordinated, and they combine to form the same universe [order]. For there is one universe made up of all things, and one god who pervades all things, and one substance, and one law, [one] common reason in all intelligent animals, and one truth; if indeed there is also one perfection for all animals which are of the same stock and participate in the same reason.

10. Everything material soon disappears in the substance of the whole; and everything formal [causal] is very soon taken back into the universal reason; and the memory of everything is very soon overwhelmed in time.

11. To the rational animal the same act is according to nature and according to reason.

12. Be thou erect, or be made erect (iii. 5).

13. Just as it is with the members in those bodies which are united in one, so it is with rational beings which exist separate, for they have been constituted for one co-operation. And the perception of this will be more apparent to thee, if thou often sayest to thyself that I am a member [μέλος] of the system of rational beings. But if [using the letter *r*] thou sayest that thou art a part [μέρος], thou

dost not yet love men from thy heart; beneficence does not yet delight thee for its own sake; thou still doest it barely as a thing of propriety, and not yet as doing good to thyself.

14. Let there fall externally what will on the parts which can feel the effects of this fall. For those parts which have felt will complain, if they choose. But I, unless I think that what has happened is an evil, am not injured. And it is in my power not to think so.

15. Whatever any one does or says, I must be good, just as if the gold, or the emerald, or the purple were always saying this: Whatever any one does or says, I must be emerald and keep my colour.

16. The ruling faculty does not disturb itself; I mean, does not frighten itself or cause itself pain. But if any one else can frighten or pain it, let him do so. For the faculty itself will not by its own opinion turn into such ways. Let the body itself take care, if it can, that it suffer nothing, and let it speak, if it suffers. But the soul itself, that which is subject to fear, to pain, which has completely the power of forming an opinion about these things, will suffer nothing, for it will never deviate into such a judgment. The leading principle in itself wants nothing, unless it makes a want for itself; and therefore it is both free from perturbation and unimpeded, if it does not disturb and impede itself.

17. Eudæmonia [happiness] is a good dæmon, or a good thing. What then art thou doing here, O imagination? go away, I entreat thee by the gods, as thou didst come, for I want thee not. But thou art come according to thy old fashion. I am not angry with thee: only go away.

18. Is any man afraid of change? Why, what can take place without change? What then is more pleasing or more suitable to the universal nature? And canst thou take a bath unless the wood undergoes a change? And canst thou be nourished unless the food undergoes a change? And can anything else that is useful be accomplished without change? Dost thou not see then that for thyself also to change is just the same, and equally necessary for the universal nature?

19. Through the universal substance as through a furious torrent all bodies are carried, being by their nature united with and cooperating with the whole, as the parts of our body with one another.

How many a Chrysippus, how many a Socrates, how many an Epictetus has time already swallowed up? And let the same thought occur to thee with reference to every man and thing (v. 23; vi. 15).

20. One thing only troubles me, lest I should do something which the constitution of man does not allow, or in the way which it does not allow, or what it does not allow now.

21. Near is thy forgetfulness of all things; and near the forgetfulness of thee by all.

22. It is peculiar to man to love even those who do wrong. And this happens, if when they do wrong it occurs to thee that they are kinsmen, and that they do wrong through ignorance and unintentionally, and that soon both of you will die; and above all, that the wrong-doer has done thee no harm, for he has not made thy ruling faculty worse than it was before.

23. The universal nature out of the universal substance, as if it were wax, now moulds a horse, and when it has broken this up, it uses the material for a tree, then for a man, then for something else; and each of these things subsists for a very short time. But it is no hardship for the vessel to be broken up, just as there was none in its being fastened together (viii. 50).

24. A scowling look is altogether unnatural; when it is often assumed, the result is that all comeliness dies away, and at last is so completely extinguished that it cannot be again lighted up at all. Try to conclude from this very fact that it is contrary to reason. For if even the perception of doing wrong shall depart, what reason is there for living any longer?

25. Nature which governs the whole will soon change all things which thou seest, and out of their substance will make other things, and again other things from the substance of them, in order that the world may be ever new (xii. 23).

26. When a man has done thee any wrong, immediately consider with what opinion about good or evil he has done wrong. For when thou hast seen this, thou wilt pity him, and wilt neither wonder nor be angry. For either thou thyself thinkest the same thing to be good that he does, or another thing of the same kind. It is thy duty then to pardon him. But if thou dost not think such things to be good or

evil, thou wilt more readily be well-disposed to him who is in error.

27. Think not so much of what thou hast not as of what thou hast: but of the things which thou hast select the best, and then reflect how eagerly they would have been sought, if thou hadst them not. At the same time, however, take care that thou dost not through being so pleased with them accustom thyself to overvalue them, so as to be disturbed if ever thou shouldst not have them.

28. Retire into thyself. The rational principle which rules has this nature, that it is content with itself when it does what is just, and so secures tranquillity.

29. Wipe out the imagination. Stop the pulling of the strings. Confine thyself to the present. Understand well what happens either to thee or to another. Divide and distribute every object into the causal [formal] and the material. Think of thy last hour. Let the wrong which is done by a man stay there where the wrong was done (viii. 29).

30. Direct thy attention to what is said. Let thy understanding enter into the things that are doing and the things which do them (vii. 4).

31. Adorn thyself with simplicity and modesty and with indifference towards the things which lie between virtue and vice. Love mankind. Follow God. The poet says that Law rules all. And it is enough to remember that law rules all.[1]

32. About death: whether it is a dispersion, or a resolution into atoms, or annihilation, it is either extinction or change.

33. About pain: the pain which is intolerable carries us off; but that which lasts a long time is tolerable; and the mind maintains its own tranquillity by retiring into itself, and the ruling faculty is not made worse. But the parts which are harmed by pain, let them, if they can, give their opinion about it.

34. About fame: look at the minds [of those who seek fame], observe what they are, and what kind of things they avoid, and what kind of things they pursue. And consider that as the heaps of sand piled on one another hide the former sands, so in life the events which go before are soon covered by those which come after.

[1]The end of this section is unintelligible.

35. From Plato: the man who has an elevated mind and takes a view of all time and of all substance, dost thou suppose it possible for him to think that human life is anything great? It is not possible, he said. Such a man then will think that death also is no evil. Certainly not.

36. From Antisthenes: It is royal to do good and to be abused.

37. It is a base thing for the countenance to be obedient and to regulate and compose itself as the mind commands, and for the mind not to be regulated and composed by itself.

38. It is not right to vex ourselves at things,
For they care nought about it.

39. To the immortal gods and us give joy.

40. Life must be reaped like the ripe ears of corn:
One man is born; another dies.

41. If gods care not for me and for my children,
There is a reason for it.

42. For the good is with me, and the just.

43. No joining others in their wailing, no violent emotion.

44. From Plato: But I would make this man a sufficient answer, which is this: Thou sayest not well, if thou thinkest that a man who is good for anything at all ought to compute the hazard of life or death, and should not rather look to this only in all that he does, whether he is doing what is just or unjust, and the works of a good or a bad man.

45. For thus it is, men of Athens, in truth: wherever a man has placed himself thinking it the best place for him, or has been placed by a commander, there in my opinion he ought to stay and to abide the hazard, taking nothing into the reckoning, either death or anything else, before the baseness [of deserting his post].

46. But, my good friend, reflect whether that which is noble and good is not something different from saving and being saved; for as to a man living such or such a time, at least one who is really a man, consider if this is not a thing to be dismissed from the thoughts: and there must be no love of life: but as to these matters a man must intrust them to the deity and believe what the women say, that no man can escape his destiny, the next inquiry being how he may best live the time that he has to live.

47. Look round at the courses of the stars, as if thou wert going along with them; and constantly consider the changes of the elements into one another; for such thoughts purge away the filth of the terrene life.

48. This is a fine saying of Plato: That he who is discoursing about men should look also at earthly things as if he viewed them from some higher place; should look at them in their assemblies, armies, agricultural labours, marriages, treaties, births, deaths, noise of the courts of justice, desert places, various nations of barbarians, feasts, lamentations, markets, a mixture of all things and an orderly combination of contraries.

49. Consider the past; such great changes of political supremacies. Thou mayest foresee also the things which will be. For they will certainly be of like form, and it is not possible that they should deviate from the order of the things which take place now: accordingly to have contemplated human life for forty years is the same as to have contemplated it for ten thousand years. For what more wilt thou see?

50. That which has grown from the earth to the earth,
But that which has sprung from heavenly seed,
Back to the heavenly realms returns.

This is either a dissolution of the mutual involution of the atoms, or a similar dispersion of the unsentient elements.

51. With food and drinks and cunning magic arts
Turning the channel's course to 'scape from death.
The breeze which heaven has sent
We must endure, and toil without complaining.

52. Another may be more expert in casting his opponent; but he is not more social, nor more modest, nor better disciplined to meet all that happens, nor more considerate with respect to the faults of his neighbours.

53. Where any work can be done conformably to the reason which is common to gods and men, there we have nothing to fear; for where we are able to get profit by means of the activity which is successful and proceeds according to our constitution, there no harm is to be suspected.

54. Everywhere and at all times it is in thy power piously to

acquiesce in thy present condition, and to behave justly to those who are about thee, and to exert thy skill upon thy present thoughts, that nothing shall steal into them without being well examined.

55. Do not look around thee to discover other men's ruling principles, but look straight to this, to what nature leads thee, both the universal nature through the things which happen to thee, and thy own nature through the acts which must be done by thee. But every being ought to do that which is according to its constitution; and all other things have been constituted for the sake of rational beings, just as among irrational things the inferior for the sake of the superior, but the rational for the sake of one another.

The prime principle then in man's constitution is the social. And the second is not to yield to the persuasions of the body, for it is the peculiar office of the rational and intelligent motion to circumscribe itself, and never to be overpowered either by the motion of the senses or of the appetites, for both are animal; but the intelligent motion claims superiority and does not permit itself to be overpowered by the others. And with good reason, for it is formed by nature to use all of them. The third thing in the rational constitution is freedom from error and from deception. Let then the ruling principle holding fast to these things go straight on, and it has what is its own.

56. Consider thyself to be dead, and to have completed thy life up to the present time; and live according to nature the remainder which is allowed thee.

57. Love that only which happens to thee and is spun with the thread of thy destiny. For what is more suitable?

58. In everything which happens keep before thy eyes those to whom the same things happened, and how they were vexed, and treated them as strange things, and found fault with them: and now where are they? Nowhere. Why then dost thou too choose to act in the same way? and why dost thou not leave these agitations which are foreign to nature, to those who cause them and those who are moved by them? And why art thou not altogether intent upon the right way of making use of the things which happen to thee? for then thou wilt use them well, and they will be a material for thee [to work on]. Only attend to thyself, and resolve to be a good man in every act which thou doest; and remember . . .

59. Look within. Within is the fountain of good, and it will ever bubble up, if thou wilt ever dig.

60. The body ought to be compact, and to show no irregularity either in motion or attitude. For what the mind shows in the face by maintaining in it the expression of intelligence and propriety, that ought to be required also in the whole body. But all these things should be observed without affectation.

61. The art of life is more like the wrestler's art than the dancer's, in respect of this, that it should stand ready and firm to meet onsets which are sudden and unexpected.

62. Constantly observe who those are whose approbation thou wishest to have, and what ruling principles they possess. For then thou wilt neither blame those who offend involuntarily, nor wilt thou want their approbation, if thou lookest to the sources of their opinions and appetites.

63. Every soul, the philosopher says, is involuntarily deprived of truth; consequently in the same way it is deprived of justice and temperance and benevolence and everything of the kind. It is most necessary to bear this constantly in mind, for thus thou wilt be more gentle towards all.

64. In every pain let this thought be present, that there is no dishonour in it, nor does it make the governing intelligence worse, for it does not damage the intelligence either so far as the intelligence is rational or so far as it is social. Indeed in the case of most pains let this remark of Epicurus aid thee, that pain is neither intolerable nor everlasting, if thou bearest in mind that it has its limits, and if thou addest nothing to it in imagination: and remember this too, that we do not perceive that many things which are disagreeable to us are the same as pain, such as excessive drowsiness, and the being scorched by heat, and the having no appetite. When then thou art discontented about any of these things, say to thyself that thou art yielding to pain.

65. Take care not to feel towards the inhuman as they feel towards men.

66. How do we know if Telauges was not superior in character to Socrates? for it is not enough that Socrates died a more noble death, and disputed more skilfully with the sophists, and passed the night in

the cold with more endurance, and that when he was bid to arrest Leon of Salamis, he considered it more noble to refuse, and that he walked in a swaggering way in the streets—though as to this fact one may have great doubts if it was true. But we ought to inquire, what kind of a soul it was that Socrates possessed, and if he was able to be content with being just towards men and pious towards the gods, neither idly vexed on account of men's villainy, nor yet making himself a slave to any man's ignorance, nor receiving as strange anything that fell to his share out of the universal, nor enduring it as intolerable, nor allowing his understanding to sympathize with the affects of the miserable flesh.

67. Nature has not so mingled [the intelligence] with the composition of the body, as not to have allowed thee the power of circumscribing thyself and of bringing under subjection to thyself all that is thy own; for it is very possible to be a divine man and to be recognized as such by no one. Always bear this in mind; and another thing too, that very little indeed is necessary for living a happy life. And because thou hast despaired of becoming a dialectician and skilled in the knowledge of nature, do not for this reason renounce the hope of being both free and modest and social and obedient to God.

68. It is in thy power to live free from all compulsion in the greatest tranquillity of mind, even if all the world cry out against thee as much as they choose, and even if wild beasts tear in pieces the members of this kneaded matter which has grown around thee. For what hinders the mind in the midst of all this from maintaining itself in tranquillity, and in a just judgment of all surrounding things, and in a ready use of the objects which are presented to it, so that the judgment may say to the thing which falls under its observation: This thou art in substance [reality], though in men's opinion thou mayest appear to be of a different kind; and the use shall say to that which falls under the hand: Thou art the thing that I was seeking; for to me that which presents itself is always a material for virtue, both rational and political, and, in a word, for the exercise of art, which belongs to man or God. For everything which happens has a relationship either to God or man, and is neither new nor difficult to handle, but usual and apt matter to work on.

69. The perfection of moral character consists in this, in passing every day as the last, and in being neither violently excited, nor torpid, nor playing the hypocrite.

70. The gods who are immortal are not vexed because during so long a time they must tolerate continually men such as they are and so many of them bad; and besides this, they also take care of them in all ways. But thou, who art destined to end so soon, art thou wearied of enduring the bad, and this too when thou art one of them?

71. It is a ridiculous thing for a man not to fly from his own badness, which is indeed possible, but to fly from other men's badness, which is impossible.

72. Whatever the rational and political [social] faculty finds to be neither intelligent nor social, it properly judges to be inferior to itself.

73. When thou hast done a good act and another has received it, why dost thou still look for a third thing besides these, as fools do, either to have the reputation of having done a good act or to obtain a return?

74. No man is tired of receiving what is useful. But it is useful to act according to nature. Do not then be tired of receiving what is useful by doing it to others.

75. The nature of the All moved to make the universe. But now either everything that takes place comes by way of consequence or [continuity]; or even the chief things towards which the ruling power of the universe directs its own movement are governed by no rational principle. If this is remembered it will make thee more tranquil in many things (vi. 44; ix. 28).

VIII

THIS reflection also tends to the removal of the desire of empty fame, that it is no longer in thy power to have lived the whole of thy life, or at least thy life from thy youth upwards, like a philosopher; but both to many others and to thyself it is plain that thou art far from philosophy. Thou hast fallen into disorder then, so that it is no longer easy for thee to get the reputation of a philosopher; and thy plan of life also opposes it. If then thou hast truly seen where the matter lies, throw away the thought, How thou shalt seem [to others], and be content if thou shalt live the rest of thy life in such wise as thy nature wills. Observe then what it wills, and let nothing else distract thee; for thou hast had experience of many wanderings without having found happiness anywhere, not in syllogisms, nor in wealth, nor in reputation, nor in enjoyment, nor anywhere. Where is it then? In doing what man's nature requires. How then shall a man do this? If he has principles from which come his affects and his acts. What principles? Those which relate to good and bad: the belief that there is nothing good for man, which does not make him just, temperate, manly, free; and that there is nothing bad, which does not do the contrary to what has been mentioned.

2. On the occasion of every act ask thyself, How is this with respect to me? Shall I repent of it? A little time and I am dead, and all is gone. What more do I seek, if what I am doing now is the work of an intelligent living being, and a social being, and one who is under the same law with God?

3. Alexander and Caius and Pompeius, what are they in comparison with Diogenes and Heraclitus and Socrates? For they were acquainted with things, and their causes [forms], and their matter, and the ruling principles of these men were the same [or conformable to their pursuits]. But as to the others, how many things had they to care for, and to how many things were they slaves.

4. [Consider] that men will do the same things nevertheless, even though thou shouldst burst.

5. This is the chief thing: Be not perturbed, for all things are according to the nature of the universal; and in a little time thou wilt be nobody and nowhere, like Hadrianus and Augustus. In the next place having fixed thy eyes steadily on thy business look at it, and at the same time remembering that it is thy duty to be a good man, and what man's nature demands, do that without turning aside; and speak as it seems to thee most just, only let it be with a good disposition and with modesty and without hypocrisy.

6. The nature of the universal has this work to do, to remove to that place the things which are in this, to change them, to take them away hence, and to carry them there. All things are change, yet we need not fear anything new. All things are familiar [to us]; but the distribution of them still remains the same.

7. Every nature is contented with itself when it goes on its way well; and a rational nature goes on its way well, when in its thoughts it assents to nothing false or uncertain, and when it directs its movements to social acts only, and when it confines its desires and aversions to the things which are in its power, and when it is satisfied with everything that is assigned to it by the common nature. For of this common nature every particular nature is a part, as the nature of the leaf is a part of the nature of the plant; except that in the plant the nature of the leaf is part of a nature which has not perception or reason, and is subject to be impeded; but the nature of man is part of a nature which is not subject to impediments, and is intelligent and just, since it gives to everything in equal portions and according to its worth, times, substance, cause [form], activity, and incident. But examine, not to discover that any one thing compared with any other single thing is equal in all respects, but by taking all the parts together of one thing and comparing them with all the parts together of another.

8. Thou hast not leisure [or ability] to read. But thou hast leisure [or ability] to check arrogance: thou hast leisure to be superior to pleasure and pain: thou hast leisure to be superior to love of fame, and not to be vexed at stupid and ungrateful people, nay even to care for them.

9. Let no man any longer hear thee finding fault with the court life or with thy own (v. 16).

10. Repentance is a kind of self-reproof for having neglected something useful; but that which is good must be something useful, and the perfect good man should look after it. But no such man would ever repent of having refused any sensual pleasure. Pleasure then is neither good nor useful.

11. This thing, what is it in itself, in its own constitution? What is its substance and material? And what its causal nature [or form]? And what is it doing in the world? And how long does it subsist?

12. When thou risest from sleep with reluctance, remember that it is according to thy constitution and according to human nature to perform social acts, but sleeping is common also to irrational animals. But that which is according to each individual's nature is also more

peculiarly its own, and more suitable to its nature, and indeed also more agreeable (v. 1).

13. Constantly and, if it be possible, on the occasion of every impression on the soul, apply to it the principles of Physic, of Ethic, and of Dialectic.

14. Whatever man thou meetest with, immediately say to thyself: What opinions has this man about good and bad? For if with respect to pleasure and pain and the causes of each, and with respect to fame and ignominy, death and life, he has such and such opinions, it will seem nothing wonderful or strange to me, if he does such and such things; and I shall bear in mind that he is compelled to do so.

15. Remember that as it is a shame to be surprised if the fig-tree produces figs, so it is to be surprised if the world produces such and such things of which it is productive; and for the physician and the helmsman it is a shame to be surprised, if a man has a fever, or if the wind if unfavourable.

16. Remember that to change thy opinion and to follow him who corrects thy error is as consistent with freedom as it is to persist in thy error. For it is thy own, the activity which is exerted according to thy own movement and judgment, and indeed according to thy own understanding too.

17. If a thing is in thy own power, why dost thou do it? but if it is in the power of another, whom dost thou blame? the atoms [chance] or the gods? Both are foolish. Thou must blame nobody. For if thou canst, correct [that which is the cause]; but if thou canst not do this, correct at least the thing itself; but if thou canst not do even this, of what use is it to thee to find fault? for nothing should be done without a purpose.

18. That which has died falls not out of the universe. If it stays here, it also changes here, and is dissolved into its proper parts, which are elements of the universe and of thyself. And these too change, and they murmur not.

19. Everything exists for some end, a horse, a vine. Why dost thou wonder? Even the sun will say, I am for some purpose, and the rest of the gods will say the same. For what purpose then art thou? to enjoy pleasure? See if common sense allows this.

20. Nature has had regard in everything no less to the end than to the beginning and the continuance, just like the man who throws up a ball. What good is it then for the ball to be thrown up, or harm for it to come down, or even to have fallen? and what good is it to the bubble while it holds together, or what harm when it is burst? The same may be said of a light also.

21. Turn it [the body] inside out, and see what kind of thing it is; and when it has grown old, what kind of thing it becomes, and when it is diseased.

Short-lived are both the praiser and the praised, and the rememberer and the remembered: and all this in a nook of this part of the world; and not even here do all agree, no, not any one with himself: and the whole earth too is a point.

22. Attend to the matter which is before thee, whether it is an opinion or an act or a word.

Thou sufferest this justly: for thou choosest rather to become good to-morrow than to be good to-day.

23. Am I doing anything? I do it with reference to the good of mankind. Does anything happen to me? I receive it and refer it to the gods, and the source of all things, from which all that happens is derived.

24. Such as bathing appears to thee—oil, sweat, dirt, filthy water, all things disgusting—so is every part of life and everything.

25. Lucilla saw Verus die, and then Lucilla died. Secunda saw Maximus die, and then Secunda died. Epitynchanus saw Diotimus die, and then Epitynchanus died. Antoninus saw Faustina die, and then Antoninus died. Such is everything. Celer saw Hadrianus die, and then Celer died. And those sharp-witted men, either seers or men inflated with pride, where are they? for instance, the sharp-witted men, Charax and Demetrius the Platonist and Eudæmon, and any one else like them. All ephemeral, dead long ago. Some indeed have not been remembered even for a short time, and others have become the heroes of fables, and again others have disappeared even from fables. Remember this, then, that this little compound, thyself, must either be dissolved, or thy poor breath must be extinguished, or be removed and placed elsewhere.

26. It is satisfaction to a man to do the proper works of a man.

Now it is a proper work of a man to be benevolent to his own kind, to despise the movements of the senses, to form a just judgment of plausible appearances, and to take a survey of the nature of the universe and of the things which happen in it.

27. There are three relations [between thee and other things]: the one to the body which surrounds thee; the second to the divine cause from which all things come to all; and the third to those who live with thee.

28. Pain is either an evil to the body—then let the body say what it thinks of it—or to the soul; but it is in the power of the soul to maintain its own serenity and tranquillity, and not to think that pain is an evil. For every judgment and movement and desire and aversion is within, and no evil ascends so high.

29. Wipe out thy imaginations by often saying to thyself: now it is in my power to let no badness be in this soul, nor desire, nor any perturbation at all; but looking at all things I see what is their nature, and I use each according to its value.—Remember this power which thou hast from nature.

30. Speak both in the senate and to every man, whoever he may be, appropriately, not with any affectation: use plain discourse.

31. Augustus' court, wife, daughter, descendants, ancestors, sister, Agrippa, kinsmen, intimates, friends, Areius, Mæcenas, physicians and sacrificing priests—the whole court is dead. Then turn to the rest, not considering the death of a single man, [but of a whole race], as of the Pompeii; and that which is inscribed on the tombs—the last of his race. Then consider what trouble those before them have had that they might leave a successor; and then, that of necessity some one must be the last. Again here consider the death of a whole race.

32. It is thy duty to order thy life well in every single act; and if every act does its duty, as far as is possible, be content; and no one is able to hinder thee so that each act shall not do its duty.—But something external will stand in the way.—Nothing will stand in the way of thy acting justly and soberly and considerately, but perhaps some other active power will be hindered. Well, but by acquiescing in the hindrance and by being content to transfer thy efforts to that which is allowed, another opportunity of action is immediately put before

thee in place of that which was hindered, and one which will adapt itself to this ordering of which we are speaking.

33. Receive [wealth or prosperity] without arrogance; and be ready to let it go.

34. If thou didst ever see a hand cut off, or a foot, or a head, lying anywhere apart from the rest of the body, such does a man make himself, as far as he can, who is not content with what happens, and separates himself from others, or does anything unsocial. Suppose that thou hast detached thyself from the natural unity—for thou wast made by nature a part, but now thou hast cut thyself off—yet here there is this beautiful provision, that it is in thy power again to unite thyself. God has allowed this to no other part, after it has been separated and cut asunder, to come together again. But consider the kindness by which he has distinguished man, for he has put it in his power not to be separated at all from the universal; and when he has been separated, he has allowed him to return and to be united and to resume his place as a part.

35. As the nature of the universal has given to every rational being all the other powers that it has, so we have received from it this power also. For as the universal nature converts and fixes in its predestined place everything which stands in the way and opposes it, and makes such things a part of itself, so also the rational animal is able to make every hindrance its own material, and to use it for such purposes as it may have designed.

36. Do not disturb thyself by thinking of the whole of thy life. Let not thy thoughts at once embrace all the various troubles which thou mayest expect to befall thee: but on every occasion ask thyself, What is there in this which is intolerable and past bearing? for thou wilt be ashamed to confess. In the next place remember that neither the future nor the past pains thee, but only the present. But this is reduced to a very little, if thou only circumscribest it, and chidest thy mind, if it is unable to hold out against even this.

37. Does Panthea or Pergamus now sit by the tomb of Verus? Does Chaurias or Diotimus sit by the tomb of Hadrianus? That would be ridiculous. Well, suppose they did sit there, would the dead be conscious of it? and if the dead were conscious, would they be pleased? and if they were pleased, would that make them im-

mortal? Was it not in the order of destiny that these persons too should first become old women and old men and then die? What then would those do after these were dead? All this is foul smell and blood in a bag.

38. If thou canst see sharp, look and judge wisely, says the philosopher.

39. In the constitution of the rational animal I see no virtue which is opposed to justice; but I see a virtue which is opposed to love of pleasure, and that is temperance.

40. If thou takest away thy opinion about that which appears to give thee pain, thou thyself standest in perfect security. Who is this self? The reason. But I am not reason. Be it so. Let then the reason itself not trouble itself. But if any other part of thee suffers, let it have its own opinion about itself (vii. 16).

41. Hindrance to the perceptions of sense is an evil to the animal nature. Hindrance to the movements [desires] is equally an evil to the animal nature. And something else also is equally an impediment and evil to the constitution of plants. So then that which is a hindrance to the intelligence is an evil to the intelligent nature. Apply all these things then to thyself. Does pain or sensuous pleasure affect thee? The senses will look to that. Has any obstacle opposed thee in thy efforts towards an object? if indeed thou wast making this effort absolutely [unconditionally, or without any reservation], certainly this obstacle is an evil to thee considered as a rational animal. But if thou takest [into consideration] the usual course of things, thou hast not yet been injured nor even impeded. The things however which are proper to the understanding no other man is used to impede, for neither fire, nor iron, nor tyrant, nor abuse, touches it in any way. When it has been made a sphere, it continues a sphere (xi. 12).

42. It is not fit that I should give myself pain, for I have never intentionally given pain even to another.

43. Different things delight different people. But it is my delight to keep the ruling faculty sound without turning away either from any man or from any of the things which happen to men, but looking at and receiving all with welcome eyes and using everything according to its value.

44. See that thou secure this present time to thyself; for those who rather pursue posthumous fame do not consider that the men of after-time will be exactly such as these whom they cannot bear now; and both are mortal. And what is it in any way to thee if these men of after-time utter this or that sound, or have this or that opinion about thee?

45. Take me and cast me where thou wilt; for there I shall keep my divine part tranquil, that is, content, if it can feel and act conformably to its proper constitution. Is this [change of place] sufficient reason why my soul should be unhappy and worse than it was, depressed, expanded, shrinking, affrighted? and what wilt thou find which is sufficient reason for this?

46. Nothing can happen to any man which is not human accident, nor to an ox which is not according to the nature of an ox, nor to a vine which is not according to the nature of a vine, nor to a stone which is not proper to a stone. If then there happens to each thing both what is usual and natural, why shouldst thou complain? For the common nature brings nothing which may not be borne by thee.

47. If thou art pained by any external thing, it is not this that disturbs thee, but thy own judgment about it. And it is in thy power to wipe out this judgment now. But if anything in thy own disposition gives thee pain, who hinders thee from correcting thy opinion? And even if thou art pained because thou art not doing some particular thing which seems to thee to be right, why dost thou not rather act than complain? But some insuperable obstacle is in the way? Do not be grieved then, for the cause of its not being done depends not on thee. But it is not worth while to live, if this cannot be done. Take thy departure then from life contentedly, just as he dies who is in full activity, and well pleased too with the things which are obstacles.

48. Remember that the ruling faculty is invincible, when self-collected it is satisfied with itself, if it does nothing which it does not choose to do, even if it resist from mere obstinacy. What then will it be when it forms a judgment about anything aided by reason and deliberately? Therefore the mind which is free from passions is a citadel, for man has nothing more secure to which he can fly for

refuge and for the future be inexpugnable. He then who has not seen this is an ignorant man; but he who has seen it and does not fly to this refuge is unhappy.

49. Say nothing more to thyself than what the first appearances report. Suppose that it has been reported to thee that a certain person speaks ill of thee. This has been reported; but that thou hast been injured, that has not been reported. I see that my child is sick. I do see; but that he is in danger, I do not see. Thus then always abide by the first appearances, and add nothing thyself from within, and then nothing happens to thee. Or rather add something, like a man who knows everything that happens in the world.

50. A cucumber is bitter.—Throw it away.—There are briars in the road.—Turn aside from them.—This is enough. Do not add, And why were such things made in the world? For thou wilt be ridiculed by a man who is acquainted with nature, as thou wouldst be ridiculed by a carpenter and shoemaker if thou didst find fault because thou seest in their workshop shavings and cuttings from the things which they make. And yet they have places into which they can throw these shavings and cuttings, and the universal nature has no external space; but the wondrous part of her art is that though she has circumscribed herself, everything within her which appears to decay and to grow old and to be useless she changes into herself, and again makes other new things from these very same, so that she requires neither substance from without nor wants a place into which she may cast that which decays. She is content then with her own space, and her own matter, and her own art.

51. Neither in thy actions be sluggish, nor in thy conversation without method, nor wandering in thy thoughts, nor let there be in thy soul inward contention nor external effusion, nor in life be so busy as to have no leisure.

Suppose that men kill thee, cut thee in pieces, curse thee. What then can these things do to prevent thy mind from remaining pure, wise, sober, just? For instance, if a man should stand by a limpid pure spring, and curse it, the spring never ceases sending up potable water; and if he should cast clay into it or filth, it will speedily disperse them and wash them out, and will not be at all polluted. How then shalt thou possess a perpetual fountain [and not a mere well]? By forming thyself hourly to freedom conjoined with contentment, simplicity and modesty.

52. He who does not know what the world is, does not know where he is. And he who does not know for what purpose the world exists, does not know who he is, nor what the world is. But he who has failed in any one of these things could not even say for what purpose he exists himself. What then dost thou think of him who [avoids or] seeks the praise of those who applaud, of men who know not either where they are or who they are?

53. Dost thou wish to be praised by a man who curses himself thrice every hour? Wouldst thou wish to please a man who does not please himself? Does a man please himself who repents of nearly everything that he does?

54. No longer let thy breathing only act in concert with the air which surrounds thee, but let thy intelligence also now be in harmony with the intelligence which embraces all things. For the intelligent power is no less diffused in all parts and pervades all things for him who is willing to draw it to him than the aërial power for him who is able to respire it.

55. Generally, wickedness does no harm at all to the universe; and particularly, the wickedness [of one man] does no harm to another. It is only harmful to him who has it in his power to be released from it, as soon as he shall choose.

56. To my own free will the free will of my neighbour is just as indifferent as his poor breath and flesh. For though we are made especially for the sake of one another, still the ruling power of each of us has its own office, for otherwise my neighbour's wickedness would be my harm, which God has not willed in order that my unhappiness may not depend on another.

57. The sun appears to be poured down, and in all directions indeed it is diffused, yet it is not effused. For this diffusion is extension: Accordingly its rays are called Extensions [ἀκτῖνες] because they are extended [ἀπό τοῦ ἐκτείνεσθαι]. But one may judge what kind of a thing a ray is, if he looks at the sun's light passing through a narrow opening into a darkened room, for it is extended in a right line, and, as it were, is divided when it meets with any solid body which stands in the way and intercepts the air beyond; but there the light

remains fixed and does not glide or fall off. Such then ought to be the outpouring and diffusion of the understanding, and it should in no way be an effusion, but an extension, and it should make no violent or impetuous collision with the obstacles which are in its way; nor yet fall down, but be fixed and enlighten that which receives it. For a body will deprive itself of the illumination, if it does not admit it.

58. He who fears death either fears the loss of sensation or a different kind of sensation. But if thou shalt have no sensation, neither wilt thou feel any harm; and if thou shalt acquire another kind of sensation, thou wilt be a different kind of living being, and thou wilt not cease to live.

59. Men exist for the sake of one another. Teach them then or bear with them.

60. In one way an arrow moves, in another way the mind. The mind, indeed, both when it exercises caution and when it is employed about inquiry, moves straight onward not the less, and to its object.

61. Enter into every man's ruling faculty; and also let every other man enter into thine.

IX

HE who acts unjustly acts impiously. For since the universal nature has made rational animals for the sake of one another to help one another according to their deserts, but in no way to injure one another, he who transgresses her will, is clearly guilty of impiety towards the highest divinity. And he too who lies is guilty of impiety to the same divinity; for the universal nature is the nature of things that are; and things that are have a relation to all things that come into existence. And further, this universal nature is named truth, and is the prime cause of all things that are true. He then who lies intentionally is guilty of impiety inasmuch as he acts unjustly by deceiving; and he also who lies unintentionally, inasmuch as he is at variance with the universal nature, and inasmuch as he disturbs the order by fighting against the nature of the world; for he fights against it, who is moved of himself to that which is contrary to truth, for he had received powers from nature through the neglect of which he is not able now to distinguish falsehood from truth. And indeed he who pursues pleasure as good, and avoids pain as evil, is guilty of impiety. For of necessity such a man must often find fault with the universal nature, alleging that it assigns things to the bad and the good contrary to their deserts, because frequently the bad are in the enjoyment of pleasure and possess the things which procure pleasure, but the good have pain for their share and the things which cause pain. And further, he who is afraid of pain will sometimes also be afraid of some of the things which will happen in the world, and even this is impiety. And he who pursues pleasure will not abstain from injustice, and this is plainly impiety. Now with respect to the things towards which the universal nature is equally affected—for it would not have made both, unless it was equally affected towards both—towards these they who wish to follow nature should be of the same mind with it, and equally affected. With respect to pain, then, and pleasure, or death and life, or honour and dishonour, which the universal nature employs equally, whoever is not equally affected is manifestly acting impiously. And I say that the universal nature employs them equally, instead of saying that they happen alike to those who are produced in continuous series and to those who come after them by virtue of a certain original movement of Providence, according to which it moved from a certain beginning to this ordering of things, having conceived certain principles of the things which were to be, and having determined powers productive of beings and of changes and of suchlike successions (vii. 75).

2. It would be a man's happiest lot to depart from mankind without having had any taste of lying and hypocrisy and luxury and pride. However to breathe out one's life when a man has had enough of these things is the next best voyage, as the saying is. Hast thou determined to abide with vice, and has not experience yet induced thee to fly from this pestilence? For the destruction of the understanding is a pestilence, much more indeed than any such corruption and change of this atmosphere which surrounds us. For this corruption is a pestilence of animals so far as they are animals; but the other is a pestilence of men so far as they are men.

3. Do not despise death, but be well content with it, since this too

is one of those things which nature wills. For such as it is to be young and to grow old, and to increase and to reach maturity, and to have teeth and beard and gray hairs, and to beget, and to be pregnant, and to bring forth, and all the other natural operations which the seasons of thy life bring, such also is dissolution. This, then, is consistent with the character of a reflecting man, to be neither careless nor impatient nor contemptuous with respect to death, but to wait for it as one of the operations of nature. As thou now waitest for the time when the child shall come out of thy wife's womb, so be ready for the time when thy soul shall fall out of this envelope. But if thou requirest also a vulgar kind of comfort which shall reach thy heart, thou wilt be made best reconciled to death by observing the objects from which thou art going to be removed, and the morals of those with whom thy soul will no longer be mingled. For it is no way right to be offended with men, but it is thy duty to care for them and to bear with them gently; and yet to remember that thy departure will be not from men who have the same principles as thyself. For this is the only thing, if there be any, which could draw us the contrary way and attach us to life, to be permitted to live with those who have the same principles as ourselves. But now thou seest how great is the trouble arising from the discordance of those who live together, so that thou mayst say, Come quick, O death, lest perchance I, too, should forget myself.

4. He who does wrong does wrong against himself. He who acts unjustly acts unjustly to himself, because he makes himself bad.

5. He often acts unjustly who does not do a certain thing; not only he who does a certain thing.

6. Thy present opinion founded on understanding, and thy present conduct directed to social good, and thy present disposition of contentment with everything which happens—that is enough.

7. Wipe out imagination: check desire: extinguish appetite: keep the ruling faculty in its own power.

8. Among the animals which have not reason one life is distributed; but among reasonable animals one intelligent soul is distributed: just as there is one earth of all things which are of an earthy nature, and we see by one light, and breathe one air, all of us that have the faculty of vision and all that have life.

9. All things which participate in anything which is common to them all move towards that which is of the same kind with themselves. Everything which is earthy turns towards the earth, everything which is liquid flows together, and everything which is of an aërial kind does the same, so that they require something to keep them asunder, and the application of force. Fire indeed moves upwards on account of the elemental fire, but it is so ready to be kindled together with all the fire which is here, that even every substance which is somewhat dry, is easily ignited, because there is less mingled with it of that which is a hindrance to ignition. Accordingly then everything also which participates in the common intelligent nature moves in like manner towards that which is of the same kind with itself, or moves even more. For so much as it is superior in comparison with all other things, in the same degree also is it more ready to mingle with and to be fused with that which is akin to it. Accordingly among animals devoid of reason we find swarms of bees, and herds of cattle, and the nurture of young birds, and in a manner, loves; for even in animals there are souls, and that power which brings them together is seen to exert itself in the superior degree, and in such a way as never has been observed in plants nor in stones nor in trees. But in rational animals there are political communities and friendships, and families and meetings of people; and in wars, treaties and armistices. But in the things which are still superior, even though they are separated from one another, unity in a manner exists, as in the stars. Thus the ascent to the higher degree is able to produce a sympathy even in things which are separated. See then what now takes place. For only intelligent animals have now forgotten this mutual desire and inclination, and in them alone the property of flowing together is not seen. But still, though men strive to avoid [this union], they are caught and held by it, for their nature is too strong for them; and thou wilt see what I say, if thou only observest. Sooner then will one find anything earthy which comes in contact with no earthy thing than a man altogether separated from other men.

10. Both man and God and the universe produce fruit; at the proper seasons each produces it. But if usage has especially fixed these terms to the vine and like things, this is nothing. Reason

produces fruit both for all and for itself, and there are produced from it other things of the same kind as reason itself.

11. If thou art able, correct by teaching those who do wrong; but if thou canst not, remember that indulgence is given to thee for this purpose. And the gods, too, are indulgent to such persons; and for some purposes they even help them to get health, wealth, reputation; so kind they are. And it is in thy power also; or say, who hinders thee?

12. Labour not as one who is wretched, nor yet as one who would be pitied or admired; but direct thy will to one thing only, to put thyself in motion and to check thyself, as the social reason requires.

13. To-day I have got out of all trouble, or rather I have cast out all trouble, for it was not outside, but within and in my opinions.

14. All things are the same, familiar in experience, and ephemeral in time, and worthless in the matter. Everything now is just as it was in the time of those whom we have buried.

15. Things stand outside of us, themselves by themselves, neither knowing aught of themselves, nor expressing any judgment. What is it, then, which does judge about them? The ruling faculty.

16. Not in passivity, but in activity, lie the evil and the good of the rational social animal, just as his virtue and his vice lie not in passivity, but in activity.

17. For the stone which has been thrown up it is no evil to come down, nor indeed any good to have been carried up (viii. 20).

18. Penetrate inwards into men's leading principles, and thou wilt see what judges thou art afraid of, and what kind of judges they are of themselves.

19. All things are changing; and thou thyself art in continuous mutation and in a manner in continuous destruction, and the whole universe too.

20. It is thy duty to leave another man's wrongful act there where it is (vii. 29; ix. 38).

21. Termination of activity, cessation from movement and opinion, and in a sense their death, is no evil. Turn thy thoughts now to the consideration of thy life, thy life as a child, as a youth, thy manhood, thy old age, for in these also every change was a death. Is this anything to fear? Turn thy thoughts now to thy life under thy

grandfather, then to thy life under thy mother, then to thy life under thy father; and as thou findest many other differences and changes and terminations, ask thyself, Is this anything to fear? In like manner, then, neither are the termination and cessation and change of thy whole life a thing to be afraid of.

22. Hasten [to examine] thy own ruling faculty and that of the universe and that of thy neighbour: thy own, that thou mayst make 't just; and that of the universe, that thou mayst remember of what thou art a part; and that of thy neighbour, that thou mayst know whether he has acted ignorantly or with knowledge, and that thou mayst also consider that his ruling faculty is akin to thine.

23. As thou thyself art a component part of a social system, so let every act of thine be a component part of social life. Whatever act of thine then has no reference, either immediately or remotely, to a social end, this tears asunder thy life, and does not allow it to be one, and it is of the nature of a mutiny, just as when in a popular assembly a man acting by himself stands apart from the general agreement.

24. Quarrels of little children and their sports, and poor spirits carrying about dead bodies [such is everything]; and so what is exhibited in the representation of the mansions of the dead strikes our eyes more clearly.

25. Examine into the quality of the form of an object, and detach it altogether from its material part, and then contemplate it; then determine the time, the longest which a thing of this peculiar form is naturally made to endure.

26. Thou hast endured infinite troubles through not being contented with thy ruling faculty, when it does the things which it is constituted by nature to do. But enough [of this].

27. When another blames thee or hates thee, or when men say about thee anything injurious, approach their poor souls, penetrate within, and see what kind of men they are. Thou wilt discover that there is no reason to take any trouble that these men may have this or that opinion about thee. However thou must be well-disposed towards them, for by nature they are friends. And the gods too aid them in all ways, by dreams, by signs, towards the attainment of those things on which they set a value.

28. The periodic movements of the universe are the same, up and

down from age to age. And either the universal intelligence puts itself in motion for every separate effect, and if this is so, be thou content with that which is the result of its activity; or it puts itself in motion once, and everything else comes by way of sequence in a manner; or indivisible elements are the origin of all things. In a word, if there is a god, all is well; and if chance rules, do not thou also be governed by it (vi. 44; vii. 75).

Soon will the earth cover us all: then the earth, too, will change, and the things also which result from change will continue to change forever, and these again forever. For if a man reflects on the changes and transformations which follow one another like wave after wave and their rapidity, he will despise everything which is perishable (xii. 21).

29. The universal cause is like a winter torrent: it carries everything along with it. But how worthless are all these poor people who are engaged in matters political, and, as they suppose, are playing the philosopher! All drivelers. Well then, man: do what nature now requires. Set thyself in motion, if it is in thy power, and do not look about thee to see if any one will observe it; nor yet expect Plato's Republic: but be content if the smallest thing goes on well, and consider such an event to be no small matter. For who can change men's opinions? And without a change of opinions what else is there than the slavery of men who groan while they pretend to obey? Come now and tell me of Alexander and Philippus and Demetrius and Phalerum. They themselves shall judge whether they discovered what the common nature required, and trained themselves accordingly. But if they acted like tragedy heroes, no one has condemned me to imitate them. Simple and modest is the work of philosophy. Draw me not aside to insolence and pride.

30. Look down from above on the countless herds of men and their countless solemnities, and the infinitely varied voyagings in storms and calms, and the differences among those who are born, who live together, and die. And consider, too, the life lived by others in olden time, and the life of those who will live after thee, and the life now lived among barbarous nations, and how many know not even thy name, and how many will soon forget it, and how they who perhaps now are praising thee will very soon blame thee, and that

neither a posthumous name is of any value, nor reputation, nor anything else.

31. Let there be freedom from perturbations with respect to the things which come from the external cause; and let there be justice in the things done by virtue of the internal cause, that is, let there be movement and action terminating in this, in social acts, for this is according to thy nature.

32. Thou canst remove out of the way many useless things among those which disturb thee, for they lie entirely in thy opinion; and thou wilt then gain for thyself ample space by comprehending the whole universe in thy mind, and by contemplating the eternity of time, and observing the rapid change of every several thing, how short is the time from birth to dissolution, and the illimitable time before birth as well as the equally boundless time after dissolution.

33. All that thou seest will quickly perish, and those who have been spectators of its dissolution will very soon perish too. And he who dies at the extremest old age will be brought into the same condition with him who died prematurely.

34. What are these men's leading principles, and about what kind of things are they busy, and for what kind of reasons do they love and honour? Imagine that thou seest their poor souls laid bare. When they think that they do harm by their blame or good by their praise, what an idea!

35. Loss is nothing else than change. But the universal nature delights in change, and in obedience to her all things are now done well, and from eternity have been done in like form, and will be such to time without end. What then dost thou say? That all things have been and all things always will be bad, and that no power has ever been found in so many gods to rectify these things, but the world has been condemned to be bound in never-ceasing evil? (iv. 45; vii. 18).

36. The rottenness of the matter which is the foundation of everything! water, dust, bones, filth; or again, marble rocks, the callosities of the earth; and gold and silver, the sediments; and garments, only bits of hair; and purple dye, blood; and everything else is of the same kind. And that which is of the nature of breath, is also another thing of the same kind, changing from this to that.

37. Enough of this wretched life and murmuring and apish tricks. Why art thou disturbed? What is there new in this? What unsettles thee? Is it the form of the thing? Look at it. Or is it the matter? Look at it. But besides these there is nothing. Towards the gods, then, now become at last more simple and better. It is the same whether we examine these things for a hundred years or three.

38. If any man has done wrong, the harm is his own. But perhaps he has not done wrong.

39. Either all things proceed from one intelligent source and come together as in one body, and the part ought not to find fault with what is done for the benefit of the whole; or there are only atoms, and nothing else than mixture and dispersion. Why, then, art thou disturbed? Say to the ruling faculty, Art thou dead, art thou corrupted, art thou playing the hypocrite, art thou become a beast, dost thou herd and feed with the rest?

40. Either the gods have no power or they have power. If, then, they have no power, why dost thou pray to them? But if they have power, why dost thou not pray for them to give thee the faculty of not fearing any of the things which thou fearest, or of not desiring any of the things which thou desirest, or not being pained at anything, rather than pray that any of these things should not happen or happen? for certainly if they can co-operate with men, they can co-operate for these purposes. But perhaps thou wilt say, the gods have placed them in thy power. Well, then, is it not better to use what is in thy power like a free man than to desire in a slavish and abject way what is not in thy power? And who has told thee that the gods do not aid us even in the things which are in our power? Begin, then, to pray for such things, and thou wilt see. One man prays thus: How shall I be able to lie with that woman? Do thou pray thus: How shall I not desire to lie with her? Another prays thus: How shall I be released from this? Another prays: How shall I not desire to be released? Another thus: How shall I not lose my little son? Thou thus: How shall I not be afraid to lose him? In fine, turn thy prayers this way, and see what comes.

41. Epicurus says, In my sickness my conversation was not about my bodily sufferings, nor, says he, did I talk on such subjects to those who visited me; but I continued to discourse on the nature of things

as before, keeping to this main point, how the mind, while participating in such movements as go on in the poor flesh, shall be free from perturbations and maintain its proper good. Nor did I, he says, give the physicians an opportunity of putting on solemn looks, as if they were doing something great, but my life went on well and happily. Do, then, the same that he did both in sickness, if thou art sick, and in any other circumstances; for never to desert philosophy in any events that may befall us, nor to hold trifling talk either with an ignorant man or with one unacquainted with nature, is a principle of all schools of philosophy; but to be intent only on that which thou art now doing and on the instrument by which thou doest it.

42. When thou art offended with any man's shameless conduct, immediately ask thyself, Is it possible, then, that shameless men should not be in the world? It is not possible. Do not, then, require what is impossible. For this man also is one of those shameless men who must of necessity be in the world. Let the same considerations be present to thy mind in the case of the knave, and the faithless man, and of every man who does wrong in any way. For at the same time that thou dost remind thyself that it is impossible that such kind of men should not exist, thou wilt become more kindly disposed towards every one individually. It is useful to perceive this, too, immediately when the occasion arises, what virtue nature has given to man to oppose to every wrongful act. For she has given to man, as an antidote against the stupid man, mildness, and against another kind of man some other power. And in all cases it is possible for thee to correct by teaching the man who is gone astray; for every man who errs misses his object and is gone astray. Besides wherein hast thou been injured? For thou wilt find that no one among those against whom thou art irritated has done anything by which thy mind could be made worse; but that which is evil to thee and harmful has its foundation only in the mind. And what harm is done or what is there strange, if the man who has not been instructed does the acts of an uninstructed man? Consider whether thou shouldst not rather blame thyself, because thou didst not expect such a man to err in such a way. For thou hadst means given thee by thy reason to suppose that it was likely that he would commit this error, and yet thou hast forgotten and art amazed that he has

erred. But most of all when thou blamest a man as faithless or ungrateful, turn to thyself. For the fault is manifestly thy own, whether thou didst trust that a man who had such a disposition would keep his promise, or when conferring thy kindness thou didst not confer it absolutely, nor yet in such way as to have received from thy very act all the profit. For what more dost thou want when thou hast done a man a service? Art thou not content that thou hast done something conformable to thy nature, and dost thou seek to be paid for it? Just as if the eye demanded a recompense for seeing, or the feet for walking. For as these members are formed for a particular purpose, and by working according to their several constitutions obtain what is their own; so also as man is formed by nature to acts of benevolence, when he has done anything benevolent or in any other way conducive to the common interest, he has acted conformably to his constitution, and he gets what is his own.

X

WILT thou then, my soul, never be good and simple and one and naked, more manifest than the body which surrounds thee? Wilt thou never enjoy an affectionate and contented disposition? Wilt thou never be full and without a want of any kind, longing for nothing more, nor desiring anything, either animate or inanimate, for the enjoyment of pleasures? nor yet desiring time wherein thou shalt have longer enjoyment, or place, or pleasant climate, or society of men with whom thou mayst live in harmony? but wilt thou be satisfied with thy present condition, and pleased with all that is about thee, and wilt thou convince thyself that thou hast everything and that it comes from the gods, that everything is well for thee, and will be well whatever shall please them, and whatever they shall give for the conservation of the perfect living being, the good and just and beautiful, which generates and holds together all things, and contains and embraces all things which are dissolved for the production of other like things? Wilt thou never be such that thou shalt so dwell in community with gods and men as neither to find fault with them at all, nor to be condemned by them?

2. Observe what thy nature requires, so far as thou art governed by nature only; then do it and accept it, if thy nature, so far as thou art a living being, shall not be made worse by it. And next thou must observe what thy nature requires so far as thou art a living being. And all this thou mayst allow thyself, if thy nature, so far as thou art a rational animal, shall not be made worse by it. But the rational animal is consequently also a political [social] animal. Use these rules then, and trouble thyself about nothing else.

3. Everything which happens either happens in such wise as thou art formed by nature to bear it, or as thou art not formed by nature to bear it. If then it happens to thee in such way as thou art formed by nature to bear it, do not complain, but bear it as thou art formed by nature to bear it. But if it happens in such wise as thou art not formed by nature to bear it, do not complain, for it will perish after it has consumed thee. Remember, however, that thou art formed by nature to bear everything, with respect to which it depends on thy own opinion to make it endurable and tolerable, by thinking that it is either thy interest or thy duty to do this.

4. If a man is mistaken, instruct him kindly and show him his error. But if thou art not able, blame thyself, or blame not even thyself.

5. Whatever may happen to thee, it was prepared for thee from all eternity; and the implication of causes was from eternity spinning the thread of thy being, and of that which is incident to it (iii. 11; iv. 26).

6. Whether the universe is [a concourse of] atoms, or nature [is a system], let this first be established, that I am a part of the whole which is governed by nature; next, I am in a manner intimately related to the parts which are of the same kind with myself. For remembering this, inasmuch as I am a part, I shall be discontented with none of the things which are assigned to me out of the whole; for nothing is injurious to the part, if it is for the advantage of the whole. For the whole contains nothing which is not for its advantage; and all natures indeed have this common principle, but the nature of the universe has this principle besides, that it cannot be compelled even by any external cause to generate anything harmful to itself. By remembering then that I am a part of such a whole, I

shall be content with everything that happens. And inasmuch as I am in a manner intimately related to the parts which are of the same kind with myself, I shall do nothing unsocial, but I shall rather direct myself to the things which are of the same kind with myself, and I shall turn all my efforts to the common interest, and divert them from the contrary. Now, if these things are done so, life must flow on happily, just as thou mayst observe that the life of a citizen is happy, who continues a course of action which is advantageous to his fellow-citizens, and is content with whatever the state may assign to him.

7. The parts of the whole, everything, I mean, which is naturally comprehended in the universe, must of necessity perish; but let this be understood in this sense, that they must undergo change. But if this is naturally both an evil and a necessity for the parts, the whole would not continue to exist in a good condition, the parts being subject to change and constituted so as to perish in various ways. For whether did nature herself design to do evil to the things which are parts of herself, and to make them subject to evil and of necessity fall into evil, or have such results happened without her knowing it? Both these suppositions, indeed, are incredible. But if a man should even drop the term Nature [as an efficient power], and should speak of these things as natural, even then it would be ridiculous to affirm at the same time that the parts of the whole are in their nature subject to change, and at the same time to be surprised or vexed as if something were happening contrary to nature, particularly as the dissolution of things is into those things of which each thing is composed. For there is either a dispersion of the elements out of which everything has been compounded, or a change from the solid to the earthy and from the airy to the aërial, so that these parts are taken back into the universal reason, whether this at certain periods is consumed by fire or renewed by eternal changes. And do not imagine that the solid and the airy part belong to thee from the time of generation. For all this received its accretion only yesterday, and the day before, as one may say, from the food and the air which is inspired. This, then, which has received [the accretion], changes, not that which thy mother brought forth. But suppose that this [which thy mother brought forth] implicates thee very much with

that other part, which has the peculiar quality [of change], this is nothing in fact in the way of objection to what is said.

8. When thou hast assumed these names, good, modest, true, rational, a man of equanimity, and magnanimous, take care thou dost not change these names; and if thou shouldst lose them, quickly return to them. And remember that the term Rational was intended to signify a discriminating attention to every several thing and freedom from negligence; and that Equanimity is the voluntary acceptance of the things which are assigned to thee by the common nature; and that Magnanimity is the elevation of the intelligent part above the pleasurable or painful sensations of the flesh, and above that poor thing called fame, and death, and all such things. If, then, thou maintainest thyself in the possession of these names, without desiring to be called by these names by others, thou wilt be another person and wilt enter on another life. For to continue to be such as thou hast hitherto been, and to be torn in pieces and defiled in such a life, is the character of a very stupid man and one overfond of his life, and like those half-devoured fighters with wild beasts, who, though covered with wounds and gore, still entreat to be kept to the following day, though they will be exposed in the same state to the same claws and bites. Therefore fix thyself in the possession of these few names: and if thou art able to abide in them, abide as if thou wast removed to certain islands of the Happy. But if thou shalt perceive that thou fallest out of them and dost not maintain thy hold, go courageously into some nook where thou shalt maintain them, or even depart at once from life, not in passion, but with simplicity and freedom and modesty, after doing this one [laudable] thing at least in thy life, to have gone out of it thus. In order, however, to the remembrance of these names, it will greatly help thee, if thou rememberest the gods, and that they wish not to be flattered, but wish all reasonable beings to be made like themselves; and if thou rememberest that what does the work of a fig-tree is a fig-tree, and that what does the work of a dog is a dog, and that what does the work of a bee is a bee, and that what does the work of a man is a man.

9. Mimi, war, astonishment, torpor, slavery, will daily wipe out those holy principles of thine. How many things without studying

nature dost thou imagine, and how many dost thou neglect? But it is thy duty so to look on and so to do everything, that at the same time the power of dealing with circumstances is perfected, and the contemplative faculty is exercised, and the confidence which comes from the knowledge of each several thing is maintained without showing it, but yet not concealed. For when wilt thou enjoy simplicity, when gravity, and when the knowledge of every several thing, both what it is in substance, and what place it has in the universe, and how long it is formed to exist, and of what things it is compounded, and to whom it can belong, and who are able both to give it and take it away?

10. A spider is proud when it has caught a fly, and another when he has caught a poor hare, and another when he has taken the little fish in a net, and another when he has taken wild boars, and another when he has taken bears, and another when he has taken Sarmatians. Are not these robbers, if thou examinest their opinions?

11. Acquire the contemplative way of seeing how all things change into one another, and constantly attend to it, and exercise thyself about this part [of philosophy]. For nothing is so much adapted to produce magnanimity. Such a man has put off the body, and as he sees that he must, no one knows how soon, go away from among men and leave everything here, he gives himself up entirely to just doing in all his actions, and in everything else that happens he resigns himself to the universal nature. But as to what any man shall say or think about him, or do against him, he never even thinks of it, being himself contented with these two things, with acting justly in what he now does, and being satisfied with what is now assigned to him; and he lays aside all distracting and busy pursuits, and desires nothing else than to accomplish the straight course through the law, and by accomplishing the straight course to follow God.

12. What need is there of suspicious fear, since it is in thy power to inquire what ought to be done? And if thou seest clear, go by this way content, without turning back: but if thou dost not see clear, stop and take the best advisers. But if any other things oppose thee, go on according to thy powers with due consideration, keeping to that which appears to be just. For it is best to reach this object, and if thou dost fail, let thy failure be in attempting this. He who follows

reason in all things is both tranquil and active at the same time, and also cheerful and collected.

13. Inquire of thyself as soon as thou wakest from sleep whether it will make any difference to thee, if another does what is just and right. It will make no difference (vi. 32; viii. 55).

Thou hast not forgotten, I suppose, that those who assume arrogant airs in bestowing their praise or blame on others, are such as they are at bed and at board, and thou hast not forgotten what they do, and what they avoid and what they pursue, and how they steal and how they rob, not with hands and feet, but with their most valuable part, by means of which there is produced, when a man chooses, fidelity, modesty, truth, law, a good dæmon [happiness]? (vii. 17.)

14. To her who gives and takes back all, to nature, the man who is instructed and modest says, Give what thou wilt; take back what thou wilt. And he says this not proudly, but obediently and well pleased with her.

15. Short is the little which remains to thee of life. Live as on a mountain. For it makes no difference whether a man lives there or here, if he lives everywhere in the world as in a state [political community]. Let men see, let them know a real man who lives according to nature. If they cannot endure him, let them kill him. For that is better than to live thus [as men do].

16. No longer talk at all about the kind of man that a good man ought to be, but be such.

17. Constantly contemplate the whole of time and the whole of substance, and consider that all individual things as to substance are a grain of a fig, and as to time the turning of a gimlet.

18. Look at everything that exists, and observe that it is already in dissolution and in change, and as it were putrefaction or dispersion, or that everything is so constituted by nature as to die.

19. Consider what men are when they are eating, sleeping, generating, easing themselves and so forth. Then what kind of men they are when they are imperious and arrogant, or angry and scolding from their elevated place. But a short time ago to how many they were slaves and for what things: and after a little time consider in what a condition they will be.

20. That is for the good of each thing, which the universal nature brings to each. And it is for its good at the time when nature brings it.

21. "The earth loves the shower"; and "the solemn æther loves": and the universe loves to make whatever is about to be. I say then to the universe, that I love as thou lovest. And is not this too said, that "this or that loves [is wont] to be produced"?

22. Either thou livest here and hast already accustomed thyself to it, or thou art going away, and this was thy own will; or thou art dying and hast discharged thy duty. But besides these things there is nothing. Be of good cheer, then.

23. Let this always be plain to thee, that this piece of land is like any other; and that all things here are the same with things on the top of a mountain, or on the sea-shore, or wherever thou choosest to be. For thou wilt find just what Plato says, Dwelling within the walls of a city as in a shepherd's fold on a mountain. [The three last words are omitted in the translation.]

24. What is my ruling faculty now to me? and of what nature am I now making it? and for what purpose am I now using it? is it void of understanding? is it loosed and rent asunder from social life? is it melted into and mixed with the poor flesh so as to move together with it?

25. He who flies from his master is a runaway; but the law is master, and he who breaks the law is a runaway. And he also who is grieved or angry or afraid, is dissatisfied because something has been or is or shall be of the things which are appointed by him who rules all things, and he is Law, and assigns to every man what is fit. He then who fears or is grieved or is angry is a runaway.

26. A man deposits seed in a womb and goes away, and then another cause takes it, and labours on it and makes a child. What a thing from such a material! Again, the child passes food down through the throat, and then another cause takes it and makes perception and motion, and in fine life and strength and other things; how many and how strange! Observe then the things which are produced in such a hidden way, and see the power just as we see the power which carries things downwards and upwards, not with the eyes, but still no less plainly (vii. 75).

27. Constantly consider how all things such as they now are, in time past also were; and consider that they will be the same again. And place before thy eyes entire dramas and stages of the same form, whatever thou hast learned from thy experience or from older history; for example, the whole court of Hadrianus, and the whole court of Antoninus, and the whole court of Philippus, Alexander, Crœsus; for all those were such dramas as we see now, only with different actors.

28. Imagine every man who is grieved at anything or discontented to be like a pig which is sacrificed and kicks and screams.

Like this pig also is he who on his bed in silence laments the bonds in which we are held. And consider that only to the rational animal is it given to follow voluntarily what happens; but simply to follow is a necessity imposed on all.

29. Severally on the occasion of everything that thou doest, pause and ask thyself, if death is a dreadful thing because it deprives thee of this.

30. When thou art offended at any man's fault, forthwith turn to thyself and reflect in what like manner thou dost err thyself; for example, in thinking that money is a good thing, or pleasure, or a bit of reputation, and the like. For by attending to this thou wilt quickly forget thy anger, if this consideration also is added, that the man is compelled; for what else could he do? or, if thou art able, take away from him the compulsion.

31. When thou hast seen Satyron the Socratic, think of either Eutyches or Hymen, and when thou hast seen Euphrates, think of Eutychion or Silvanus, and when thou hast seen Alciphron, think of Tropæophorus, and when thou hast seen Xenophon, think of Crito or Severus, and when thou hast looked on thyself, think of any other Cæsar, and in the case of every one do in like manner. Then let this thought be in thy mind, Where then are those men? Nowhere, or nobody knows where. For thus continuously thou wilt look at human things as smoke and nothing at all; especially if thou reflectest at the same time that what has once changed will never exist again in the infinite duration of time. But thou, in what a brief space of time is thy existence? And why art thou not content to pass through this short time in an orderly way? What matter and oppor-

tunity [for thy activity] art thou avoiding? For what else are all these things, except exercises for the reason, when it has viewed carefully and by examination into their nature the things which happen in life? Persevere then until thou shalt have made these things thy own, as the stomach which is strengthened makes all things its own, as the blazing fire makes flame and brightness out of everything that is thrown into it.

32. Let it not be in any man's power to say truly of thee that thou art not simple or that thou art not good; but let him be a liar whoever shall think anything of this kind about thee; and this is altogether in thy power. For who is he that shall hinder thee from being good and simple? Do thou only determine to live no longer, unless thou shalt be such. For neither does reason allow [thee to live], if thou art not such.

33. What is that which as to this material [our life] can be done or said in the way most conformable to reason? For whatever this may be, it is in thy power to do it or to say it, and do not make excuses that thou art hindered. Thou wilt not cease to lament till thy mind is in such a condition that, what luxury is to those who enjoy pleasure, such shall be to thee, in the matter which is subjected and presented to thee, the doing of the things which are conformable to man's constitution; for a man ought to consider as an enjoyment everything which it is in his power to do according to his own nature. And it is in his power everywhere. Now, it is not given to a cylinder to move everywhere by its own motion, nor yet to water nor to fire nor to anything else which is governed by nature or an irrational soul, for the things which check them and stand in the way are many. But intelligence and reason are able to go through everything that opposes them, and in such manner as they are formed by nature and as they choose. Place before thy eyes this facility with which the reason will be carried through all things, as fire upwards, as a stone downwards, as a cylinder down an inclined surface, and seek for nothing further. For all other obstacles either affect the body only which is a dead thing; or, except through opinion and the yielding of the reason itself, they do not crush nor do any harm of any kind; for if they did, he who felt it would im-

mediately become bad. Now, in the case of all things which have a certain constitution, whatever harm may happen to any of them, that which is so affected becomes consequently worse; but in the like case, a man becomes both better, if one may say so, and more worthy of praise by making a right use of these accidents. And finally remember that nothing harms him who is really a citizen, which does not harm the state; nor yet does anything harm the state which does not harm law [order]; and of these things which are called misfortunes not one harms law. What then does not harm law does not harm either state or citizen.

34. To him who is penetrated by true principles even the briefest precept is sufficient, and any common precept, to remind him that he should be free from grief and fear. For example:

> Leaves, some the wind scatters on the ground—
> So is the race of men.

Leaves, also, are thy children; and leaves, too, are they who cry out as if they were worthy of credit and bestow their praise, or on the contrary curse, or secretly blame and sneer; and leaves, in like manner, are those who shall receive and transmit a man's fame to aftertimes. For all such things as these "are produced in the season of spring," as the poet says; then the wind casts them down; then the forest produces other leaves in their places. But a brief existence is common to all things, and yet thou avoidest and pursuest all things as if they would be eternal. A little time, and thou shalt close thy eyes; and him who has attended thee to thy grave another soon will lament.

35. The healthy eye ought to see all visible things and not to say, I wish for green things; for this is the condition of a diseased eye. And the healthy hearing and smelling ought to be ready to perceive all that can be heard and smelled. And the healthy stomach ought to be with respect to all food just as the mill with respect to all things which it is formed to grind. And accordingly the healthy understanding ought to be prepared for everything which happens; but that which says, Let my dear children live, and let all men praise whatever I may do, is an eye which seeks for green things, or teeth which seek for soft things.

36. There is no man so fortunate that there shall not be by him when he is dying some who are pleased with what is going to happen. Suppose that he was a good and wise man, will there not be at last some one to say to himself, Let us at last breathe freely, being relieved from this schoolmaster? It is true that he was harsh to none of us, but I perceived that he tacitly condemns us.—This is what is said of a good man. But in our own case how many other things are there for which there are many who wish to get rid of us. Thou wilt consider this then when thou art dying, and thou wilt depart more contentedly by reflecting thus: I am going away from such a life, in which even my associates in behalf of whom I have striven so much, prayed, and cared, themselves wish me to depart, hoping perchance to get some little advantage by it. Why, then, should a man cling to a longer stay here? Do not, however, for this reason go away less kindly disposed to them, but preserving thy own character, and friendly and benevolent and mild, and on the other hand not as if thou wast torn away; but as when a man dies a quiet death, the poor soul is easily separated from the body, such also ought thy departure from men to be, for nature united thee to them and associated thee. But does she now dissolve the union? Well, I am separated as from kinsmen, not, however, dragged resisting, but without compulsion; for this too is one of the things according to nature.

37. Accustom thyself as much as possible on the occasion of anything being done by any person to inquire with thyself, For what object is this man doing this? but begin with thyself, and examine thyself first.

38. Remember that this which pulls the strings is the thing which is hidden within: this is the power of persuasion, this is life; this, if one may so say, is man. In contemplating thyself never include the vessel which surrounds thee, and these instruments which are attached about it. For they are like to an ax, differing only in this, that they grow to the body. For indeed there is no more use in these parts without the cause which moves and checks them than in the weaver's shuttle, and the writer's pen, and the driver's whip.

XI

THESE are the properties of the rational soul: it sees itself, analyzes itself, and makes itself such as it chooses; the fruit which it bears itself enjoys—for the fruits of plants and that in animals which corresponds to fruits others enjoy—it obtains its own end, wherever the limit of life may be fixed. Not as in a dance and in a play and in suchlike things, where the whole action is incomplete, if anything cuts it short; but in every part and wherever it may be stopped, it makes what has been set before it full and complete, so that it can say, I have what is my own. And further it traverses the whole universe, and the surrounding vacuum, and surveys its form, and it extends itself into the infinity of time, and embraces and comprehends the periodical renovation of all things, and it comprehends that those who come after us will see nothing new, nor have those before us seen anything more, but in a manner he who is forty years old, if he has any understanding at all, has seen by virtue of the uniformity that prevails all things which have been and all that will be. This toc is a property of the rational soul, love of one's neighbour, and truth and modesty, and to value nothing more than itself, which is also the property of Law. Thus then right reason differs not at all from the reason of justice.

2. Thou wilt set little value on pleasing song and dancing and the pancratium, if thou wilt distribute the melody of the voice into its several sounds, and ask thyself as to each, if thou art mastered by this; for thou wilt be prevented by shame from confessing it: and in the matter of dancing, if at each movement and attitude thou wilt do the same; and the like also in the matter of the pancratium. In all things, then, except virtue and the acts of virtue, remember to apply thyself to their several parts, and by this division to come to value them little: and apply this rule also to thy whole life.

3. What a soul that is which is ready, if at any moment it must be separated from the body, and ready either to be extinguished or dispersed or continue to exist; but so that this readiness comes from a man's own judgment, not from mere obstinacy, as with the Christians, but considerately and with dignity and in a way to persuade another, without tragic show.

4. Have I done something for the general interest? Well, then, I have had my reward. Let this always be present to thy mind, and never stop [doing such good].

5. What is thy art? to be good. And how is this accomplished well except by general principles, some about the nature of the universe, and others about the proper constitution of man?

6. At first tragedies were brought on the stage as means of reminding men of the things which happen to them, and that it is according to nature for things to happen so, and that, if you are delighted with what is shown on the stage, you should not be troubled with that which takes place on the larger stage. For you see that these things must be accomplished thus, and that even they bear them who cry out, "O Cithæron." And, indeed, some things are said well by the dramatic writers, of which kind is the following especially—

> Me and my children if the gods neglect,
> This has its reason too.

And again—

> We must not chafe and fret at that which happens.

And—

> Life's harvest reap like the wheat's fruitful ear.

And other things of the same kind.

After tragedy the old comedy was introduced, which had a magisterial freedom of speech, and by its very plainness of speaking was useful in reminding men to beware of insolence; and for this purpose too Diogenes used to take from these writers.

But as to the middle comedy which came next, observe what it was, and again, for what object the new comedy was introduced, which gradually sunk down into a mere mimic artifice. That some good things are said even by these writers, everybody knows: but the whole plan of such poetry and dramaturgy, to what end does it look!

7. How plain does it appear that there is not another condition of life so well suited for philosophizing as this in which thou now happenest to be.

8. A branch cut off from the adjacent branch must of necessity

be cut off from the whole tree also. So too a man when he is separated from another man has fallen off from the whole social community. Now as to a branch, another cuts it off, but a man by his own act separates himself from his neighbour when he hates him and turns away from him, and he does not know that he has at the same time cut himself off from the whole social system. Yet he has this privilege certainly from Zeus who framed society, for it is in our power to grow again to that which is near to us, and again to become a part which helps to make up the whole. However, if it often happens, this kind of separation, it makes it difficult for that which detaches itself to be brought to unity and to be restored to its former condition. Finally, the branch, which from the first grew together with the tree, and has continued to have one life with it, is not like that which after being cut off is then ingrafted, for this is something like what the gardeners mean when they say that it grows with the rest of the tree, but that it has not the same mind with it.

9. As those who try to stand in thy way when thou art proceeding according to right reason, will not be able to turn thee aside from thy proper action, so neither let them drive thee from thy benevolent feelings towards them, but be on thy guard equally in both matters, not only in the matter of steady judgment and action, but also in the matter of gentleness towards those who try to hinder or otherwise trouble thee. For this also is a weakness, to be vexed at them, as well as to be diverted from thy course of action and to give way through fear; for both are equally deserters from their post, the man who does it through fear, and the man who is alienated from him who is by nature a kinsman and a friend.

10. There is no nature which is inferior to art, for the arts imitate the natures of things. But if this is so, that nature which is the most perfect and the most comprehensive of all natures, cannot fall short of the skill of art. Now all arts do the inferior things for the sake of the superior; therefore the universal nature does so too. And, indeed, hence is the origin of justice, and in justice the other virtues have their foundation: for justice will not be observed, if we either care for middle things [things indifferent], or are easily deceived and careless and changeable (v. 16, 30; vii. 55).

11. If the things do not come to thee, the pursuits and avoidances of which disturb thee, still in a manner thou goest to them. Let then thy judgment about them be at rest, and they will remain quiet, and thou wilt not be seen either pursuing or avoiding.

12. The spherical form of the soul maintains its figure, when it is neither extended towards any object, nor contracted inwards, nor dispersed nor sinks down, but is illuminated by light, by which it sees the truth, the truth of all things and the truth that is in itself (viii. 41, 45; xii. 3).

13. Suppose any man shall despise me. Let him look to that himself. But I will look to this, that I be not discovered doing or saying anything deserving of contempt. Shall any man hate me? Let him look to it. But I will be mild and benevolent towards every man, and ready to show even him his mistake, not reproachfully, nor yet as making a display of my endurance, but nobly and honestly, like the great Phocion, unless indeed he only assumed it. For the interior [parts] ought to be such, and a man ought to be seen by the gods neither dissatisfied with anything nor complaining. For what evil is it to thee, if thou art now doing what is agreeable to thy own nature, and art satisfied with that which at this moment is suitable to the nature of the universe, since thou art a human being placed at thy post in order that what is for the common advantage may be done in some way?

14. Men despise one another and flatter one another; and men wish to raise themselves above one another, and crouch before one another.

15. How unsound and insincere is he who says, I have determined to deal with thee in a fair way.—What art thou doing, man? There is no occasion to give this notice. It will soon show itself by acts. The voice ought to be plainly written on the forehead. Such as a man's character is, he immediately shows it in his eyes, just as he who is beloved forthwith reads everything in the eyes of lovers. The man who is honest and good ought to be exactly like a man who smells strong, so that the bystander as soon as he comes near him must smell whether he choose or not. But the affectation of simplicity is like a crooked stick. Nothing is more disgraceful than a wolfish

friendship [false friendship]. Avoid this most of all. The good and simple and benevolent show all these things in the eyes, and there is no mistaking.

16. As to living in the best way, this power is in the soul, if it be indifferent to things which are indifferent. And it will be indifferent, if it looks on each of these things separately and all together, and if it remembers that not one of them produces in us an opinion about itself, nor comes to us; but these things remain immovable, and it is we ourselves who produce the judgments about them, and, as we may say, write them in ourselves, it being in our power not to write them, and it being in our power, if perchance these judgments have imperceptibly got admission to our minds, to wipe them out; and if we remember also that such attention will only be for a short time, and then life will be at an end. Besides, what trouble is there at all in doing this? For if these things are according to nature, rejoice in them, and they will be easy to thee: but if contrary to nature, seek what is conformable to thy own nature, and strive towards this, even if it bring no reputation; for every man is allowed to seek his own good.

17. Consider whence each thing is come, and of what it consists, and into what it changes, and what kind of a thing it will be when it has changed, and that it will sustain no harm.

18. [If any have offended against thee, consider first]: What is my relation to men, and that we are made for one another; and in another respect, I was made to be set over them, as a ram over the flock or a bull over the herd. But examine the matter from first principles, from this: If all things are not mere atoms, it is nature which orders all things: if this is so, the inferior things exist for the sake of the superior, and these for the sake of one another (ii. 1; ix. 39; v. 16; iii. 4).

Second, consider what kind of men they are at table, in bed, and so forth; and particularly, under what compulsions in respect of opinions they are; and as to their acts, consider with what pride they do what they do (viii. 14; ix. 34).

Third, that if men do rightly what they do, we ought not to be displeased; but if they do not right, it is plain that they do so involuntarily and in ignorance. For as every soul is unwillingly deprived of the truth, so also is it unwillingly deprived of the power of behaving to each man according to his deserts. Accordingly men are pained when they are called unjust, ungrateful, and greedy, and in a word wrong-doers to their neighbours (vii. 62, 63; ii. 1; vii. 26; viii. 29).

Fourth, consider that thou also doest many things wrong, and that thou art a man like others; and even if thou dost abstain from certain faults, still thou hast the disposition to commit them, though either through cowardice, or concern about reputation or some such mean motive, thou dost abstain from such faults (i. 17).

Fifth, consider that thou dost not even understand whether men are doing wrong or not, for many things are done with a certain reference to circumstances. And, in short, a man must learn a great deal to enable him to pass a correct judgment on another man's acts (ix. 38; iv. 51).

Sixth, consider when thou art much vexed or grieved, that man's life is only a moment, and after a short time we are all laid out dead (vii. 58; iv. 48).

Seventh, that it is not men's acts which disturb us, for those acts have their foundation in men's ruling principles, but it is our own opinions which disturb us. Take away these opinions then, and resolve to dismiss thy judgment about an act as if it were something grievous, and thy anger is gone. How then shall I take away these opinions? By reflecting that no wrongful act of another brings shame on thee: for unless that which is shameful is alone bad, thou also must of necessity do many things wrong, and become a robber and everything else (v. 25; vii. 16).

Eighth, consider how much more pain is brought on us by the anger and vexation caused by such acts than by the acts themselves, at which we are angry and vexed (iv. 39, 49; vii. 24).

Ninth, consider that a good disposition is invincible, if it be genuine, and not an affected smile and acting a part. For what will the most violent man do to thee, if thou continuest to be of a kind disposition towards him, and if, as opportunity offers, thou gently admonishest him and calmly correctest his errors at the very time when he is trying to do thee harm, saying, Not so, my child: we are constituted by nature for something else: I shall certainly not be injured, but thou art injuring thyself, my child.—And show him with gentle tact and by general principles that this is so, and that even bees do not do as he does, nor any animals which are formed by nature to be gregarious. And thou must do this neither with any double meaning nor in the way of reproach, but affectionately and without any rancour in thy soul; and not as if thou wert lecturing him, nor yet that any bystander may admire, but either when he is alone, and if others are present. . .[1]

Remember these nine rules, as if thou hadst received them as a gift from the Muses, and begin at last to be a man while thou livest. But thou must equally avoid flattering men and being vexed at them, for both are unsocial and lead to harm. And let this truth be present to thee in the excitement of anger, that to be moved by passion is not manly, but that mildness and gentleness, as they are more agreeable to human nature, so also are they more manly; and he who possesses these qualities possesses strength, nerves and courage, and not the man who is subject to fits of passion and discontent. For in the same degree in which a man's mind is nearer to freedom from all passion, in the same degree also is it nearer to strength: and as the sense of pain is a characteristic of weakness, so also is anger. For he who yields to pain and he who yields to anger, both are wounded and both submit.

But if thou wilt, receive also a tenth present from the leader of the [Muses, Apollo], and it is this—that to expect bad men not to do wrong is madness, for he who expects this desires an impossibility. But to allow men to behave so to others, and to expect them not to do thee any wrong, is irrational and tyrannical.

19. There are four principal aberrations of the superior faculty against which thou shouldst be constantly on thy guard, and when thou hast detected them, thou shouldst wipe them out and say on each occasion thus: this thought is not necessary: this tends to destroy social union: this which thou art going to say comes not from the real thoughts; for thou shouldst consider it among the most absurd of things for a man not to speak from his real thoughts. But the fourth is when thou shalt reproach thyself for anything, for this is an evidence of the diviner part within thee being overpowered and

[1] It appears that there is a defect in the text here.

yielding to the less honourable and to the perishable part, the body, and to its gross pleasures (iv. 24; ii. 16).

20. Thy aërial part and all the fiery parts which are mingled in thee, though by nature they have an upward tendency, still in obedience to the disposition of the universe they are overpowered here in the compound mass [the body]. And also the whole of the earthy part in thee and the watery, though their tendency is downwards, still are raised up and occupy a position which is not their natural one. In this manner then the elemental parts obey the universal, for when they have been fixed in any place perforce they remain there until again the universal shall sound the signal for dissolution. Is it not then strange that thy intelligent part only should be disobedient and discontented with its own place? And yet no force is imposed on it, but only those things which are conformable to its nature: still it does not submit, but is carried in the opposite direction. For the movement towards injustice and intemperance and to anger and grief and fear is nothing else than the act of one who deviates from nature. And also when the ruling faculty is discontented with anything that happens, then too it deserts its post: for it is constituted for piety and reverence towards the gods no less than for justice. For these qualities also are comprehended under the generic term of contentment with the constitution of things, and indeed they are prior to acts of justice.

21. He who has not one and always the same object in life, cannot be one and the same all through his life. But what I have said is not enough, unless this also is added, what this object ought to be. For as there is not the same opinion about all the things which in some way or other are considered by the majority to be good, but only about some certain things, that is, things which concern the common interest; so also ought we to propose to ourselves an object which shall be of a common kind [social] and political. For he who directs all his own efforts to this object, will make all his acts alike, and thus will always be the same.

22. Think of the country mouse and of the town mouse, and of the alarm and trepidation of the town mouse.

23. Socrates used to call the opinions of the many by the name of Lamiæ, bugbears to frighten children.

24. The Lacedæmonians at their public spectacles used to set seats in the shade for strangers, but themselves sat down anywhere.

25. Socrates excused himself to Perdiccas for not going to him, saying, It is because I would not perish by the worst of all ends, that is, I would not receive a favour and then be unable to return it.

26. In the writings of the [Ephesians] there was this precept, constantly to think of some one of the men of former times who practised virtue.

27. The Pythagoreans bid us in the morning look to the heavens that we may be reminded of those bodies which continually do the same things and in the same manner perform their work, and also be reminded of their purity and nudity. For there is no veil over a star.

28. Consider what a man Socrates was when he dressed himself in a skin, after Xanthippe had taken his cloak and gone out, and what Socrates said to his friends who were ashamed of him and drew back from him when they saw him dressed thus.

29. Neither in writing nor in reading wilt thou be able to lay down rules for others before thou shalt have first learned to obey rules thyself. Much more is this so in life.

30. A slave thou art: free speech is not for thee.

31. —And my heart laughed within (Od. ix. 413).

32. And virtue they will curse speaking harsh words (Hesiod, "Works and Days," 184).

33. To look for the fig in winter is a madman's act: such is he who looks for his child when it is no longer allowed (Epictetus, iii. 24, 87).

34. When a man kisses his child, said Epictetus, he should whisper to himself, "To-morrow perchance thou wilt die."—But those are words of bad omen.—"No word is a word of bad omen," said Epictetus, "which expresses any work of nature; or if it is so, it is also a word of bad omen to speak of the ears of corn being reaped" (Epictetus, iii. 24, 88).

35. The unripe grape, the ripe bunch, the dried grape all are changes, not into nothing, but into something which exists not yet (Epictetus, iii. 24).

36. No man can rob us of our free will (Epictetus, iii. 22, 105).

37. Epictetus also said, a man must discover an art [or rules]

with respect to giving his assent; and in respect to his movements he must be careful that they be made with regard to circumstances, that they be consistent with social interests, that they have regard to the value of the object; and as to sensual desire, he should altogether keep away from it; and as to avoidance [aversion], he should not show it with respect to any of the things which are not in our power.

38. The dispute then, he said, is not about any common matter, but about being mad or not.

39. Socrates used to say, What do you want? Souls of rational men or irrational?—Souls of rational men.—Of what rational men? Sound or unsound?—Sound.—Why then do you not seek for them? —Because we have them.—Why then do you fight and quarrel?

XII

ALL those things at which thou wishest to arrive by a circuitous road, thou canst have now, if thou dost not refuse them to thyself. And this means, if thou wilt take no notice of all the past, and trust the future to providence, and direct the present only conformably to piety and justice. Conformably to piety, that thou mayest be content with the lot which is assigned to thee, for nature designed it for thee and thee for it. Conformably to justice, that thou mayest always speak the truth freely and without disguise, and do the things which are agreeable to law and according to the worth of each. And let neither another man's wickedness hinder thee, nor opinion nor voice, nor yet the sensations of the poor flesh which has grown about thee; for the passive part will look to this. If then, whatever the time may be when thou shalt be near to thy departure, neglecting everything else thou shalt respect only thy ruling faculty and the divinity within thee, and if thou shalt be afraid not because thou must sometime cease to live, but if thou shalt fear never to have begun to live according to nature—then thou wilt be a man worthy of the universe which has produced thee, and thou wilt cease to be a stranger in thy native land, and to wonder at things which happen daily as if they were something unexpected, and to be dependent on this or that.

2. God sees the minds [ruling principles] of all men bared of the material vesture and rind and impurities. For with his intellec-

tual part alone he touches the intelligence only which has flowed and been derived from himself into these bodies. And if thou also usest thyself to do this, thou wilt rid thyself of thy much trouble. For he who regards not the poor flesh which envelops him, surely will not trouble himself by looking after raiment and dwelling and fame and suchlike externals and show.

3. The things are three of which thou art composed, a little body, a little breath [life], intelligence. Of these the first two are thine, so far as it is thy duty to take care of them; but the third alone is properly thine. Therefore, if thou shalt separate from thyself, that is, from thy understanding, whatever others do or say, and whatever thou hast done or said thyself, and whatever future things trouble thee because they may happen, and whatever in the body which envelops thee, or in the breath [life], which is by nature associated with the body, is attached to thee independent of thy will, and whatever the external circumfluent vortex whirls round, so that the intellectual power exempt from the things of fate can live pure and free by itself, doing what is just and accepting what happens and saying the truth: if thou wilt separate, I say, from this ruling faculty the things which are attached to it by the impressions of sense, and the things of time to come and of time that is past, and wilt make thyself like Empedocles' sphere—

All round, and in its joyous rest reposing;

and if thou shalt strive to live only what is really thy life, that is, the present, then thou wilt be able to pass that portion of life which remains for thee up to the time of thy death, free from perturbations, nobly, and obedient to thy own dæmon [to the god that is within thee] (ii. 13, 17; iii. 5, 6; xi. 12).

4. I have often wondered how it is that every man loves himself more than all the rest of men, but yet sets less value on his own opinion of himself than on the opinion of others. If then a god or a wise teacher should present himself to a man and bid him to think of nothing and to design nothing which he would not express as soon as he conceived it, he could not endure it even for a single day. So much more respect have we to what our neighbours shall think of us than to what we shall think of ourselves.

5. How can it be that the gods, after having arranged all things well and benevolently for mankind, have overlooked this alone, that some men and very good men, and men who, as we may say, have had most communion with the divinity, and through pious acts and religious observances have been most intimate with the divinity, when they have once died should never exist again, but should be completely extinguished?

But if this is so, be assured that if it ought to have been otherwise, the gods would have done it. For if it were just, it would also be possible; and if it were according to nature, nature would have had it so. But because it is not so, if in fact it is not so, be thou convinced that it ought not to have been so:—for thou seest even of thyself that in this inquiry thou art disputing with the deity; and we should not thus dispute with the gods, unless they were most excellent and most just;—but if this is so, they would not have allowed anything in the ordering of the universe to be neglected unjustly and irrationally.

6. Practise thyself even in the things which thou despairest of accomplishing. For even the left hand, which is ineffectual for all other things for want of practice, holds the bridle more vigorously than the right hand; for it has been practised in this.

7. Consider in what condition, both in body and soul, a man should be when he is overtaken by death; and consider the shortness of life, the boundless abyss of time, past and future, the feebleness of all matter.

8. Contemplate the formative principles [forms] of things bare of their coverings; the purposes of actions; consider what pain is, what pleasure is, and death, and fame; who is to himself the cause of his uneasiness; how no man is hindered by another; that everything is opinion.

9. In the application of thy principles thou must be like the pancratiast, not like the gladiator; for the gladiator lets fall the sword which he uses and is killed; but the other always has his hand, and needs to do nothing else than use it.

10. See what things are in themselves, dividing them into matter, form and purpose.

11. What a power man has to do nothing except what God will approve, and to accept all that God may give him.

12. With respect to that which happens conformably to nature, we ought to blame neither gods, for they do nothing wrong either voluntarily or involuntarily, nor men, for they do nothing wrong except involuntarily. Consequently we should blame nobody (ii. 11, 12, 13; vii. 62; viii. 17).

13. How ridiculous and what a stranger he is who is surprised at anything which happens in life.

14. Either there is a fatal necessity and invincible order, or a kind providence, or a confusion without a purpose and without a director (iv. 27). If then there is an invincible necessity, why dost thou resist? But if there is a providence which allows itself to be propitiated, make thyself worthy of the help of the divinity. But if there is a confusion without a governor, be content that in such a tempest thou hast in thyself a certain ruling intelligence. And even if the tempest carry thee away, let it carry away the poor flesh, the poor breath, everything else; for the intelligence at least it will not carry away.

15. Does the light of the lamp shine without losing its splendour until it is extinguished; and shall the truth which is in thee and justice and temperance be extinguished [before thy death]?

16. When a man has presented the appearance of having done wrong, [say], How then do I know if this is a wrongful act? And even if he has done wrong, how do I know that he has not condemned himself? and so this is like tearing his own face. Consider that he who would not have the bad man do wrong, is like the man who would not have the fig-tree to bear juice in the figs and infants to cry and the horse to neigh, and whatever else must of necessity be. For what must a man do who has such a character? If then thou art irritable, cure this man's disposition.

17. If it is not right, do not do it: if it is not true, do not say it. [For let thy efforts be.—][1]

18. In everything always observe what the thing is which produces for thee an appearance, and resolve it by dividing it into the

[1]There is something wrong here, or incomplete.

formal, the material, the purpose, and the time within which it must end.

19. Perceive at last that thou hast in thee something better and more divine than the things which cause the various effects, and as it were pull thee by the strings. What is there now in my mind? is it fear, or suspicion, or desire, or anything of the kind? (v. 11.)

20. First, do nothing inconsiderately, nor without a purpose. Second, make thy acts refer to nothing else than to a social end.

21. Consider that before long thou wilt be nobody and nowhere, nor will any of the things exist which thou now seest, nor any of those who are now living. For all things are formed by nature to change and be turned and to perish in order that other things in continuous succession may exist (ix. 28).

22. Consider that everything is opinion, and opinion is in thy power. Take away then, when thou choosest, thy opinion, and like a mariner, who has doubled the promontory, thou wilt find calm, everything stable, and a waveless bay.

23. Any one activity, whatever it may be, when it has ceased at its proper time, suffers no evil because it has ceased; nor he who has done this act, does he suffer any evil for this reason that the act has ceased. In like manner then the whole which consists of all the acts, which is our life, if it cease at its proper time, suffers no evil for this reason that it has ceased; nor he who has terminated this series at the proper time, has he been ill dealt with. But the proper time and the limit nature fixes, sometimes as in old age the peculiar nature of man, but always the universal nature, by the change of whose parts the whole universe continues ever young and perfect. And everything which is useful to the universal is always good and in season. Therefore the termination of life for every man is no evil, because neither is it shameful, since it is both independent of the will and not opposed to the general interest, but it is good, since it is seasonable and profitable to and congruent with the universal. For thus too he is moved by the deity who is moved in the same manner with the deity and moved towards the same things in his mind.

24. These three principles thou must have in readiness. In the things which thou doest do nothing either inconsiderately or otherwise than as justice herself would act; but with respect to what may

happen to thee from without, consider that it happens either by chance or according to providence, and thou must neither blame chance nor accuse providence. Second, consider what every being is from the seed to the time of its receiving a soul, and from the reception of a soul to the giving back of the same, and of what things every being is compounded and into what things it is resolved. Third, if thou shouldst suddenly be raised up above the earth, and shouldst look down on human beings, and observe the variety of them how great it is, and at the same time also shouldst see at a glance how great is the number of beings who dwell all around in the air and the æther, consider that as often as thou shouldst be raised up, thou wouldst see the same things, sameness of form and shortness of duration. Are these things to be proud of?

25. Cast away opinion: thou art saved. Who then hinders thee from casting it away?

26. When thou art troubled about anything, thou hast forgotten this, that all things happen according to the universal nature; and forgotten this, that a man's wrongful act is nothing to thee; and further thou hast forgotten this, that everything which happens, always happened so and will happen so, and now happens so everywhere; forgotten this too, how close is the kinship between a man and the whole human race, for it is a community, not of a little blood or seed, but of intelligence. And thou hast forgotten this too, that every man's intelligence is a god, and is an efflux of the deity; and forgotten this, that nothing is a man's own, but that his child and his body and his very soul came from the deity; forgotten this, that everything is opinion; and lastly thou hast forgotten that every man lives the present time only, and loses only this.

27. Constantly bring to thy recollection those who have complained greatly about anything, those who have been most conspicuous by the greatest fame or misfortunes or enmities or fortunes of any kind: then think where are they all now? Smoke and ash and a tale, or not even a tale. And let there be present to thy mind also everything of this sort, how Fabius Catullinus lived in the country, and Lucius Lupus in his gardens, and Stertinius at Baiæ, and Tiberius at Capreæ, and Velius Rufus [or Rufus at Velia]; and in fine think of the eager pursuit of anything conjoined with

pride; and how worthless everything is after which men violently strain; and how much more philosophical it is for a man in the opportunities presented to him to show himself just, temperate, obedient to the gods, and to do this with all simplicity: for the pride which is proud of its want of pride is the most intolerable of all.

28. To those who ask, Where hast thou seen the gods or how dost thou comprehend that they exist and so worshipest them? I answer, in the first place, they may be seen even with the eyes; in the second place, neither have I seen even my own soul and yet I honour it. Thus then with respect to the gods, from what I constantly experience of their power, from this I comprehend that they exist and I venerate them.

29. The safety of life is this, to examine everything all through, what it is itself, what is its material, what the formal part; with all thy soul to do justice and to say the truth. What remains except to enjoy life by joining one good thing to another so as not to leave even the smallest intervals between?

30. There is one light of the sun, though it is interrupted by walls, mountains, and other things infinite. There is one common substance, though it is distributed among countless bodies which have their several qualities. There is one soul, though it is distributed among infinite natures and individual circumscriptions [or individuals]. There is one intelligent soul, though it seems to be divided. Now in the things which have been mentioned all the other parts, such as those which are air and matter, are without sensation and have no fellowship: and yet even these parts the intelligent principle holds together, and the gravitation towards the same. But intellect in a peculiar manner tends to that which is of the same kin, and combines with it, and the feeling for communion is not interrupted.

31. What dost thou wish? to continue to exist? Well, dost thou wish to have sensation? movement? growth? and then again to cease to grow? to use thy speech? to think? What is there of all these things which seem to thee worth desiring? But if it is easy to set little value on all these things, turn to that which remains, which is to follow reason and god. But it is inconsistent with honouring reason and god to be troubled because by death a man will be deprived of the other things.

32. How small a part of the boundless and unfathomable time is assigned to every man! for it is very soon swallowed up in the eternal. And how small a part of the whole substance! and how small a part of the universal soul! and on what a small clod of the whole earth thou creepest! Reflecting on all this, consider nothing to be great, except to act as thy nature leads thee, and to endure that which the common nature brings.

33. How does the ruling faculty make use of itself? for all lies in this. But everything else, whether it is in the power of thy will or not, is only lifeless ashes and smoke.

34. This reflection is most adapted to move us to contempt of death, that even those who think pleasure to be a good and pain an evil still have despised it.

35. The man to whom that only is good which comes in due season, and to whom it is the same thing whether he has done more or fewer acts conformable to right reason, and to whom it makes no difference whether he contemplates the world for a longer or a shorter time—for this man neither is death a terrible thing (iii. 7; vi. 23; x. 20; xii. 23).

36. Man, thou hast been a citizen in this great state [the world]: what difference does it make to thee whether for five years [or three]? for that which is conformable to the laws is just for all. Where is the hardship then, if no tyrant nor yet an unjust judge sends thee away from the state, but nature who brought thee into it? the same as if a prætor who has employed an actor dismisses him from the stage.—"But I have not finished the five acts, but only three of them."—Thou sayest well, but in life the three acts are the whole drama; for what shall be a complete drama is determined by him who was once the cause of its composition, and now of its dissolution: but thou art the cause of neither. Depart then satisfied, for he also who releases thee is satisfied.

M. AURELIUS ANTONINUS

BY GEORGE LONG, M.A.

M. ANTONINUS was born at Rome A.D. 121, on the 26th of April. His father Annius Verus died while he was prætor. His mother was Domitia Calvilla, also named Lucilla. The Emperor T. Antoninus Pius married Annia Galeria Faustina, the sister of Annius Verus, and was consequently the uncle of M. Antoninus. When Hadrian adopted Antoninus Pius and declared him his successor in the empire, Antoninus Pius adopted both L. Ceionius Commodus, the son of Ælius Cæsar, and M. Antoninus, whose original name was M. Annius Verus. Antoninus then took the name of M. Ælius Aurelius Verus, to which was added the title of Cæsar in A.D. 139: the name Ælius belonged to Hadrian's family, and Aurelius was the name of Antoninus Pius. When M. Antoninus became Augustus, he dropped the name of Verus and took the name of Antoninus. Accordingly he is generally named M. Aurelius Antoninus or simply M. Antoninus.

The youth was most carefully brought up. He thanks the gods (I. 17) that he had good grandfathers, good parents, a good sister, good teachers, good associates, good kinsmen and friends, nearly everything good. He had the happy fortune to witness the example of his uncle and adoptive father Antoninus Pius, and he has recorded in his work (I. 16; VI. 30) the virtues of this excellent man and prudent ruler. Like many young Romans he tried his hand at poetry and studied rhetoric. Herodes Atticus and M. Cornelius Fronto were his teachers in eloquence. There are extant letters between Fronto and Marcus,[1] which show the great affection of the pupil for the master, and the master's great hopes of his industrious pupil. M. Antoninus mentions Fronto (I. 11) among those to whom he was indebted for his education.

[1] M. Cornelii Frontonis Reliquiæ, Berlin, 1816. There are a few letters between Fronto and Antoninus Pius.

When he was eleven years old, he assumed the dress of philosophers, something plain and coarse, became a hard student, and lived a most laborious, abstemious life, even so far as to injure his health. Finally, he abandoned poetry and rhetoric for philosophy, and he attached himself to the sect of the Stoics. But he did not neglect the study of law, which was a useful preparation for the high place which he was designed to fill. His teacher was L. Volusianus Mæcianus, a distinguished jurist. We must suppose that he learned the Roman discipline of arms, which was a necessary part of the education of a man who afterwards led his troops to battle against a warlike race.

Antoninus has recorded in his first book the names of his teachers and the obligations which he owed to each of them. The way in which he speaks of what he learned from them might seem to savour of vanity or self-praise, if we look carelessly at the way in which he has expressed himself; but if any one draws this conclusion, he will be mistaken. Antoninus means to commemorate the merits of his several teachers, what they taught and what a pupil might learn from them. Besides, this book, like the eleven other books, was for his own use, and if we may trust the note at the end of the first book, it was written during one of M. Antoninus' campaigns against the Quadi, at a time when the commemoration of the virtues of his illustrious teachers might remind him of their lessons and the practical uses which he might derive from them.

Among his teachers of philosophy was Sextus of Chæroneia, a grandson of Plutarch. What he learned from this excellent man is told by himself (I. 9). His favourite teacher was Q. Junius Rusticus (I. 7), a philosopher and also a man of practical good sense in public affairs. Rusticus was the adviser of Antoninus after he became emperor. Young men who are destined for high places are not often fortunate in those who are about them, their companions and teachers; and I do not know any example of a young prince having had an education which can be compared with that of M. Antoninus. Such a body of teachers distinguished by their acquirements and their character will hardly be collected again; and as to the pupil, we have not had one like him since.

Hadrian died in July, A.D. 138, and was succeeded by Antoninus Pius. M. Antoninus married Faustina, his cousin, the daughter of

Pius, probably about A.D. 146, for he had a daughter born in 147. He received from his adoptive father the title of Cæsar and was associated with him in the administration of the state. The father and the adopted son lived together in perfect friendship and confidence. Antoninus was a dutiful son, and the emperor Pius loved and esteemed him.

Antoninus Pius died in March, A.D. 161. The Senate, it is said, urged M. Antoninus to take the sole administration of the empire, but he associated with himself the other adopted son of Pius, L. Ceionius Commodus, who is generally called L. Verus. Thus Rome for the first time had two emperors. Verus was an indolent man of pleasure and unworthy of his station. Antoninus however bore with him, and it is said that Verus had sense enough to pay to his colleague the respect due to his character. A virtuous emperor and a loose partner lived together in peace, and their alliance was strengthened by Antoninus giving to Verus for wife his daughter Lucilla.

The reign of Antoninus was first troubled by a Parthian war, in which Verus was sent to command, but he did nothing, and the success that was obtained by the Romans in Armenia and on the Euphrates and Tigris was due to his generals. This Parthian war ended in A.D. 165. Aurelius and Verus had a triumph (A.D. 166) for the victories in the east. A pestilence followed which carried off great numbers in Rome and Italy, and spread to the west of Europe.

The north of Italy was also threatened by the rude people beyond the Alps from the borders of Gallia to the eastern side of the Hadriatic. These barbarians attempted to break into Italy, as the Germanic nations had attempted near three hundred years before; and the rest of the life of Antoninus with some intervals was employed in driving back the invaders. In 169 Verus suddenly died, and Antoninus administered the state alone.

During the German wars Antoninus resided for three years on the Danube at Carnuntum. The Marcomanni were driven out of Pannonia and almost destroyed in their retreat across the Danube; and in A.D. 174 the emperor gained a great victory over the Quadi.

In A.D. 175 Avidius Cassius, a brave and skilful Roman commander who was at the head of the troops in Asia, revolted and declared himself Augustus. But Cassius was assassinated by some of his officers, and so the rebellion came to an end. Antoninus showed his humanity by his treatment of the family and the partisans of Cassius, and his letter to the senate in which he recommends mercy is extant. (Vulcatius, Avidius Cassius, c. 12.)

Antoninus set out for the east on hearing of Cassius' revolt. Though he appears to have returned to Rome in A.D. 174, he went back to prosecute the war against the Germans, and it is probable that he marched direct to the east from the German war. His wife, Faustina, who accompanied him into Asia, died suddenly at the foot of the Taurus to the great grief of her husband. Capitolinus, who has written the life of Antoninus, and also Dion Cassius accuse the empress of scandalous infidelity to her husband and of abominable lewdness. But Capitolinus says that Antoninus either knew it not or pretended not to know it. Nothing is so common as such malicious reports in all ages, and the history of imperial Rome is full of them. Antoninus loved his wife and he says that she was "obedient, affectionate and simple." The same scandal had been spread about Faustina's mother, the wife of Antoninus Pius, and yet he too was perfectly satisfied with his wife. Antoninus Pius says after her death in a letter to Fronto that he would rather have lived in exile with his wife than in his palace at Rome without her. There are not many men who would give their wives a better character than these two emperors. Capitolinus wrote in the time of Diocletian. He may have intended to tell the truth, but he is a poor, feeble biographer. Dion Cassius, the most malignant of historians, always reports and perhaps he believed any scandal against anybody.

Antoninus continued his journey to Syria and Egypt, and on his return to Italy through Athens he was initiated into the Eleusinian mysteries. It was the practice of the emperor to conform to the established rites of the age and to perform religious ceremonies with due solemnity. We cannot conclude from this that he was a superstitious man, though we might perhaps do so, if his book did not show that he was not. But this is only one among many instances that a ruler's public acts do not always prove his real opinions. A prudent governor will not roughly oppose even the superstitions of his people, and though he may wish that they were wiser, he will know that he cannot make them so by offending their prejudices.

Antoninus and his son Commodus entered Rome in triumph, perhaps for some German victories, on the 23rd of December, A.D. 176. In the following year Commodus was associated with his father in the empire and took the name of Augustus. This year A.D. 177 is memorable in ecclesiastical history. Attalus and others were put to death at Lyon for their adherence to the Christian religion. The evidence of this persecution is a letter preserved by Eusebius (E. H. v. 1; printed in Routh's "Reliquiæ Sacræ," vol. 1., with notes). The letter is from the Christians of Vienna and Lugdunum in Gallia (Vienne and Lyon) to their Christian brethren in Asia and Phrygia; and it is preserved perhaps nearly entire. It contains a very particular description of the tortures inflicted on the Christians in Gallia, and it states that while the persecution was going on, Attalus, a Christian and a Roman citizen, was loudly demanded by the populace and brought into the amphitheatre, but the governor ordered him to be reserved with the rest who were in prison, until he had received instructions from the emperor. Many had been tortured before the governor thought of applying to Antoninus. The imperial rescript, says the letter, was that the Christians should be punished, but if they would deny their faith, they must be released. On this the work began again. The Christians who were Roman citizens were beheaded: the rest were exposed to the wild beasts in the amphitheatre. Some modern writers on ecclesiastical history, when they use this letter, say nothing of the wonderful stories of the martyrs' sufferings. Sanctus, as the letter says, was burnt with plates of hot iron till his body was one sore and had lost all human form, but on being put to the rack he recovered his former appearance under the torture, which was thus a cure instead of a punishment. He was afterwards torn by beasts, and placed on an iron chair and roasted. He died at last.

The letter is one piece of evidence. The writer, whoever he was that wrote in the name of the Gallic Christians, is our evidence both for the ordinary and the extraordinary circumstances of the story, and we cannot accept his evidence for one part and reject the other. We often receive small evidence as a proof of a thing which we believe to be within the limits of probability or possibility, and we reject exactly the same evidence, when the thing to which it refers, appears very improbable or impossible. But this is a false method of inquiry, though it is followed by some modern writers, who select what they like from a story and reject the rest of the evidence; or if they do not reject it, they dishonestly suppress it. A man can only act consistently by accepting all this letter or rejecting it all, and we cannot blame him for either. But he who rejects it may still admit that such a letter may be founded on real facts; and he would make this admission as the most probable way of accounting for the existence of the letter: but if, as he would suppose, the writer has stated some things falsely, he cannot tell what part of his story is worthy of credit.

The war on the northern frontier appears to have been uninterrupted during the visit of Antoninus to the East, and on his return the emperor again left Rome to oppose the barbarians. The Germanic people were defeated in a great battle, A.D. 179. During this campaign the emperor was seized with some contagious malady, of which he died in the camp at Sirmium (Mitrovitz) on the Save in Lower Pannonia, but at Vindobona (Vienna) according to other authorities, on the 17th March, A.D. 180, in the fifty-ninth year of his age. His son Commodus was with him. The body or the ashes probably of the emperor were carried to Rome, and he received the honour of deification. Those who could afford it had his statue or bust, and when Capitolinus wrote, many people still had statues of Antoninus among the Dei Penates or household deities. He was in a manner made a saint. Commodus erected to the memory of his father the Antonine column which is now in the Piazza Colonna at Rome. The bas reliefs which are placed in a spiral line round the shaft commemorate the victories of Antoninus over the Marcomanni and the Quadi, and the miraculous shower of rain which refreshed the Roman soldiers and discomfited their enemies. The statue of Antoninus was placed on the capital of the column, but it was removed at some time unknown, and a bronze statue of St. Paul was put in the place by Pope Sixtus the fifth.

The historical evidence for the times of Antoninus is very defective, and some of that which remains is not credible. The most curious is the story about the miracle which happened in A.D. 174 during the war with the Quadi. The Roman army was in danger of perishing by thirst, but a sudden storm drenched them with rain, while it discharged fire and hail on their enemies, and the Romans gained a great victory. All the authorities which speak of the battle speak also of the miracle. The Gentile writers assign it to their gods, and the Christians to the intercession of the Christian legion in the emperor's army. To confirm the Christian statement it is added that the emperor gave the title of Thundering to this legion; but Dacier and others who maintain the Christian report of the miracle, admit that this title of Thundering or Lightning was not given to this legion because the Quadi were struck with lightning, but because there was a figure of lightning on their shields, and that this title of the legion existed in the time of Augustus.

Scaliger also had observed that the legion was called Thundering (κεραυνοβόλος, or κεραυνοφόρος) before the reign of Antoninus. We learn this from Dion Cassius (Lib. 55, c. 23, and the note of Reimarus), who enumerates all the legions of Augustus' time. The name Thundering or Lightning also occurs on an inscription of the reign of Trajan, which was found at Trieste. Eusebius (v. 5), when he relates the miracle, quotes Apolinarius, bishop of Hierapolis, as authority for this name being given to the legion Melitene by the emperor in consequence of the success which he obtained through their prayers; from which we may estimate the value of Apolinarius' testimony. Eusebius does not say in what book of Apolinarius the statement occurs. Dion says that the Thundering legion was stationed in Cappadocia in the time of Augustus. Valesius also observes that in the Notitia of the Imperium Romanum there is mentioned under the commander of Armenia the Præfectura of the twelfth legion named "Thundering Melitene"; and this position in Armenia will agree with what Dion says of its position in Cappadocia. Accordingly Valesius concludes that Melitene was not the name of the legion, but of the town in which it was stationed. Melitene was also the name of the district in which this town was situated. The legions did not, he says, take their name from the place where they were on duty, but from the country in which they were raised, and therefore what Eusebius says about the Melitene does not seem probable to him. Yet Valesius on the authority of Apolinarius and Tertullian believed that the miracle was worked through the prayers of the Christian soldiers in the emperor's army. Rufinus does not give the name of Melitene to this legion, says Valesius, and probably he purposely omitted it, because he knew that Melitene was the name of a town in Armenia Minor, where the legion was stationed in his time.

The emperor, it is said, made a report of his victory to the Senate, which we may believe, for such was the practice; but we do not know what he said in his letter, for it is not extant. Dacier assumes that the emperor's letter was purposely destroyed by the Senate or the enemies of Christianity, that so honourable a testimony to the Christians and their religion might not be perpetuated. The critic has however not seen that he contradicts himself when he tells us the purport of the letter, for he says that it was destroyed, and even Eusebius could not find it. But there does exist a letter in Greek addressed by Antoninus to the Roman people and the sacred Senate after this memorable victory. It is sometimes printed after Justin's first Apology, but it is totally unconnected with the apologies. This letter is one of the most stupid forgeries of the many which exist, and it cannot be possibly founded even on the genuine report of Antoninus to the Senate. If it were genuine, it would free the emperor from the charge of persecuting men because they were Christians, for he says in this false letter that if a man accuse another only of being a Christian and the accused confess and there is nothing else against him, he must be set free; with this monstrous addition, made by a man inconceivably ignorant, that the informer must be burnt alive.

During the time of Antoninus Pius and Marcus Antoninus there appeared the first Apology of Justinus, and under M. Antoninus the Oration of Tatian against the Greeks, which was a fierce attack on the established religions; the address of Athenagoras to M. Antoninus on behalf of the Christians, and the Apology of Melito, bishop of Sardes, also addressed to the emperor, and that of Apolinarius. The first Apology of Justinus is addressed to T. Antoninus Pius and his two adopted sons M. Antoninus and L. Verus; but we do not know whether they read it.[2] The second Apology of Justinus is intitled "to the Roman Senate"; but this superscription is from some copyist. In the first chapter Justinus addresses the Romans. In the second chapter he speaks of an affair that had recently happened in the time of M. Antoninus and L. Verus, as it seems; and he also directly addresses the emperor, saying of a certain woman, "she addressed a petition to thee, the emperor, and thou didst grant the petition." In other passages the writer addresses the two emperors, from which we must conclude that the Apology was directed to them. Eusebius (E. H. IV. 18) states that the second Apology was addressed to the successor of Antoninus Pius, and he names him Antoninus Verus, meaning M. Antoninus. In one passage of this second Apology (c. 8), Justinus, or the writer, whoever he may be, says that even men who followed the Stoic doctrines, when they ordered their lives according to ethical reason, were hated and murdered, such as Heraclitus, Musonius in his own times, and others; for all those who in any way laboured to live according to reason and avoided wickedness were always hated; and this was the effect of the work of dæmons.

Justinus himself is said to have been put to death at Rome, because he refused to sacrifice to the gods. It cannot have been in the reign of Hadrian, as one authority states; nor in the time of Antoninus Pius, if the second Apology was written in the time of M. Antoninus; and there is evidence that this event took place under M. Antoninus and L. Verus, when Rusticus was præfect of the city.

The persecution in which Polycarp suffered at Smyrna belongs to the time of M. Antoninus. The evidence for it is the letter of the church of Smyrna to the churches of Philomelium and the other Christian churches, and it is preserved by Eusebius (E. H. IV. 15). But the critics do not agree about the time of Polycarp's death, differing in the two extremes to the amount of twelve years. The circumstances of Polycarp's martyrdom were accompanied by miracles, one of which Eusebius (IV. 15) has omitted, but it appears in the oldest Latin version of the letter, which Usher published, and it is supposed that this version was made not long after the time

[2] Orosius, vii. 14, says that Justinus the philosopher presented to Antoninus Pius his work in defence of the Christian religion, and made him merciful to the Christians.

of Eusebius. The notice at the end of the letter states that it was transcribed by Caius from the copy of Irenæus, the disciple of Polycarp, then transcribed by Socrates at Corinth; "after which I, Pionius, again wrote it out from the copy above mentioned, having searched it out by the revelation of Polycarp, who directed me to it, etc." The story of Polycarp's martyrdom is embellished with miraculous circumstances which some modern writers on ecclesiastical history take the liberty of omitting.[3]

In order to form a proper notion of the condition of the Christians under M. Antoninus we must go back to Trajan's time. When the younger Pliny was governor of Bithynia, the Christians were numerous in those parts, and the worshippers of the old religion were falling off. The temples were deserted, the festivals neglected, and there were no purchasers of victims for sacrifice. Those who were interested in the maintenance of the old religion thus found that their profits were in danger. Christians of both sexes and of all ages were brought before the governor, who did not know what to do with them. He could come to no other conclusion than this, that those who confessed to be Christians and persevered in their religion ought to be punished; if for nothing else, for their invincible obstinacy. He found no crimes proved against the Christians, and he could only characterize their religion as a depraved and extravagant superstition, which might be stopped, if the people were allowed the opportunity of recanting. Pliny wrote this in a letter to Trajan (Plinius, Ep. x. 97). He asked for the emperor's directions, because he did not know what to do: He remarks that he had never been engaged in judicial inquiries about the Christians, and that accordingly he did not know what to inquire about or how far to inquire and punish. This proves that it was not a new thing to examine into a man's profession of Christianity and to punish him for it. Trajan's Rescript is extant. He approved of the governor's judgment in the matter; but he said that no search must be made after the Christians;

[3] Conyers Middleton, "An Inquiry into the Miraculous Powers," etc., p. 126. Middleton says that Eusebius omitted to mention the dove, which flew out of Polycarp's body, and Dodwell and Archbishop Wake have done the same. Wake says, "I am so little a friend to such miracles that I thought it better with Eusebius to omit that circumstance than to mention it from Bp. Usher's Manuscript," which manuscript, however, says Middleton, he afterwards declares to be so well attested that we need not any further assurance of the truth of it.

if a man was charged with the new religion and convicted, he must not be punished if he affirmed that he was not a Christian and confirmed his denial by showing his reverence to the heathen gods. He added that no notice must be taken of anonymous informations, for such things were of bad example. Trajan was a mild and sensible man, and both motives of mercy and policy probably also induced him to take as little notice of the Christians as he could; to let them live in quiet, if it were possible. Trajan's Rescript is the first legislative act of the head of the Roman state with reference to Christianity which is known to us. It does not appear that the Christians were further disturbed under his reign. The martyrdom of Ignatius by the order of Trajan himself is not universally admitted to be an historical fact.[4]

In the time of Hadrian it was no longer possible for the Roman government to overlook the great increase of the Christians and the hostility of the common sort to them. If the governors in the provinces were willing to let them alone, they could not resist the fanaticism of the heathen community, who looked on the Christians as atheists. The Jews, too, who were settled all over the Roman Empire, were as hostile to the Christians as the Gentiles were.[5] With the time of Hadrian begin the Christian Apologies, which show plainly what the popular feeling towards the Christians then was. A rescript of Hadrian to Minucius Fundanus, the Proconsul of Asia, which stands at the end of Justin's first Apology,[6] instructs the governor that innocent people must not be troubled and false accusers must not be allowed to extort money from them; the charges against the Christians must be made in due form, and no attention

[4] The Martyrium Ignatii, first published in Latin by Archbishop Usher, is the chief evidence for the circumstances of Ignatius' death.

[5] We have the evidence of Justinus (ad Diognetum, c. 5) to this effect: "the Christians are attacked by the Jews as if they were men of a different race, and are persecuted by the Greeks; and those who hate them cannot give the reason of their enmity."

[6] And in Eusebius, E. H. iv. 8, 9. Orosius (vii. 13) says that Hadrian sent this rescript to Minucius Fundanus, proconsul of Asia, after being instructed in books written on the Christian religion by Quadratus, a disciple of the Apostles, and Aristides, an Athenian, an honest and wise man, and Serenus Granius. In the Greek text of Hadrian's Rescript there is mentioned Serenius Granianus, the predecessor of Minucius Fundanus in the government of Asia.

This rescript of Hadrian has clearly been added to the Apology by some editor. The Apology ends with the words: ὃ φίλον τῷ θεῷ, τοῦτο γενέσθω.

must be paid to popular clamours; when Christians were regularly prosecuted and convicted of illegal acts, they must be punished according to their deserts; and false accusers also must be punished. Antoninus Pius is said to have published Rescripts to the same effect. The terms of Hadrian's Rescript seem very favourable to the Christians; but if we understand it in this sense, that they were only to be punished like other people for illegal acts, it would have had no meaning, for that could have been done without asking the emperor's advice. The real purpose of the Rescript is that Christians must be punished if they persisted in their belief, and would not prove their renunciation of it by acknowledging the heathen religion. This was Trajan's rule, and we have no reason for supposing that Hadrian granted more to the Christians than Trajan did. There is also printed at the end of Justin's first Apology a Rescript of Antoninus Pius to the Commune of Asia (τὸ κοινὸν τῆς Ἀσίας), and it is also in Eusebius (E. H. IV. 13). The date of the Rescript is the third consulship of Antoninus Pius. The Rescript declares that the Christians, for they are meant, though the name Christians does not occur in the Rescript, were not to be disturbed unless they were attempting something against the Roman rule, and no man was to be punished simply for being a Christian. But this Rescript is spurious. Any man moderately acquainted with Roman history will see by the style and tenor that it is a clumsy forgery.

In the time of M. Antoninus the opposition between the old and the new belief was still stronger, and the adherents of the heathen religion urged those in authority to a more regular resistance to the invasions of the Christian faith. Melito in his apology to M. Antoninus represents the Christians of Asia as persecuted under new imperial orders. Shameless informers, he says, men who were greedy after the property of others, used these orders as a means of robbing those who were doing no harm. He doubts if a just emperor could have ordered anything so unjust; and if the last order was really not from the emperor, the Christians entreat him not to give them up to their enemies. We conclude from this that there were at least imperial Rescripts or Constitutions of M. Antoninus, which were made the foundation of these persecutions. The fact of being a Christian was now a crime and punished, unless the accused denied their religion. Then come the persecutions at Smyrna, which some modern critics place in A.D. 167, ten years before the persecution of Lyon. The governors of the provinces under M. Antoninus might have found enough even in Trajan's Rescript to warrant them in punishing Christians, and the fanaticism of the people would drive them to persecution, even if they were unwilling. But besides the fact of the Christians rejecting all the heathen ceremonies, we must not forget that they plainly maintained that all the heathen religions were false. The Christians thus declared war against the heathen rites, and it is hardly necessary to observe that this was a declaration of hostility against the Roman government, which tolerated all the various forms of superstition that existed in the empire, and could not consistently tolerate another religion, which declared that all the rest were false and all the splendid ceremonies of the empire only a worship of devils.

If we had a true ecclesiastical history, we should know how the Roman emperors attempted to check the new religion, how they enforced their principle of finally punishing Christians, simply as Christians, which Justin in his Apology affirms that they did, and I have no doubt that he tells the truth; how far popular clamour and riots went in this matter, and how far many fanatical and ignorant Christians, for there were many such, contributed to excite the fanaticism on the other side and to embitter the quarrel between the Roman government and the new religion. Our extant ecclesiastical histories are manifestly falsified, and what truth they contain is grossly exaggerated; but the fact is certain that in the time of M. Antoninus the heathen populations were in open hostility to the Christians, and that under Antoninus' rule men were put to death because they were Christians. Eusebius in the preface to his fifth book remarks that in the seventeenth year of Antoninus' reign, in some parts of the world the persecution of the Christians became more violent and that it proceeded from the populace in the cities; and he adds in his usual style of exaggeration, that we may infer from what took place in a single nation that myriads of martyrs were made in the habitable earth. The nation which he alludes to is Gallia; and he then proceeds to give the letter of the churches of Vienna and Lugdunum. It is probable that he has assigned the true cause of the persecutions, the fanaticism of the populace, and that both governors and emperor had a great deal of trouble with these disturbances. How far Marcus was cognizant of these cruel proceedings we do not know, for the historical records of his reign are very defective. He did not make the rule against the Christians, for Trajan did that; and if we admit that he would have been willing to let the Christians alone, we cannot affirm that it was in his power, for it would be a great mistake to suppose that Antoninus had the unlimited authority, which some modern sovereigns have had. His power was limited by certain constitutional forms, by the senate, and by the precedents of his predecessors. We cannot admit that such a man was an active persecutor, for there is no evidence that he was,[7] though it is certain that he had no good opinion of the Christians, as appears from his own words. But he knew nothing of them except their hostility to the Roman religion, and he probably thought that they were dangerous to the state, notwithstanding the professions false or true of some of the Apologists. So much I have said, because it would be unfair not to state all that can be urged against a man whom his contemporaries and subsequent ages venerated as a model of virtue and benevolence. If I admitted the genuineness of some documents, he would be altogether clear from the charge of even allowing any persecutions; but as I seek the truth and am sure that they are false, I leave him to bear whatever blame is his due.[8] I add that it is quite certain that Antoninus did not derive any of his Ethical principles from a religion of which he knew nothing.[9]

There is no doubt that the Emperor's "Reflections," or his "Meditations," as they are generally named, is a genuine work. In the first book he speaks of himself, his family, and his teachers; and in other books he mentions himself. Suidas (v. Μάρκος) notices a work of

[7] Except that of Orosius (VII. 15), who says that during the Parthian war there were grievous persecutions of the Christians in Asia and Gallia under the orders of Marcus (præcepto ejus), and "many were crowned with the martyrdom of saints."

[8] Dr. F. C. Baur, in his work entitled "Das Christenthum und die Christliche Kirche der drei ersten Jahrhunderte," etc., has examined this question with great good sense and fairness, and I believe he has stated the truth as near as our authorities enable us to reach it.

[9] In the Digest, 48, 19, 30, there is the following excerpt from Modestinus: "Si quis aliquid fecerit, quo leves hominum animi superstitione numinis terrerentur, divus Marcus hujusmodi homines in insulam relegari rescripsit."

Antoninus in twelve books, which he names the "conduct of his own life"; and he cites the book under several words in his Dictionary, giving the emperor's name, but not the title of the work. There are also passages cited by Suidas from Antoninus without mention of the emperor's name. The true title of the work is unknown. Xylander, who published the first edition of this book (Zürich, 1558, 8vo.) with a Latin version, used a manuscript, which contained the twelve books, but it is not known where the manuscript is now. The only other complete manuscript which is known to exist is in the Vatican library, but it has no title and no inscriptions of the several books: the eleventh only has the inscription Μάρκου αὐτοκράτορος marked with an asterisk. The other Vatican manuscripts and the three Florentine contain only excerpts from the emperor's book. All the titles of the excerpts nearly agree with that which Xylander prefixed to his edition, Μάρκου 'Αντωνίνου Αὐτοκράτορος τῶν εἰς ἑαυτὸν βιβλία ιβ. This title has been used by all subsequent editors. We cannot tell whether Antoninus divided his work into books or somebody else did it. If the inscriptions at the end of the first and second books are genuine, he may have made the division himself.

It is plain that the emperor wrote down his thoughts or reflections as the occasions arose; and since they were intended for his own use, it is no improbable conjecture that he left a complete copy behind him written with his own hand; for it is not likely that so diligent a man would use the labour of a transcriber for such a purpose, and expose his most secret thoughts to any other eye. He may have also intended the book for his son Commodus, who however had no taste for his father's philosophy. Some careful hand preserved the precious volume; and a work by Antoninus is mentioned by other late writers besides Suidas.

Many critics have laboured on the text of Antoninus. The most complete edition is that by Thomas Gataker, 1652, 4to. The second edition of Gataker was superintended by George Stanhope, 1697, 4to. There is also an edition of 1704. Gataker made and suggested many good corrections, and he also made a new Latin version, which is not a very good specimen of Latin, but it generally expresses the sense of the original and often better than some of the more recent translations. He added in the margin opposite to each paragraph references to the other parallel passages; and he wrote a commentary, one of the most complete that has been written on any ancient author. This commentary contains the editor's exposition of the more difficult passages, and quotations from all the Greek and Roman writers for the illustration of the text. It is a wonderful monument of learning and labour, and certainly no Englishman has yet done anything like it. At the end of his preface the editor says that he wrote it at Rotherhithe near London in a severe winter, when he was in the seventy-eighth year of his age, 1651, a time when Milton, Selden, and other great men of the Commonwealth time were living; and the great French scholar Saumaise (Salmasius), with whom Gataker corresponded and received help from him for his edition of Antoninus. The Greek text has also been edited by J. M. Schultz, Leipzig, 1802, 8vo.; and by the learned Greek Adamantinus Coraïs, Paris, 1816, 8vo. The text of Schultz was republished by Tauchnitz, 1821.

There are English, German, French, Italian, and Spanish translations of M. Antoninus, and there may be others. I have not seen all the English translations. There is one by Jeremy Collier, 1702, 8vo., a most coarse and vulgar copy of the original. The latest French translation by Alexis Pierron in the collection of Charpentier is better than Dacier's, which has been honoured with an Italian version (Udine, 1772). There is an Italian version (1675) which I have not seen. It is by a cardinal. "A man illustrious in the church, the Cardinal Francis Barberini the elder, nephew of Pope Urban VIII., occupied the last years of his life in translating into his native language the thoughts of the Roman emperor, in order to diffuse among the faithful the fertilizing and vivifying seeds. He dedicated this translation to his soul, to make it, as he says in his energetic style, redder than his purple at the sight of the virtues of this Gentile" (Pierron, Preface).

I have made this translation at intervals after having used the book for many years. It is made from the Greek, but I have not always followed one text; and I have occasionally compared other versions with my own. I made this translation for my own use, because I found that it was worth the labour; but it may be useful to others also and therefore I determined to print it. As the original is sometimes very difficult to understand and still more difficult to translate, it is not possible that I have always avoided error. But I believe that I have not often missed the meaning, and those who will take the trouble to compare the translation with the original should not hastily conclude that I am wrong, if they do not agree with me. Some passages do give the meaning, though at first sight they may not appear to do so; and when I differ from the translators, I think that in some places they are wrong, and in other places I am sure that they are. . . . I could have made the language more easy and flowing, but I have preferred a ruder style as being better suited to express the character of the original; and sometimes the obscurity which may appear in the version is a fair copy of the obscurity of the Greek. If I have not given the best words for the Greek, I have done the best that I could; and in the text I have always given the same translation of the same word.

The last reflection of the Stoic philosophy that I have observed is in Simplicius' "Commentary on the Enchiridion of Epictetus." Simplicius was not a Christian, and such a man was not likely to be converted at a time when Christianity was grossly corrupted. But he was a really religious man, and he concludes his commentary with a prayer to the Deity which no Christian could improve. From the time of Zeno to Simplicius, a period of about nine hundred years, the Stoic philosophy formed the characters of some of the best and greatest men. Finally it became extinct, and we hear no more of it till the revival of letters in Italy. Angelo Poliziano met with two very inaccurate and incomplete manuscripts of Epictetus' Enchiridion, which he translated into Latin and dedicated to his great patron Lorenzo de' Medici, in whose collection he had found the book. Poliziano's version was printed in the first Bâle edition of the Enchiridion, A.D. 1531 (apud And. Cratandrum). Poliziano recommends the Enchiridion to Lorenzo as a work well suited to his temper, and useful in the difficulties by which he was surrounded.

Epictetus and Antoninus have had readers ever since they were first printed. The little book of Antoninus has been the companion of some great men. Machiavelli's "Art of War" and Marcus Antoninus were the two books which were used when he was a young man by Captain John Smith, and he could not have found two writers better fitted to form the character of a soldier and a man. Smith is almost unknown and forgotten in England, his native country, but not in America, where he saved the young colony of Virginia. He was great in his heroic mind and his deeds in arms, but greater still in the nobleness of his character. For a man's greatness lies not in wealth and station, as the vulgar believe, nor yet in his intellectual capacity, which is often associated with the meanest moral character, the most abject servility to those in high places and arrogance to the poor and lowly; but a man's true greatness lies in the consciousness of an honest purpose in life, founded on a just estimate of himself and everything else, on frequent self-examination, and a steady obedience to the rule which he knows to be right, without troubling himself, as the emperor says he should not, about what others may think or say, or whether they do or do not do that which he thinks and says and does.

THE PHILOSOPHY OF ANTONINUS

BY GEORGE LONG, M.A.

IT has been said that the Stoic philosophy first showed its real value when it passed from Greece to Rome. The doctrines of Zeno and his successors were well suited to the gravity and practical good sense of the Romans; and even in the Republican period we have an example of a man, M. Cato Uticensis, who lived the life of a Stoic and died consistently with the opinions which he professed. He was a man, says Cicero, who embraced the Stoic philosophy from conviction; not for the purpose of vain discussion, as most did, but in order to make his life conformable to the Stoic precepts. In the wretched times from the death of Augustus to the murder of Domitian, there was nothing but the Stoic philosophy which could console and support the followers of the old religion under imperial tyranny and amidst universal corruption. There were even then noble minds that could dare and endure, sustained by a good conscience and an elevated idea of the purposes of man's existence. Such were Pætus Thrasea, Helvidius Priscus, Cornutus, C. Musonius Rufus,[1] and the poets Persius and Juvenal, whose energetic language and manly thoughts may be as instructive to us now as they might have been to their contemporaries. Persius died under Nero's bloody reign, but Juvenal had the good fortune to survive the tyrant Domitian and to see the better times of Nerva, Trajan, and Hadrian.[2] His best precepts are derived from the Stoic school, and they are

[1] I have omitted Seneca, Nero's preceptor. He was in a sense a Stoic and he has said many good things in a very fine way. There is a judgment of Gellius (XII. 2) on Seneca, or rather a statement of what some people thought of his philosophy, and it is not favourable. His writings and his life must be taken together, and I have nothing more to say of him here. The reader will find a notice of Seneca and his philosophy in "Seekers after God," by the Rev. F. W. Farrar. Macmillan and Co.

[2] Ribbeck has laboured to prove that those Satires which contain philosophical precepts are not the work of the real, but of a false Juvenal, a Declamator. Still the verses exist, and were written by somebody who was acquainted with the Stoic doctrines.

enforced in his finest verses by the unrivalled vigour of the Latin language.

The two best expounders of the later Stoical philosophy were a Greek slave and a Roman emperor. Epictetus, a Phrygian Greek, was brought to Rome, we know not how, but he was there the slave and afterwards the freedman of an unworthy master, Epaphroditus by name, himself a freedman and a favourite of Nero. Epictetus may have been a hearer of C. Musonius Rufus, while he was still a slave, but he could hardly have been a teacher before he was made free. He was one of the philosophers whom Domitian's order banished from Rome. He retired to Nicopolis in Epirus, and he may have died there. Like other great teachers he wrote nothing, and we are indebted to his grateful pupil Arrian for what we have of Epictetus' discourses. Arrian wrote eight books of the discourses of Epictetus, of which only four remain and some fragments. We have also from Arrian's hand the small Enchiridion or Manual of the chief precepts of Epictetus. There is a valuable commentary on the Enchiridion by Simplicius, who lived in the time of the emperor Justinian.[3]

Antoninus in his first book (I. 7), in which he gratefully commemorates his obligations to his teachers, says that he was made acquainted by Junius Rusticus with the discourses of Epictetus, whom he mentions also in other passages (IV. 41; XI. 34, 36). Indeed the doctrines of Epictetus and Antoninus are the same, and Epictetus is the best authority for the explanation of the philosophical language of Antoninus and the exposition of his opinions. But the method of the two philosophers is entirely different. Epictetus addressed himself to his hearers in a continuous discourse and in a familiar and simple manner. Antoninus wrote down his reflections for his own use only, in short unconnected paragraphs, which are often obscure.

The Stoics made three divisions of philosophy, Physic (φυσικόν), Ethic (ἠθικόν), and Logic (λογικόν) (VIII. 13). This division, we are told by Diogenes, was made by Zeno of Citium, the founder of the Stoic sect, and by Chrysippus; but these philosophers placed the

[3] There is a complete edition of Arrian's Epictetus with the commentary of Simplicius by J. Schweighäuser, 6 vols. 8vo. 1799, 1800.

three divisions in the following order: Logic, Physic, Ethic. It appears, however, that this division was made before Zeno's time and acknowledged by Plato, as Cicero remarks (Acad. Post. I. 5). Logic is not synonymous with our term Logic in the narrower sense of that word.

Cleanthes, a Stoic, subdivided the three divisions, and made six: Dialectic and Rhetoric, comprised in Logic; Ethic and Politic; Physic and Theology. This division was merely for practical use, for all Philosophy is one. Even among the earliest Stoics Logic or Dialectic does not occupy the same place as in Plato: it is considered only as an instrument which is to be used for the other divisions of Philosophy. An exposition of the earlier Stoic doctrines and of their modifications would require a volume. My object is to explain only the opinions of Antoninus, so far as they can be collected from his book.

According to the subdivision of Cleanthes Physic and Theology go together, or the study of the nature of Things, and the study of the nature of the Deity, so far as man can understand the Deity, and of his government of the universe. This division or subdivision is not formally adopted by Antoninus, for, as already observed, there is no method in his book; but it is virtually contained in it.

Cleanthes also connects Ethic and Politic, or the study of the principles of morals and the study of the constitution of civil society; and undoubtedly he did well in subdividing Ethic into two parts, Ethic in the narrower sense and Politic, for though the two are intimately connected, they are also very distinct, and many questions can only be properly discussed by carefully observing the distinction. Antoninus does not treat of Politic. His subject is Ethic, and Ethic in its practical application to his own conduct in life as a man and as a governor. His Ethic is founded on his doctrines about man's nature, the Universal Nature, and the relation of every man to everything else. It is therefore intimately and inseparably connected with Physic or the Nature of Things and with Theology or the Nature of the Deity. He advises us to examine well all the impressions on our minds (*φαντασίαι*) and to form a right judgment of them, to make just conclusions, and to inquire into the meanings of words, and so far to apply Dialectic, but he has no attempt at any exposition of

Dialectic, and his philosophy is in substance purely moral and practical. He says (VIII. 13), "Constantly and, if it be possible, on the occasion of every impression on the soul, apply to it the principles of Physic, of Ethic, and of Dialectic": which is only another way of telling us to examine the impression in every possible way. In another passage (III. 11) he says, "To the aids which have been mentioned let this one still be added: make for thyself a definition or description of the object (*τὸ φανταστόν*) which is presented to thee, so as to see distinctly what kind of a thing it is in its substance, in its nudity, in its complete entirety, and tell thyself its proper name, and the names of the things of which it has been compounded, and into which it will be resolved." Such an examination implies a use of Dialectic, which Antoninus accordingly employed as a means towards establishing his Physical, Theological, and Ethical principles.

There are several expositions of the Physical, Theological, and Ethical principles, which are contained in the work of Antoninus; and more expositions than I have read. Ritter ("Geschichte der Philosophie," IV. 241), after explaining the doctrines of Epictetus, treats very briefly and insufficiently those of Antoninus. But he refers to a short essay, in which the work is done better.[4] There is also an essay on the Philosophical Principles of M. Aurelius Antoninus by J. M. Schultz, placed at the end of his German translation of Antoninus (Schleswig, 1799). With the assistance of these two useful essays and his own diligent study a man may form a sufficient notion of the principles of Antoninus; but he will find it more difficult to expound them to others. Besides the want of arrangement in the original and of connection among the numerous paragraphs, the corruption of the text, the obscurity of the language and the style, and sometimes perhaps the confusion in the writer's own ideas—besides all this there is occasionally an apparent contradiction in the emperor's thoughts, as if his principles were sometimes unsettled, as if doubt sometimes clouded his mind. A man who leads a life of tranquillity and reflection, who is not disturbed at home and meddles not with the affairs of the world, may keep his mind at ease and his thoughts in one even course. But such a man

[4] "De Marco Aurelio Antonino . . . ex ipsius Commentariis. Scriptio Philologica." Instituit Nicolaus Bachius, Lipsiæ, 1826.

has not been tried. All his Ethical philosophy and his passive virtue might turn out to be idle words, if he were once exposed to the rude realities of human existence. Fine thoughts and moral dissertations from men who have not worked and suffered may be read, but they will be forgotten. No religion, no Ethical philosophy is worth anything, if the teacher has not lived the "life of an apostle," and been ready to die "the death of a martyr." "Not in passivity [the passive affects], but in activity, lie the evil and the good of the rational social animal, just as his virtue and his vice lie not in passivity, but in activity" (ix. 16). The emperor Antoninus was a practical moralist. From his youth he followed a laborious discipline, and though his high station placed him above all want or the fear of it, he lived as frugally and temperately as the poorest philosopher. Epictetus wanted little, and it seems that he always had the little that he wanted, and he was content with it, as he had been with his servile station. But Antoninus after his accession to the empire sat on an uneasy seat. He had the administration of an empire which extended from the Euphrates to the Atlantic, from the cold mountains of Scotland to the hot sands of Africa; and we may imagine, though we cannot know it by experience, what must be the trials, the troubles, the anxiety, and the sorrows of him who has the world's business on his hands with the wish to do the best that he can, and the certain knowledge that he can do very little of the good which he wishes.

In the midst of war, pestilence, conspiracy, general corruption, and with the weight of so unwieldy an empire upon him, we may easily comprehend that Antoninus often had need of all his fortitude to support him. The best and the bravest men have moments of doubt and of weakness, but if they are the best and the bravest, they rise again from their depression by recurring to first principles, as Antoninus does. The emperor says that life is smoke, a vapour, and St. James in his Epistle is of the same mind; that the world is full of envious, jealous, malignant people, and a man might be well content to get out of it. He has doubts perhaps sometimes even about that to which he holds most firmly. There are only a few passages of this kind, but they are evidence of the struggles which even the noblest of the sons of men had to maintain against the hard realities of his daily life. A poor remark it is which I have seen somewhere, and made in a disparaging way, that the emperor's reflections show that he had need of consolation and comfort in life, and even to prepare him to meet his death. True that he did need comfort and support, and we see how he found it. He constantly recurs to his fundamental principle that the universe is wisely ordered, that every man is a part of it and must conform to that order which he cannot change, that whatever the Deity has done is good, that all mankind are a man's brethren, that he must love and cherish them and try to make them better, even those who would do him harm. This is his conclusion (II. 17): "What then is that which is able to conduct a man? One thing and only one, Philosophy. But this consists in keeping the divinity within a man free from violence and unharmed, superior to pains and pleasures, doing nothing without a purpose nor yet falsely and with hypocrisy, not feeling the need of another man's doing or not doing anything; and besides, accepting all that happens and all that is allotted, as coming from thence, wherever it is, from whence he himself came; and, finally, waiting for death with a cheerful mind as being nothing else than a dissolution of the elements of which every living being is compounded. But if there is no harm to the elements themselves in each continually changing into another, why should a man have any apprehension about the change and dissolution of all the elements [himself]? for it is according to nature; and nothing is evil that is according to nature."

The Physic of Antoninus is the knowledge of the Nature of the Universe, of its government, and of the relation of man's nature to both. He names the universe (*ἡ τῶν ὅλων οὐσία*, VI. 1) "the universal substance," and he adds that "reason" (λόγος) governs the universe. He also (VI. 9) uses the terms "universal nature" or "nature of the universe." He (VI. 25) calls the universe "the one and all, which we name Cosmus or Order" (*κόσμος*). If he ever seems to use these general terms as significant of the All, of all that man can in any way conceive to exist, he still on other occasions plainly distinguishes between Matter, Material things (*ὕλη, ὑλικόν*), and Cause, Origin, Reason (*αἰτία, αἰτιῶδες, λόγος*). This is conformable to Zeno's doctrine that there are two original principles (*ἀρχαί*) of all things, that which acts (*τὸ ποιοῦν*) and that which is acted upon (*τὸ πάσχον*). That which is acted on is the formless matter (*ὕλη*): that which acts is the reason (λόγος), God, who is eternal and operates through all matter, and produces all things. So Antoninus (v. 32) speaks of the reason (λόγος) which pervades all substance (οὐσία), and through all time by fixed periods (revolutions) administers the universe (τὸ πᾶν). God is eternal, and Matter is eternal. It is God who gives form to matter, but he is not said to have created matter. According to this view, which is as old as Anaxagoras, God and matter exist independently, but God governs matter. This doctrine is simply the expression of the fact of the existence both of matter and of God. The Stoics did not perplex themselves with the insoluble question of the origin and nature of matter. Antoninus also assumes a beginning of things, as we now know them; but his language is sometimes very obscure. I have endeavoured to explain the meaning of one difficult passage. (VII. 75, and the note.)

Matter consists of elemental parts (στοιχεῖα) of which all material objects are made. But nothing is permanent in form. The nature of the universe, according to Antoninus' expression (IV. 36), "loves nothing so much as to change the things which are, and to make new things like them. For everything that exists is in a manner the seed of that which will be. But thou art thinking only of seeds which are cast into the earth or into a womb: but this is a very vulgar notion." All things then are in a constant flux and change: some things are dissolved into the elements, others come in their places; and so the "whole universe continues ever young and perfect." (XII. 23.)

Antoninus has some obscure expressions about what he calls "seminal principles" (σπερματικοὶ λόγοι). He opposes them to the Epicurean atoms (VI. 24), and consequently his "seminal principles" are not material atoms which wander about at hazard, and combine nobody knows how. In one passage (IV. 21) he speaks of living principles, souls (ψυχαί) after the dissolution of their bodies being received into the "seminal principle of the universe." Schultz thinks that by "seminal principles Antoninus means the relations of the various elemental principles, which relations are determined by the Deity and by which alone the production of organized beings is possible." This may be the meaning, but if it is, nothing of any value can be derived from it. Antoninus often uses the word "Nature" (φύσις), and we must attempt to fix its meaning. The simple etymological sense of φύσις is "production," the birth of what we call

Things. The Romans used Natura, which also means "birth" originally. But neither the Greeks nor the Romans stuck to this simple meaning, nor do we. Antoninus says (x. 6): "Whether the universe is [a concourse of] atoms, or Nature [is a system], let this first be established, that I am a part of the whole which is governed by nature." Here it might seem as if nature were personified and viewed as an active, efficient power, as something which, if not independent of the Deity, acts by a power which is given to it by the Deity. Such, if I understand the expression right, is the way in which the word Nature is often used now, though it is plain that many writers use the word without fixing any exact meaning to it. It is the same with the expression Laws of Nature, which some writers may use in an intelligible sense, but others as clearly use in no definite sense at all. There is no meaning in this word Nature, except that which Bishop Butler assigns to it, when he says, "The only distinct meaning of that word Natural is Stated, Fixed or Settled; since what is natural as much requires and presupposes an intelligent agent to render it so, i.e. to effect it continually or at stated times, as what is supernatural or miraculous does to effect it at once." This is Plato's meaning ("De Leg.," IV. 715), when he says that God holds the beginning and end and middle of all that exists, and proceeds straight on his course, making his circuit according to nature (that is, by a fixed order); and he is continually accompanied by justice, who punishes those who deviate from the divine law, that is, from the order or course which God observes.

When we look at the motions of the planets, the action of what we call gravitation, the elemental combination of unorganized bodies and their resolution, the production of plants and of living bodies, their generation, growth, and their dissolution, which we call their death, we observe a regular sequence of phænomena, which within the limits of experience present and past, so far as we know the past, is fixed and invariable. But if this is not so, if the order and sequence of phænomena, as known to us, are subject to change in the course of an infinite progression—and such change is conceivable—we have not discovered, nor shall we ever discover, the whole of the order and sequence of phænomena, in which sequence there may be involved according to its very nature, that is, according to its fixed order, some variation of what we now call the Order or Nature of Things.

It is also conceivable that such changes have taken place, changes in the order of things, as we are compelled by the imperfection of language to call them, but which are no changes; and further it is certain that our knowledge of the true sequence of all actual phænomena, as, for instance, the phænomena of generation, growth, and dissolution, is and ever must be imperfect.

We do not fare much better when we speak of Causes and Effects than when we speak of Nature. For the practical purposes of life we may use the terms cause and effect conveniently, and we may fix a distinct meaning to them, distinct enough at least to prevent all misunderstanding. But the case is different when we speak of causes and effects as of Things. All that we know is phænomena, as the Greeks called them, or appearances which follow one another in a regular order, as we conceive it, so that if some one phænomenon should fail in the series, we conceive that there must either be an interruption of the series, or that something else will appear after the phænomenon which has failed to appear, and will occupy the vacant place; and so the series in its progression may be modified or totally changed. Cause and effect then mean nothing in the sequence of natural phænomena beyond what I have said; and the real cause, or the transcendent cause, as some would call it, of each successive phænomenon is in that which is the cause of all things which are, which have been, and which will be forever. Thus the word Creation may have a real sense if we consider it as the first, if we can conceive a first, in the present order of natural phænomena; but in the vulgar sense a creation of all things at a certain time, followed by a quiescence of the first cause and an abandonment of all sequences of phænomena to the laws of Nature, or to the other words that people may use, is absolutely absurd.[5]

Now, though there is great difficulty in understanding all the

[5] Time and space are the conditions of our thought; but time infinite and space infinite cannot be objects of thought, except in a very imperfect way. Time and space must not in any way be thought of, when we think of the Deity. Swedenborg says, "The natural man may believe that he would have no thought, if the ideas of time, of space, and of things material were taken away; for upon those is founded all the thought that man has. But let him know that the thoughts are limited and confined in proportion as they partake of time, of space, and of what is material; and that they are not limited and are extended, in proportion as they do not partake of those things; since the mind is so far elevated above the things corporeal and worldly." ("Concerning Heaven and Hell," 169.)

passages of Antoninus, in which he speaks of Nature, of the changes of things, and of the economy of the universe, I am convinced that his sense of Nature and Natural is the same as that which I have stated; and as he was a man who knew how to use words in a clear way and with strict consistency, we ought to assume, even if his meaning in some passages is doubtful, that his view of Nature was in harmony with his fixed belief in the all-pervading, ever present, and ever active energy of God. (II. 4; IV. 40; X. 1; VI. 40; and other passages. Compare Seneca, "De Benef.," iv. 7. Swedenborg, "Angelic Wisdom," 349–357.)

There is much in Antoninus that is hard to understand, and it might be said that he did not fully comprehend all that he wrote; which would, however, be in no way remarkable, for it happens now that a man may write what neither he nor anybody can understand. Antoninus tells us (XII. 10) to look at things and see what they are, resolving them into the material (ὕλη), the causal (αἴτιον), and the relation (ἀναφορά), or the purpose, by which he seems to mean something in the nature of what we call effect, or end. The word Cause (αἰτία) is the difficulty. There is the same word in the Sanscrit (*hétu*); and the subtle philosophers of India and of Greece, and the less subtle philosophers of modern times, have all used this word, or an equivalent word, in a vague way. Yet the confusion sometimes may be in the inevitable ambiguity of language rather than in the mind of the writer, for I cannot think that some of the wisest of men did not know what they intended to say. When Antoninus says (IV. 36) that "everything that exists is in a manner the seed of that which will be," he might be supposed to say what some of the Indian philosophers have said, and thus a profound truth might be converted into a gross absurdity. But he says, "in a manner," and in a manner he said true; and in another manner, if you mistake his meaning, he said false. When Plato said, "Nothing ever is, but is always becoming" (ἀεὶ γίγνεται), he delivered a text, out of which we may derive something; for he destroys by it not all practical, but all speculative notions of cause and effect. The whole series of things, as they appear to us, must be contemplated in time, that is, in succession, and we conceive or suppose intervals between one state of things and another state of things, so that there is priority and sequence, and interval, and Being, and a ceasing to Be, and beginning and ending. But there is nothing of the kind in the Nature of Things. It is an everlasting continuity. (iv. 45; vii. 75.) When Antoninus speaks of generation (x. 26), he speaks of one cause (*αἰτία*) acting, and then another cause taking up the work, which the former left in a certain state, and so on; and we might conceive that he had some notion like what has been called "the self-evolving power of nature"; a fine phrase indeed, the full import of which I believe that the writer of it did not see, and thus he laid himself open to the imputation of being a follower of one of the Hindu sects, which makes all things come by evolution out of nature or matter, or out of something which takes the place of Deity, but is not Deity. I would have all men think as they please, or as they can, and I only claim the same freedom which I give. When a man writes anything, we may fairly try to find out all that his words must mean, even if the result is that they mean what he did not mean; and if we find this contradiction, it is not our fault, but his misfortune. Now Antoninus is perhaps somewhat in this condition in what he says (x. 26), though he speaks at the end of the paragraph of the power which acts, unseen by the eyes, but still no less clearly. But whether in this passage (x. 26) he means that the power is conceived to be in the different successive causes (*αἰτίαι*), or in something else, nobody can tell. From other passages, however, I do collect that his notion of the phænomena of the universe is what I have stated. The Deity works unseen, if we may use such language, and perhaps I may, as Job did, or he who wrote the book of Job. "In him we live and move and are," said St. Paul to the Athenians, and to show his bearers that this was no new doctrine, he quoted the Greek poets. One of these poets was the Stoic Cleanthes, whose noble hymn to Zeus or God is an elevated expression of devotion and philosophy. It deprives Nature of her power and puts her under the immediate government of the Deity.

"Thee all this heaven, which whirls around the earth,
Obeys and willing follows where thou leadest.—
Without thee, God, nothing is done on earth,
Nor in the æthereal realms, nor in the sea,
Save what the wicked through their folly do."

Antoninus' conviction of the existence of a divine power and government was founded on his perception of the order of the universe. Like Socrates (Xen., "Mem.," IV. 3, 13, etc.), he says that though we cannot see the forms of divine powers we know that they exist because we see their works.

"To those who ask, Where hast thou seen the gods or how dost thou comprehend that they exist and so worshipest them? I answer, in the first place, that they may be seen even with the eyes; in the second place, neither have I seen my own soul, and yet I honour it. Thus then with respect to the gods, from what I constantly experience of their power, from this I comprehend that they exist and I venerate them." (XII. 28, and the note. Comp. Aristotle, "de Mundo," c. 6; Xen., "Mem.," I. 4, 9; Cicero, "Tuscul.," I. 28, 29; St. Paul's Epistle to the Romans, I. 19, 20; and Montaigne's "Apology for Raimond de Sebonde," II. c. 12.) This is a very old argument which has always had great weight with most people, and has appeared sufficient. It does not acquire the least additional strength by being developed in a learned treatise. It is as intelligible in its simple enunciation as it can be made. If it is rejected, there is no arguing with him who rejects it: and if it is worked out into innumerable particulars, the value of the evidence runs the risk of being buried under a mass of words.

Man being conscious that he is a spiritual power or intellectual power, or that he has such a power, in whatever way he conceives that he has it—for I wish simply to state a fact—from this power which he has in himself, he is led, as Antoninus says, to believe that there is a greater power, which, as the old Stoics tell us, pervades the whole universe as the intellect (*νοῦς*) pervades man. (Compare Epictetus' "Discourses," I. 14; and Voltaire à Mad[e]. Necker, vol. LXVII. p. 278, ed. Lequien.)

God exists then, but what do we know of his nature? Antoninus says that the soul of man is an efflux from the divinity. We have bodies like animals, but we have reason, intelligence as the gods. Animals have life (*ψυχή*), and what we call instincts or natural principles of action: but the rational animal man alone has a rational, intelligent soul (*ψυχὴ λογική, νοερά*). Antoninus insists on this continually: God is in man,[6] and so we must constantly attend to the divinity within us, for it is only in this way that we can have any knowledge of the nature of God. The human soul is in a sense a portion of the divinity; and the soul alone has any communication with the Deity, for, as he says (XII. 2): "With his intellectual part alone God touches the intelligence only which has flowed and been derived from himself into these bodies." In fact he says that which is hidden within a man is life, that is the man himself. All the rest is vesture, covering, organs, instrument, which the living man, the real man, uses for the purpose of his present existence. The air is universally diffused for him who is able to respire, and so for him who is willing to partake of it the intelligent power, which holds within it all things, is diffused as wide and free as the air. (VIII. 54.) It is by living a divine life that man approaches to a knowledge of the divinity. It is by following the divinity within, *δαίμων* or *θεός*' as Antoninus calls it, that man comes nearest to the Deity, the supreme good, for man can never attain to perfect agreement with his internal guide (*τὸ ἡγεμονικόν*). "Live with the gods. And he does live with the gods who constantly shows to them that his own soul is satisfied with that which is assigned to him, and that it does all the dæmon (*δαίμων*) wishes, which Zeus hath given to every man for his guardian and guide, a portion of himself. And this dæmon is every man's understanding and reason." (V. 27).

There is in man, that is in the reason, the intelligence, a superior faculty which if it is exercised rules all the rest. This is the ruling faculty (*τὸ ἡγεμονικόν*) which Cicero ("De Natura Deorum," II. 11) renders by the Latin word Principatus, "to which nothing can or ought to be superior." Antoninus often uses this term, and others which are equivalent. He names it (VII. 64) "the governing intelligence." The governing faculty is the master of the soul. (V. 26.) A man must reverence only his ruling faculty and the divinity within him. As we must reverence that which is supreme in the universe, so we must reverence that which is supreme in ourselves, and this is that which is of like kind with that which is supreme in the universe. (V. 21.) So, as Plotinus says, the soul of man can only know

[6] Comp. Ep. to the Corinthians, I, 3, 17, and James IV. 8, "Draw nigh to God and he will draw nigh to you."

the divine, so far as it knows itself. In one passage (XI. 19) Antoninus speaks of a man's condemnation of himself, when the diviner part within him has been overpowered and yields to the less honourable and to the perishable part, the body, and its gross pleasures. In a word, the views of Antoninus on this matter, however his expressions may vary, are exactly what Bishop Butler expresses, when he speaks of "the natural supremacy of reflection or conscience," of the faculty "which surveys, approves or disapproves the several affections of our mind and actions of our lives."

Much matter might be collected from Antoninus on the notion of the universe being one animated Being. But all that he says amounts to no more, as Schultz remarks, than this: the soul of man is most intimately united to his body, and together they make one animal, which we call man; so the Deity is most intimately united to the world or the material universe, and together they form one whole. But Antoninus did not view God and the material universe as the same, any more than he viewed the body and soul of man as one. Antoninus has no speculations on the absolute nature of the Deity. It was not his fashion to waste his time on what man cannot understand.[7] He was satisfied that God exists, that he governs all things, that man can only have an imperfect knowledge of his nature, and he must attain this imperfect knowledge by reverencing the divinity which is within him, and keeping it pure.

From all that has been said it follows that the universe is administered by the Providence of God (*πρόνοια*), and that all things are wisely ordered. There are passages in which Antoninus expresses doubts, or states different possible theories of the constitution and government of the universe, but he always recurs to his fundamental principle, that if we admit the existence of a Deity, we must also admit that he orders all things wisely and well. (IV. 27; VI. 1; IX. 28; XII. 5, and many other passages.) Epictetus says (I. 6) that we can discern the providence which rules the world, if we possess two things, the power of seeing all that happens with respect to each thing, and a grateful disposition.

But if all things are wisely ordered, how is the world so full of

[7] "God who is infinitely beyond the reach of our narrow capacities." Locke, "Essay concerning Human Understanding," II. chap. 17.

what we call evil, physical and moral? If instead of saying that there is evil in the world, we use the expression which I have used, "what we call evil," we have partly anticipated the emperor's answer. We see and feel and know imperfectly very few things in the few years that we live, and all the knowledge and all the experience of all the human race is positive ignorance of the whole, which is infinite. Now as our reason teaches us that everything is in some way related to and connected with every other thing, all notion of evil as being in the universe of things is a contradiction, for if the whole comes from and is governed by an intelligent being, it is impossible to conceive anything in it which tends to the evil or destruction of the whole. (VIII. 55; X. 6.) Everything is in constant mutation, and yet the whole subsists. We might imagine the solar system resolved into its elemental parts, and yet the whole would still subsist "ever young and perfect."

All things, all forms, are dissolved and new forms appear. All living things undergo the change which we call death. If we call death an evil, then all change is an evil. Living beings also suffer pain, and man suffers most of all, for he suffers both in and by his body, and by his intelligent part. Men suffer also from one another, and perhaps the largest part of human suffering comes to man from those whom he calls his brothers. Antoninus says (VIII. 55), "Generally, wickedness does no harm at all to the universe; and particularly, the wickedness [of one man] does no harm to another. It is only harmful to him who has it in his power to be released from it as soon as he shall choose." The first part of this is perfectly consistent with the doctrine that the whole can sustain no evil or harm. The second part must be explained by the Stoic principle that there is no evil in anything which is not in our power. What wrong we suffer from another is his evil, not ours. But this is an admission that there is evil in a sort, for he who does wrong does evil, and if others can endure the wrong, still there is evil in the wrong-doer. Antoninus (XI. 18) gives many excellent precepts with respect to wrongs and injuries, and his precepts are practical. He teaches us to bear what we cannot avoid, and his lessons may be just as useful to him who denies the being and the government of God as to him who believes in both. There is no direct answer in Antoninus to the objections which may be made to the existence and providence of God because of the moral disorder and suffering which are in the world, except this answer which he makes in reply to the supposition that even the best men may be extinguished by death. He says if it is so, we may be sure that if it ought to have been otherwise, the gods would have ordered it otherwise. (XII. 5.) His conviction of the wisdom which we may observe in the government of the world is too strong to be disturbed by any apparent irregularities in the order of things. That these disorders exist is a fact, and those who would conclude from them against the being and government of God conclude too hastily. We all admit that there is an order in the material world, a Nature, in the sense in which that word has been explained, a constitution (*κατασκευή*), what we call a system, a relation of parts to one another and a fitness of the whole for something. So in the constitution of plants and of animals there is an order, a fitness for some end. Sometimes the order, as we conceive it, is interrupted and the end, as we conceive it, is not attained. The seed, the plant, or the animal sometimes perishes before it has passed through all its changes and done all its uses. It is according to Nature, that is, a fixed order, for some to perish early and for others to do all their uses and leave successors to take their place. So man has a corporeal and intellectual and moral constitution fit for certain uses, and on the whole man performs these uses, dies, and leaves other men in his place. So society exists, and a social state is manifestly the Natural State of man, the state for which his Nature fits him; and society amidst innumerable irregularities and disorders still subsists; and perhaps we may say that the history of the past and our present knowledge give us a reasonable hope that its disorders will diminish, and that order, its governing principle, may be more firmly established. As order then, a fixed order, we may say, subject to deviations real or apparent, must be admitted to exist in the whole Nature of things, that which we call disorder or evil as it seems to us, does not in any way alter the fact of the general constitution of things having a Nature or fixed order. Nobody will conclude from the existence of disorder that order is not the rule, for the existence of order both physical and moral is proved by daily experience and all past experience. We cannot conceive how the order of the universe is maintained: we cannot even conceive how our own life from day to day is continued, nor how we perform the simplest movements of the body, nor how we grow and think and act, though we know many of the conditions which are necessary for all these functions. Knowing nothing then of the unseen power which acts in ourselves except by what is done, we know nothing of the power which acts through what we call all time and all space; but seeing that there is a Nature or fixed order in all things known to us, it is conformable to the nature of our minds to believe that this universal Nature has a cause which operates continually, and that we are totally unable to speculate on the reason of any of those disorders or evils which we perceive. This I believe is the answer which may be collected from all that Antoninus has said.[8]

The origin of evil is an old question. Achilles tells Priam ("Iliad," 24, 527) that Zeus has two casks, one filled with good things, and the other with bad, and that he gives to men out of each according to his pleasure; and so we must be content, for we cannot alter the will of Zeus. One of the Greek commentators asks how must we reconcile this doctrine with what we find in the first book of the "Odyssey," where the king of the gods says, Men say that evil comes to them from us, but they bring it on themselves through their own folly. The answer is plain enough even to the Greek commentator. The poets make both Achilles and Zeus speak appropriately to their several characters. Indeed Zeus says plainly that men do attribute their sufferings to the gods, but they do it falsely, for they are the cause of their own sorrows.

Epictetus in his Enchiridion (c. 27) makes short work of the question of evil. He says, "As a mark is not set up for the purpose of missing it, so neither does the nature of evil exist in the Universe." This will appear obscure enough to those who are not acquainted with Epictetus, but he always knows what he is talking about. We do not set up a mark in order to miss it, though we may miss it. God, whose existence Epictetus assumes, has not ordered all things so that his purpose shall fail. Whatever there may be of what we call

[8] Cleanthes says in his hymn:

> "For all things good and bad to One thou formest,
> So that One everlasting reason governs all."

See Bishop Butler's Sermons. Sermon XV, "Upon the Ignorance of Man."

evil, the Nature of evil, as he expresses it, does not exist; that is, evil is not a part of the constitution or nature of Things. If there were a principle of evil (ἀρχή) in the constitution of things, evil would no longer be evil, as Simplicius argues, but evil would be good. Simplicius (c. 34, [27]) has a long and curious discourse on this text of Epictetus, and it is amusing and instructive.

One passage more will conclude this matter. It contains all that the emperor could say (II. 11): "To go from among men, if there are gods, is not a thing to be afraid of, for the gods will not involve thee in evil; but if indeed they do not exist, or if they have no concern about human affairs, what is it to me to live in a universe devoid of gods or devoid of providence? But in truth they do exist, and they do care for human things, and they have put all the means in man's power to enable him not to fall into real evils. And as to the rest, if there was anything evil, they would have provided for this also, that it should be altogether in a man's power not to fall into it. But that which does not make a man worse, how can it make a man's life worse? But neither through ignorance nor having the knowledge, but not the power to guard against or correct these things, is it possible that the nature of the Universe has overlooked them; nor is it possible that it has made so great a mistake, either through want of power or want of skill, that good and evil should happen indiscriminately to the good and the bad. But death certainly and life, honour and dishonour, pain and pleasure, all these things equally happen to good and bad men, being things which make us neither better nor worse. Therefore they are neither good nor evil."

The Ethical part of Antoninus' Philosophy follows from his general principles. The end of all his philosophy is to live conformably to Nature, both a man's own nature and the nature of the Universe. Bishop Butler has explained what the Greek philosophers meant when they spoke of living according to Nature, and he says that when it is explained, as he has explained it and as they understood it, it is "a manner of speaking not loose and undeterminate, but clear and distinct, strictly just and true." To live according to Nature is to live according to a man's whole nature, not according to a part of it, and to reverence the divinity within him as the governor of all his actions. "To the rational animal the same act is according to nature and according to reason."[9] (VII. 11.) That which is done contrary to reason is also an act contrary to nature, to the whole nature, though it is certainly conformable to some part of man's nature, or it could not be done. Man is made for action, not for idleness or pleasure. As plants and animals do the uses of their nature, so man must do his. (V. 1.)

Man must also live conformably to the universal nature, conformably to the nature of all things of which he is one; and as a citizen of a political community he must direct his life and actions with reference to those among whom, and for whom, among other purposes, he lives.[10] A man must not retire into solitude and cut himself off from his fellow men. He must be ever active to do his part in the great whole. All men are his kin, not only in blood, but still more by participating in the same intelligence and by being a portion of the same divinity. A man cannot really be injured by his brethren, for no act of theirs can make him bad, and he must not be angry with them nor hate them: "For we are made for cooperation, like feet, like hands, like eyelids, like the rows of the upper and lower teeth. To act against one another then is contrary to nature; and it is acting against one another to be vexed and to turn away." (II. 1.)

Further he says: "Take pleasure in one thing and rest in it, in passing from one social act to another social act, thinking of God." (VI. 7.) Again: "Love mankind. Follow God." (VII. 31.) It is the characteristic of the rational soul for a man to love his neighbour. (XI. 1.) Antoninus teaches in various passages the forgiveness of injuries, and we know that he also practised what he taught. Bishop Butler remarks that "this divine precept to forgive injuries and to love our enemies, though to be met with in Gentile moralists, yet is in a peculiar sense a precept of Christianity, as our Saviour has insisted more upon it than on any other single virtue." The practice of this precept is the most difficult of all virtues. Antoninus often enforces it and gives us aid towards following it. When we are injured, we feel anger and resentment, and the feeling is natural,

[9] This is what Juvenal means when he says (XIV. 321):
"Nunquam aliud Natura aliud Sapientia dicit."

[10] See VIII. 52, and Persius, III. 66.

just, and useful for the conservation of society. It is useful that wrong-doers should feel the natural consequences of their actions, among which is the disapprobation of society and the resentment of him who is wronged. But revenge, in the proper sense of that word, must not be practised. "The best way of avenging thyself," says the emperor, "is not to become like the wrong-doer." It is plain by this that he does not mean that we should in any case practise revenge; but he says to those who talk of revenging wrongs, Be not like him who has done the wrong. Socrates in the Crito (c. 10) says the same in other words, and St. Paul (Ep. to the Romans, xii. 17). "When a man has done thee any wrong, immediately consider with what opinion about good or evil he has done wrong. For when thou hast seen this, thou wilt pity him and wilt neither wonder nor be angry." (vii. 26.) Antoninus would not deny that wrong naturally produces the feeling of anger and resentment, for this is implied in the recommendation to reflect on the nature of the man's mind who has done the wrong, and then you will have pity instead of resentment: and so it comes to the same as St. Paul's advice to be angry and sin not; which, as Butler well explains it, is not a recommendation to be angry, which nobody needs, for anger is a natural passion, but it is a warning against allowing anger to lead us into sin. In short the emperor's doctrine about wrongful acts is this: wrong-doers do not know what good and bad are: they offend out of ignorance, and in the sense of the Stoics this is true. Though this kind of ignorance will never be admitted as a legal excuse, and ought not to be admitted as a full excuse in any way by society, there may be grievous injuries, such as it is in a man's power to forgive without harm to society; and if he forgives because he sees that his enemies know not what they do, he is acting in the spirit of the sublime prayer, "Father, forgive them, for they know not what they do."

The emperor's moral philosophy was not a feeble, narrow system, which teaches a man to look directly to his own happiness, though a man's happiness or tranquillity is indirectly promoted by living as he ought to do. A man must live conformably to the universal nature, which means, as the emperor explains it in many passages, that a man's actions must be conformable to his true relations to all other human beings, both as a citizen of a political community and as a member of the whole human family. This implies, and he often expresses it in the most forcible language, that a man's words and actions, so far as they affect others, must be measured by a fixed rule, which is their consistency with the conservation and the interests of the particular society of which he is a member, and of the whole human race. To live conformably to such a rule, a man must use his rational faculties in order to discern clearly the consequences and full effect of all his actions and of the actions of others: he must not live a life of contemplation and reflection only, though he must often retire within himself to calm and purify his soul by thought, but he must mingle in the work of man and be a fellow labourer for the general good.

A man should have an object or purpose in life, that he may direct all his energies to it; of course a good object. (II. 7.) He who has not one object or purpose of life, cannot be one and the same all through his life. (XI. 21.) Bacon has a remark to the same effect, on the best means of "reducing of the mind unto virtue and good estate; which is, the electing and propounding unto a man's self good and virtuous ends of his life, such as may be in a reasonable sort within his compass to attain." He is a happy man who has been wise enough to do this when he was young and has had the opportunities; but the emperor, seeing well that a man cannot always be so wise in his youth, encourages himself to do it when he can, and not to let life slip away before he has begun. He who can propose to himself good and virtuous ends of life, and be true to them, cannot fail to live conformably to his own interest and the universal interest, for in the nature of things they are one. If a thing is not good for the hive, it is not good for the bee. (VI. 54.)

One passage may end this matter. "If the gods have determined about me and about the things which must happen to me, they have determined well, for it is not easy even to imagine a deity without forethought; and as to doing me harm, why should they have any desire towards that? For what advantage would result to them from this or to the whole, which is the special object of their providence? But if they have not determined about me individually, they have certainly determined about the whole at least; and the things which happen by way of sequence in this general arrangement I ought to accept with pleasure and to be content with them. But if they determine about nothing—which it is wicked to believe, or if we do believe it, let us neither sacrifice nor pray nor swear by them nor do anything else which we do as if the gods were present and lived with us—but if however the gods determine about none of the things which concern us, I am able to determine about myself, and I can inquire about that which is useful; and that is useful to every man which is conformable to his own constitution (*κατασκευή*) and nature. But my nature is rational and social; and my city and country, so far as I am Antoninus, is Rome; but so far as I am a man, it is the world. The things then which are useful to these cities are alone useful to me." (VI. 44.)

It would be tedious, and it is not necessary, to state the emperor's opinions on all the ways in which a man may profitably use his understanding towards perfecting himself in practical virtue. The passages to this purpose are in all parts of his book, but as they are in no order or connection, a man must use the book a long time before he will find out all that is in it. A few words may be added here. If we analyze all other things, we find how insufficient they are for human life, and how truly worthless many of them are. Virtue alone is indivisible, one, and perfectly satisfying. The notion of Virtue cannot be considered vague or unsettled, because a man may find it difficult to explain the notion fully to himself or to expound it to others in such a way as to prevent cavilling. Virtue is a whole, and no more consists of parts than man's intelligence does, and yet we speak of various intellectual faculties as a convenient way of expressing the various powers which man's intellect shows by his works. In the same way we may speak of various virtues or parts of virtue, in a practical sense, for the purpose of showing what particular virtues we ought to practise in order to the exercise of the whole of virtue, that is, as much as man's nature is capable of.

The prime principle in man's constitution is social. The next in order is not to yield to the persuasions of the body, when they are not conformable to the rational principle, which must govern. The third is freedom from error and from deception. "Let then the ruling principle holding fast to these things go straight on, and it has what is its own." (VII. 55.) The emperor selects justice as the virtue which is the basis of all the rest (x. 11), and this had been said long before his time.

It is true that all people have some notion of what is meant by justice as a disposition of the mind, and some notion about acting in conformity to this disposition; but experience shows that men's notions about justice are as confused as their actions are inconsistent with the true notion of justice. The emperor's notion of justice is clear enough, but not practical enough for all mankind. "Let there be freedom from perturbations with respect to the things which come from the external cause; and let there be justice in the things done by virtue of the internal cause, that is, let there be movement and action terminating in this, in social acts, for this is according to thy nature." (IX. 31.) In another place (IX. 1) he says that "he who acts unjustly acts impiously," which follows of course from all that he says in various places. He insists on the practice of truth as a virtue and as a means to virtue, which no doubt it is: for lying even in indifferent things weakens the understanding; and lying maliciously is as great a moral offence as a man can be guilty of, viewed both as showing an habitual disposition, and viewed with respect to consequences. He couples the notion of justice with action. A man must not pride himself on having some fine notion of justice in his head, but he must exhibit his justice in act, like St. James's notion of faith. But this is enough.

The Stoics, and Antoninus among them, call some things beautiful (καλά) and some ugly (αἰσχρά), and as they are beautiful so they are good, and as they are ugly so they are evil or bad. (II. I.) All these things good and evil are in our power absolutely, some of the stricter Stoics would say; in a manner only, as those who would not depart altogether from common sense would say; practically they are to a great degree in the power of some persons and in some circumstances, but in a small degree only in other persons and in other circumstances. The Stoics maintain man's free will as to the things which are in his power; for as to the things which are out of his power, free will terminating in action is of course excluded by the very terms of the expression. I hardly know if we can discover exactly Antoninus' notion of the free will of man, nor is the question worth the inquiry. What he does mean and does say is intelligible.

All the things which are not in our power (ἀπροαίρετα) are indifferent: they are neither good nor bad, morally. Such are life, health, wealth, power, disease, poverty, and death. Life and death are all men's portion. Health, wealth, power, disease, and poverty happen to men indifferently to the good and to the bad; to those who live according to nature and to those who do not. "Life," says the emperor, "is a warfare and a stranger's sojourn, and after-fame is oblivion." (II. 17.) After speaking of those men who have disturbed the world and then died, and of the death of philosophers such as Heraclitus and Democritus, who was destroyed by lice, and of Socrates, whom other lice (his enemies) destroyed, he says: "What means all this? Thou hast embarked, thou hast made the voyage, thou art come to shore; get out. If indeed to another life, there is no want of gods, not even there. But if to a state without sensation, thou wilt cease to be held by pains and pleasures, and to be a slave to the vessel which is as much inferior as that which serves it is superior: for the one is intelligence and deity; the other is earth and corruption." (III. 3.) It is not death that a man should fear, but he should fear never beginning to live according to nature. (XII. 1.) Every man should live in such a way as to discharge his duty, and to trouble himself about nothing else. He should live such a life that he shall always be ready for death, and shall depart content when the summons comes. For what is death? "A cessation of the impressions through the senses, and of the pulling of the strings which move the appetites, and of the discursive movements of the thoughts, and of the service to the flesh." (VI. 28.) Death is such as generation is, a mystery of nature. (IV. 5.) In another passage, the exact meaning of which is perhaps doubtful (IX. 3), he speaks of the child which leaves the womb, and so he says the soul at death leaves its envelope. As the child is born or comes into life by leaving the womb, so the soul may on leaving the body pass into another existence which is perfect. I am not sure if this is the emperor's meaning. Butler compares it with a passage in Strabo (p. 713), about the Brachmans' notion of death being the birth into real life and a happy life to those who have philosophized; and he thinks that Antoninus may allude to this opinion.

Antoninus' opinion of a future life is nowhere clearly expressed.

His doctrine of the nature of the soul of necessity implies that it does not perish absolutely, for a portion of the divinity cannot perish. The opinion is at least as old as the time of Epicharmus and Euripides; what comes from earth goes back to earth, and what comes from heaven, the divinity, returns to him who gave it. But I find nothing clear in Antoninus as to the notion of the man existing after death so as to be conscious of his sameness with that soul which occupied his vessel of clay. He seems to be perplexed on this matter, and finally to have rested in this, that God or the gods will do whatever is best and consistent with the university of things.

Nor I think does he speak conclusively on another Stoic doctrine, which some Stoics practised, the anticipating the regular course of nature by a man's own act. The reader will find some passages in which this is touched on, and he may make of them what he can. But there are passages in which the emperor encourages himself to wait for the end patiently and with tranquillity; and certainly it is consistent with all his best teaching that a man should bear all that falls to his lot and do useful acts as long as he lives. He should not therefore abridge the time of his usefulness by his own act. Whether he contemplates any possible cases in which a man should die by his own hand, I cannot tell, and the matter is not worth a curious inquiry, for I believe it would not lead to any certain result as to his opinion on this point. I do not think that Antoninus, who never mentions Seneca, though he must have known all about him, would have agreed with Seneca when he gives as a reason for suicide, that the eternal law, whatever he means, has made nothing better for us than this, that it has given us only one way of entering into life and many ways of going out of it. The ways of going out indeed are many, and that is a good reason for a man taking care of himself.

Happiness was not the direct object of a Stoic's life. There is no rule of life contained in the precept that a man should pursue his own happiness. Many men think that they are seeking happiness when they are only seeking the gratification of some particular passion, the strongest that they have. The end of a man is, as already explained, to live conformably to nature, and he will thus obtain happiness, tranquillity of mind, and contentment. (III. 12; VIII. 1, and other places.) As a means of living conformably to nature he must study the four chief virtues, each of which has its proper sphere: wisdom, or the knowledge of good and evil; justice, or the giving to every man his due; fortitude, or the enduring of labour and pain; and temperance, which is moderation in all things. By thus living conformably to nature the Stoic obtained all that he wished or expected. His reward was in his virtuous life, and he was satisfied with that. Some Greek poet long ago wrote:

> For virtue only of all human things
> Takes her reward not from the hands of others.
> Virtue herself rewards the toils of virtue.

Some of the Stoics indeed expressed themselves in very arrogant, absurd terms about the wise man's self-sufficiency: they elevated him to the rank of a deity. But these were only talkers and lecturers, such as those in all ages who utter fine words, know little of human affairs, and care only for notoriety. Epictetus and Antoninus both by precept and example laboured to improve themselves and others; and if we discover imperfections in their teaching, we must still honour these great men who attempted to show that there is in man's nature and in the constitution of things sufficient reason for living a virtuous life. It is difficult enough to live as we ought to live, difficult even for any man to live in such a way as to satisfy himself, if he exercises only in a moderate degree the power of reflecting upon and reviewing his own conduct; and if all men cannot be brought to the same opinions in morals and religion, it is at least worth while to give them good reasons for as much as they can be persuaded to accept.